LANDING

MW00526255

101 HOURS
IN A ZEPPELIN

ERNST AUGUST LEHMANN AND THE DREAM OF TRANSATLANTIC FLIGHT, 1917

Robert S. Pohl

SCHIFFER MILITARY

4880 Lower Valley Road   Atglen, PA 19310

Other Schiffer Books on related subjects

Zeppelin: The Story of the Zeppelin Airships, Hans G. Knäusel, ISBN 978-0-7643-4478-7

The Zeppelin in Combat: A History of the German Naval Airship Division, Douglas H. Robinson, ISBN 978-0-88740-510-5

Designed by Christopher Bower
Cover design by Ashley Millhouse
Type set in Abolition/Garamond Premier Pro

ISBN: 978-0-7643-6641-3
Printed in China

Published by Schiffer Publishing, Ltd.
4880 Lower Valley Road
Atglen, PA 19310
Phone: (610) 593-1777; Fax: (610) 593-2002
Email: Info@schifferbooks.com
Web: www.schifferbooks.com

For our complete selection of fine books on this and related subjects, please visit our website at www.schifferbooks.com. You may also write for a free catalog.

Schiffer Publishing's titles are available at special discounts for bulk purchases for sales promotions or premiums. Special editions, including personalized covers, corporate imprints, and excerpts, can be created in large quantities for special needs. For more information, contact the publisher.

We are always looking for people to write books on new and related subjects. If you have an idea for a book, please contact us at proposals@schifferbooks.com.

To my father, Robert Otto Pohl

> Und wenn vielleicht, nach fünfzig Jahren,
> Ein Luftschiff voller Griechenwein
> Durch's Morgenroth käm' hergefahren —
> Wer möchte da nicht Fährmann sein?

And if maybe in fifty years
An airship full of Greek wine
Flies through the red morning
Who would not want to steer this?

Penultimate stanza of the poem "Justinius Kerner, Erwiderung auf sein Lied: Unter dem Himmel" (1845) by Gottfried Keller. Full text including translation appears in the appendix.

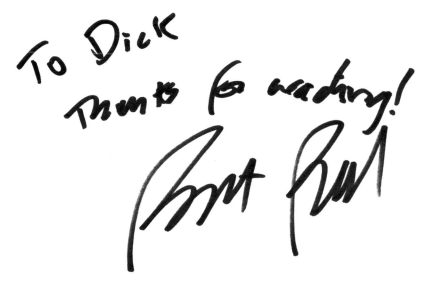

CONTENTS

ACKNOWLEDGMENTS

First and foremost, I must thank my grandfather Robert Wichard Pohl for being such a good son and diligent letter writer. His weekly letters home give a broad and deep look at his life from 1903 until the late 1920s. He seems to have been aware of the value of his letters, mentioning in one that he hoped his mother would add a note in the stack that a number of letters had gotten lost at this point, as he had failed to write for a couple of weeks. In fact, his mother did collect them, and they eventually made their way to her son's attic. So, thanks to both son and mother in creating and saving these pieces of history.

Second, thanks go to my father, Robert Otto Pohl, who, after his retirement, took on the job of typing up the letters written by his father. Having discovered them in the attic of his father's house, he worked his way through all of them, leaving an electronic record that has made the current work a far easier job. Furthermore, his ability to read the old German script that his father wrote in—called Sütterlin, and not taught in German schools since the Second World War—was crucial to the project's success.

Hand in hand with that go thanks to my mother, Karin Pohl, for ensuring that I could speak German—and also read and write it. As good as electronic means of translation have become of late, nothing beats being able to read the original sources, both those of my grandfather and the many other books and articles written about Zeppelins. I thank her in particular for working through my translation of the Kerner and Keller poems, keeping me from making some major mistakes.

Next, three archives must be thanked: First, that of the Aeronauticum Nordholz, a museum built adjacent to the former Zeppelin airbase in northwestern Germany. The information in their archives about the flight of added a precision that was lacking in both my grandfather's letters and the various stories that Captain Lehmann later wrote down. The day spent looking through their material was fruitful indeed.

Second, the Library of Congress, which contains an enormous amount of historical data, both electronic and on paper. Beginning with their newspaper collection and continuing with the books on Zeppelins and genealogical data available at the institution itself, I was able to refine and find evidence for many of the stories I had read about in other sources.

Finally, the online archives at the District of Columbia Public Library, through which I had access to a number of newspapers still in copyright, as well as further genealogical databases.

Along with these three main sources, thanks also to the many people who have put some part of the Zeppelin story online, whether Harry Redner, who as Luftschiffharry put together an overview over German army airships during the war, or the many people at the Puget Sound Airship Society who put a broad overview of Zeppelins on their website, or Andreas Krug, with his small but well-researched website covering Zeppelin history. Each contained important information and hints as to where to focus my research.

Not to be ignored here are the online archives: Google Books, Archive.org, and the HathiTrust, who allow for searches through old books and magazines, giving an incredibly rich source of data about not only the airships and their technology, but the times and places in which Robert Wichard Pohl lived.

In writing this book, I have had the invaluable support of my writing friends: Jennifer Howard, Jonathan Lewis, and Louis Bayard. Beyond that, my coffee buddies: Tim Krepp, Eric Zakim, Frank Pietrucha, Maggie Hall, Sam Fromartz, Heather Pfahl, Mike Showalter, Nadine Henderson, Sheldon Harris, Larry Slagle, Jen Graham, and Mark Shlien. Thanks for believing in me, guys!

Finally, no thanks would be complete without thanking my wife, Antonia Herzog, and son, Ian Herzog-Pohl, who have spent way too much time hearing me go on about some arcane detail of Zeppelin history and have allowed an ever-growing number of Zeppelin pictures to grace the walls of our house.

To all these, and to all readers, thank you!

Robert Stephan Pohl
Washington, DC, April 2020

INTRODUCTION

THE ZEPPELIN RAIDS : THE VOW OF VENGEANCE
Drawn for 'The Daily Chronicle' by Frank Brangwyn ARA

'DAILY CHRONICLE' READERS ARE
COVERED AGAINST THE RISKS OF
BOMBARDMENT BY ZEPPELIN OR
AEROPLANE

1915 poster featuring a drawing by the Anglo-Welsh artist Frank Brangwyn for the London *Daily Chronicle* and printed by the Avenue Press, Bouverie St. London. E.C. Brangwyn, who had been born in Belgium, was particularly incensed by German atrocities during the war. The *Chronicle*, known for its independent editorial stance, had been published since 1872. Its editor, Robert Donald, had been in that position since 1904. *Library of Congress*

J uly 1917. For almost three years, the world has been at war. All around the world, newspaper editors are preparing greater or lesser articles marking the upcoming anniversary.

Three years earlier, the world had held its breath for two days and seventeen hours, the time between Serbia's answer to the Austro-Hungarian ultimatum and Austria-Hungary's reply—in the form of a declaration of war—thereto. Since both countries had mobilized, and the Serbian answer had not been the complete capitulation demanded by Austria-Hungary, it was clear that war was imminent.

The exact start of the war was a question that the newspapers were divided on. Some saw it as the date of the Austro-Hungarian ultimatum to Serbia, delivered on July 23; others declared it to be the twenty-eighth, when Austria formally declared war, while still others felt that the twenty-ninth was more appropriate, as this was the day that Belgrade was shelled by the Austro-Hungarian empire. Germans tended to see the beginning as August 1, on which day they had declared war on Russia, while French newspapers dated the beginning to August 3, the day the French had mobilized their army.

However you saw it, there was no doubt that the world had just completed three full years of unimaginable carnage.

It was a time to look back. In New York, Ogden Mills Reid, editor of the *Tribune*, finalized plans for an elaborate special section to be published two days hence. Included was a full-page timeline of the war, stretching back to June 28, 1914, when Gavrilo Princip assassinated Franz Ferdinand, Archduke of Austria.[1]

Across the ocean, in France, *Le Matin* was not interested in rehashing the war, as they instead contented themselves with running articles about the seeds of war and who was responsible for it.[2]

Others looked ahead, like *Le Figaro*, who were waiting for the day that they reckoned the war from—the day of the French mobilization—and were not planning on mentioning the anniversary until August 3.[3]

Others looked even farther ahead, past whatever fighting that would inevitably still occur. To a future where there was, once again, unhindered international travel, a world where the rich and powerful were prepared to pay dearly for a comfortable means of reaching their destination. A world where a fleet of giant airships crisscrossed the globe.

It was this world that lieutenant of the naval reserves Ernst August Lehmann dreamed of. This young airship officer, already one of the great veterans of not only combat but also civilian flying, was about to close out one chapter of this life and embark on a new one—one that required a clear-eyed and hopeful view of the future.

Lehmann had been flying Zeppelins into combat since the first days of the war, when it looked as if Germany and the rest of the Central Powers would be able to prosecute the fight the way they wanted to. The sweep into Belgium went as planned, as did the turn down into France and toward Paris, a victory that would allow them to concentrate their might on the real enemy: Russia.

In the east, French pressure convinced Russia to attack German East Prussia, culminating in the battles of Gumbinnen and Stallupönen, and with the Russian army sweeping well into German territory. However, then the German army reassembled itself and fought back, and by the end of 1914 had swept their enemy back into their own territory.

At the same time, the movement on the western front was bogging down. The combined French and British armies had fought back at the Marne River just outside of Paris and halted the German advance. There followed a series of flanking maneuvers to the northeast, ending with the battle lines stretching all the way to the English Channel. At this point, both sides began to dig trenches on their side of a swath of land nobody could—or wanted to—enter, and the war, at least on this front, settled down into a series of bloody but inconclusive attempts to push back the enemy.

While movement on the eastern front tended toward greater distances, the results were much the same—large numbers of soldiers dead for gains of territory that tended to be lost within a few months. A bloody stalemate had set in.

There were other fronts: Austria-Hungary had invaded Serbia immediately at the beginning of the war, though after much bloody fighting and the loss of Belgrade, the Serbs had regrouped and driven the enemy back to their original borders.

In early 1915, the British attacked Turkey, in an attempt to reopen the Dardanelles and thus the lifeline to Russia. The attacks, which stretched out over much of 1915, failed, though the allies did end up with two beachheads on or near these important straits. Much like on the western front, a stalemate ensued, and only nine months later did the Allies break off the fight and evacuate all soldiers from there.

The attack on Turkey opened up two further fronts, or, more accurately, reopened one and opened another. The Austro-Hungarian Empire took on Serbia again, this time with greater success, especially when the Bulgarians joined in the fight.

South of them, the Greeks, who had remained neutral up to this point, found themselves overrun by Serbian soldiers fleeing the combined attack on their country. A new front opened up on the border of Greece, further complicated by the chaotic nature of Greek politics at the time.

To the west of Greece, Italy, which had managed to remain neutral for about the first year of the war, and Austria-Hungary had fought a series of battles that had done little to change the effective borders between the countries.

In the Middle East, British Empire attacks on Turkey were smaller, but more effective than at Gallipoli. The Ottoman Empire did little to counter the attacks that spread all across the Mesopotamian region.

Even Africa had its share of fighting, with German colonies defending themselves against both invasions and uprisings from locals.

The biggest news of the past year had, however, been the declaration of war by the United States. In spite of having campaigned and won with the slogan "He kept us out of war," Woodrow Wilson on April 2, 1917, asked for a declaration of war against Germany. His reasons were the recently resumed unrestricted submarine warfare, as well as the interception of a telegram to Mexico, in which Germany promised to help that country regain lands lost during the Mexican-American War more than fifty years earlier. In his speech, Wilson used the phrases "make to world safe for democracy" and that this was a "war to end war." The declarations passed both houses over the next four days with only token opposition, and on April 6, Wilson formally declared war.

The direct consequences of this vote were hardly to be felt at this time. Only a few thousand US troops had arrived in France, and none of them were at the front yet. However, on June 5, the first draft registration had occurred, and some ten million young men between the ages of twenty-one and thirty had registered and were preparing to be inducted into the army. There was still the hope on the German side that they would be able to slow the Americans' transatlantic movement by using their U-boats.

Right now, however, none of this mattered to Lehmann and his crew. They found themselves in a quiet part of the German Empire, and though they knew it could not last, that they would soon be forced by recent decisions of the German high command to go elsewhere, they were ready for one last peaceful trip.[4]

CHAPTER 1
JULY 26, 11:40 P.M.–JULY 27, 6:00 A.M.

The Seerappen hangar as seen from the air. The door on the left is cracked open to allow entrance from the other end. The 240-meter-long double hangar was built in 1916–17.

"Luftschiff, hoch!" comes the order. The men whose combined weight is holding the giant airship down let go, and slowly, too slowly, the ship rises. In the front gondola, the captain of the airship, Ernst August Lehmann, anxiously watches the altimeter. He knows the airship is filled close to its maximum with provisions, gear, and, most importantly, fuel,[1] but nonetheless, the vertical progress is not what he is hoping for.[2]

Lehmann looks at the thermometer and sees that the outside temperature is rising, and not falling, as would be expected as their altitude increases: they are in a temperature inversion; the upper levels of the air are warmer than lower ones. Lehmann knows that for every degree centigrade that the air warms, he will lose about 200 kilograms in lifting capacity, and the last thing he wants to do right now is to dump the precious water ballast that he has on board, even before the flight has begun in earnest.

After a final check that no one is still holding on to a line and hanging on for dear life, a circumstance that happened too often and required an immediate landing to rescue them,[3] Lehmann signals for the engines to be turned up to full, and slowly the airship makes its way out of the valley in which its hangar and the town of Seerappen stand. Reaching the crest of the hill that surrounds it, they find themselves not over but next to a building. The occupants look out in shock into the windows of the Zeppelin. Finally, the airship makes its way into the air, above any potentially dangerous obstacles. Lehmann and the rest of the crew in the gondola of the Zeppelin breathe a little easier. It would not have done to start what they hoped would be a record-breaking trip with a mishap, especially as they might never be given permission to try a similar flight. He orders the radio antennas be lowered so that they can stay in touch with the ground.[4]

The gondola, which is attached well forward on the airship and below the bulk of the airship, sways with each gust of wind. It is necessary to be aware at all times of a good handhold nearby, to grab at when the next gust hits. The first officer abandons his spot at the table in back and sits down on the wide ledge below the windows that surround the front of the gondola, a spot where he can still keep a close eye on the compass while still having a good view out the front.

Above Lehmann's head, and a few meters forward, another desperate struggle is taking place. Professor Robert Wichard Pohl, ostensibly on board to do further radio experiments, is attempting to get settled for the night. His bed is a hammock slung up between the girders that make up the skeleton of the airship, hanging parallel to the catwalk that stretches along the keel of the airship from front to back. What worries him most is the floor below, which consists of a thin sheet of canvas. Pohl is distinctly aware of the frailty of this cloth, knowing that it is built to break free if a container of water or fuel has to be suddenly ditched, and has no interest in showing that the same fate can befall a human. He also knows that he tends to thrash about in his sleep, something that usually just leads to badly mussed bedsheets, but in this case can have far more deadly consequences.

He struggles quietly and despairingly with his two blankets, hoping not to disturb those in the other nineteen hammocks around him, hammocks that represent the only available sleeping accommodation aboard the enormous airship. Pohl finally wedges himself into the hammock in a way that precludes being ejected therefrom and goes to sleep.[5]

Around him, half of the crew is similarly engaged. Lehmann had given orders that the flight would be crewed in shifts, that enlisted men would switch off every eight hours while officers would do so every six. He is interested to see if there is any difference in these two rhythms, and which schedule might be better at keeping the crew alert and prepared at all times.[6]

In the driver's gondola, the weather continues to be an issue. While at takeoff the sky had been clear, it has begun to cloud over as they head over the Baltic shore. For the first three hours, they motor west, making 80 km/h—below the maximum speed that airship can go, but given the time they are hoping to stay aloft, a prudent choice.[7]

As they reach Rixhöft, a cape on the other side of the Bay of Danzig that they have been flying over since about midnight, the weather begins to worsen. Below, they can only vaguely make out the lighthouse. As they cross over the shore, the weather is cloudy, foggy, and surprisingly warm.[8]

An hour and a half later, now over the Garder Lake that is just inland from the south coast of the Baltic, the wind kicks up and Lehmann finds himself flying backward briefly.[9] Lehmann also finds himself continually adjusting his heading to avoid thunderstorms that block his passage. The storms do at least cool down the ship a bit, and Lehmann steers the ship back over the Baltic Sea and follows the coast to the west, relaxing a bit as the weather begins to improve.[10]

For Pohl, the previous days had been no less hectic. The planning had begun earlier that month when he had received word, via Susanne Lehmann, that her husband was to attempt a long-distance flight in his Zeppelin. Lehmann requested that Pohl join him, ostensibly for further tests, but in reality simply as an opportunity to spend some time with an old friend.[11]

Unfortunately, the state of army airships meant that nobody was particularly interested in giving Pohl the requisite papers to go. Pohl therefore had to attempt to convince various officers in the Inspektion der Luftschiffertruppen (Iluft; Inspectorate for Airship Troops), as well as the Inspektion für Technische

Angelegenheiten (Itechang; Inspectorate for Technical Affairs), and the Technical Section for Technische Abteilung der Funkertruppen (Tafunk; Technical Section for Radio Communication) of the importance of his mission. For a while, the only offer he could get was a suggestion that he wait until winter, when the navy would need help with their tests in Potsdam, near Pohl's home in Berlin. But, as Pohl wrote in a letter written a few hours before the flight was to begin, "What good are the naval experiments in winter when Seerappen is near Wien's estate and the sun is shining now?"

In the end, the best he was able to pry loose from a major in the Iluft was a telegram that stated that "Experiments on *LZ 120* will begin again on Wednesday the twenty-fifth; we have no reason to oppose the detachment of Chief Engineer Pohl to observe these." This was enough to generate the needed invitation for him.[12]

Lehmann's decision to make this flight was a little more straightforward. He and his airship had been stationed in the east since March, when it was determined that it was too dangerous to fly against targets in England. Their job here was to watch over naval movements in the Baltic. This meant looking for foreign naval ships anywhere there, and in particular the Russo-English submarine base on the Äland Islands at the entrance of the Gulf of Bothnia that separated Finland and Sweden. Beyond that, they were to look for mines, and several of the flights taken early June had been made with this as their primary purpose. Finally, they were to keep an eye on merchant vessels, particularly along the Swedish coast.[13]

The flights tended to take up a full twenty-four hours, and the crew would thereafter be given a day off. In between, the weather could keep them in the hangar for a week or ten days. When the weather was good, however, the schedule was punishing, in spite of there being no actual military incidents worthy of report. Lehmann began to wonder if there might not be a better way to operate. After all, they were spending a considerable time simply getting into position. The Äland Islands, for instance, were almost 600 kilometers from their base, and required at least four hours just to get there, eight for the round trip—which represented one-third of their total time aloft. Would it not make more sense, Lehmann thought, to stay aloft for longer periods of time, three or four days at a stretch, in order to maximize the time the Zeppelin was on patrol? A discussion in this direction in the mess one evening brought the question to a head. The biggest issue that others brought up was the quality of the engines, which needed continual maintenance and would not be able to run for this length of time. Beyond that was the question of the ability of the men to get enough rest while underway to ensure their continued ability to do their jobs.[14]

There was only one way to find out if this would work, Lehmann decided: To try it. And soon. The army was getting out of the airship business, and Lehmann himself was ending his time as a military Zeppelin captain. He was to report to the headquarters of the Zeppelin firm in Friedrichshafen, in the distant south of Germany on the Lake of Constance, as soon as possible.[15]

Remarkably, the army acquiesced. Whether they hoped to help the navy in their efforts with any newfound knowledge or simply wanted to see Lehmann off with a parting gift, they gave permission for an extended flight. Lehmann immediately set about working out the details, what combination of crew members, and the amount of supplies, both for the airship and the crew, that he would have to bring on board. Part of the planning was passing on the word, via his wife, to Pohl that this flight was going to happen. The last week before the flight was quiet, with no flights scheduled.[16] Lehmann took the opportunity to take the train to Berlin for two days while his crew prepared the airship.[17]

The evening of his departure from Berlin, Pohl and friends celebrated a military victory that was, at the time, thought to be the beginning of the end: a Russian attack in Galicia on Austro-Hungarian and German troops, ordered in early July by Russian war minister Alexander Kerensky and led by General Aleksei Brusilov, had been turned by the Germans into a rout. The friends had met in the wood-paneled dining room of Louis Mitscher's wine bar to celebrate over a bottle of the Moselle wine the establishment was renowned for[18] and had ended the evening by writing a postcard to Pohl's sister. Pohl tucked the postcard in his pocket and headed out, up Friedrichstrasse and across Unter den Linden, Berlin's main avenue, and to the train station.[19]

By 9:30, Pohl was in the train leaving Berlin. Lehmann was already on board and had saved a seat for him. It was a quiet trip, though, with Pohl wrapping himself into a special sleeping jacket his sister had made for him and nodding off for at least part of the time. It was a long trip: 500 kilometers to the northeast. They arrived the next morning in Königsberg in East Prussia, where they were picked up and taken by car west to their hangar in Seerappen, and the Zeppelin.[20]

In the evening, after Pohl had taken a nap, they had taken the Zeppelin up for a quick spin that they put down as a test flight, to make sure that all systems were working. After their takeoff from Seerappen, they headed east to Königsberg. Pohl was particularly interested in this city, as it was where his great-grandfather Daniel Gotthilf Pohl had moved as a young man and where his grandfather Robert Pohl and his grandmother Louise Marie Schmidt had been born.[21] The city had grown considerably since his grandfather had left there and now had more than 200,000 inhabitants. It was the capitol of East Prussia and had been an important fortress since its founding in 1255, when the castle that Pohl could see below had been built.[22] From above, the shape of the fortress—a rectangle with one of the longer sides slightly bent to the outside, with a church tower on the opposite corner—could be seen clearly. Pohl knew the church from his father, who had shown him the tickets for the coronation that had taken place there in 1861, tickets that a friend of his father's had given him. Outside the palace to the north was the palace pond, a half-kilometer-long finger pointing northeast; to the south were the famous islands Kneiphof and Lomse, whose seven bridges had been used to set a problem by Leonhard Euler[23] that had been used to badger Pohl as a student.[24]

Lehmann had pictures taken of the city as they flew over; Pohl asked for copies to remind him of the flight.

From Königsberg they flew north across Samland, the peninsula north of that city and jutting out into the Baltic Sea. While north and south of the peninsula, lengthy spits and lagoons separated the mainland from the water, here the interface between the two was more direct with the land rising to sandy cliffs in its northwest corner. The land below was covered with trees and agriculture, taking advantage of the fertile soil.[25]

They traveled north about 25 kilometers, covering the whole peninsula north to south, and arrived at the (in the words of Karl Baedeker) "city-like village" of Kranz, a seaside town at the base of the Curonian Spit, which had drawn visitors since 1816.[26] From the air, they could see the large hotels that lined the promenade, and the piers projecting well into the Baltic Sea, as well as a number of smaller breakwaters evenly spaced along the shore. Just looking at the elegant hotels made it clear why it was the most-visited resort on the Sambian Peninsula, and while it only had three thousand inhabitants, it welcomed five times that many visitors per year.[27] At Kranz they turned back south and toward Seerappen, finishing their 60-kilometer flight in about two and a half hours. The airship had performed as hoped; now there was only one thing that could hold up departure—the weather.

Thus the following day was spent in the study of the local weather patterns, in particular a red flag outside the window at which Pohl sat and wrote a letter, which depending on how much or little it flapped would indicate the likelihood of a flight. Lehmann himself divided his time between newly produced weather maps and his 1914 income tax return. Others kept themselves busy deciding what food was to be brought on board. Pohl was horrified to hear that they were considering 150 liters of coffee—and no alcohol. Otherwise, his only challenge was to find a fur coat to keep him warm during the flight; fortunately there was another Zeppelin, the navy *L 30*, in the hangar, and they were currently not flying and had coats to spare.

Across Germany, it was a busy day for Zeppelins. Eight hundred kilometers due west, in Ahlhorn, three airships were aloft that day: *L 44* and *L 46* patrolling the North Sea, while *L 50* was testing out its motors. In Tondern, 200 kilometers due north of Ahlhorn, *L 45* was sweeping for mines. In between, in the large airship station in Nordholz, *L 16* was on a training flight, while *L 51* was being transferred from Friedrichshafen, where it had been completed and launched some three weeks earlier. Closer to home, the only other army airship in the air, *LZ 111*, had flown from Seddin on a patrol mission but had had to return back, and *L 37* had departed from its hangar in Wainoden, 200 kilometers to the north, and was still on patrol somewhere in the Baltic Sea.[28]

Before departure, Captain Lehmann also had to fill out a flight report, on which all details of the circumstances of the flight, the twenty-seventh since the ship was built and the twenty-fourth since being taken on by the army, were listed. Beginning at the top, with the name of the airship, the orders were simple: reconnaissance flight.

Below that were the names of the twenty-nine members of the crew, beginning with Lehmann himself, including three names that had been part of his crew for several years by now: Buczilowski, Grözinger, and Hölzemann. While the first was listed, as so often before, as pilot, the latter two were slotted in as machine gun operators, although they were experienced mechanics. Lehmann felt that having more people able to attend to the engines was more important than gunners needed only in the extremely unlikely event of an enemy attack. Lehmann's list ended with two passengers: Professor Pohl and a navy ensign named Bügel.

Far more important were the following entries, which also gave an indication why Lehmann's start had been so difficult. The heaviest item—beyond the weight of the airship itself—was the fuel. For the fifty-six-hour flight that Lehmann had announced, this meant 23,000 liters that weighed 16,900 kilograms—far more than the 2,500 kilograms that the men aboard weighed. Beyond that, there were 1,000 kilograms of oil and 4,100 kilograms of water as both ballast and for cooling the engines. While he had no intention of getting into any fights, there were still 1,500 kilograms of munitions, both bombs and machine guns on board, and even the observation car and its winch, which took up another 400 kilograms of lift away from the airship's capacity. Finally, 1,500 kilograms of supplies rounded out the airship's cargo.

Countering this were 55,000 cubic meters of hydrogen in the nineteen bags crowded throughout the length of the airship. While they were in good shape, and the outer covering was dry, it was this sheer amount brought on board which threatened to drag down the airship at takeoff, especially as the hydrogen that had taken on was far from pure, delivering about 10 percent less lift than it should have. This left exactly 200 kilograms of lift available to

Lehmann, and explained why he had had such a difficult time getting the airship up and out of its valley at takeoff.[29]

For now, all is well. The thunderstorms that had previously threatened the airship have subsided, and although the weather is still far from clear, the bit of haze in the air does nothing to hinder the airship's progress and those on the bridge can relax and begin to enjoy the prospect of a few days sailing over the Baltic Sea with no chance of coming into danger from enemy action.

CHAPTER 2
GRAF VON ZEPPELIN

1863 picture by Alexander Gardner at Fairfax Courthouse of Count Zeppelin, Ulric Dahlgren, and others. The men are studying *The Art of War*, though not the famous work by Sun Tzu, but rather an 1838 work by the Baron de Jomini.[*] The work was translated into English in 1854[**] and 1862,[***] and was the principal tactical work taught at the US Military Academy before the Civil War.[****] Dahlgren, who was the son of the Washington Navy Yard commander John Dahlgren, would lose his leg, and later his life, in the Civil War. *Library of Congress*

[*] Jomini, Le Baron de. *Précis de l'Art de la Guerre: Des Principales Combinaisons de la Stratégie, de la Grande Tactique et de la Politique Militaire.* Brussels: Meline, Cans et Copagnie, 1838.

[**] Jomini, Le Baron de. Translated from the French by Maj. Oscar. F. Winship and Lt. Eugene E. McLean. *Summary of the Art of War, or, A New Analytical Compend of the Principal Combinations of Strategy, of Grand Tactics and of Military Policy.* New York: Putnam, 1854.

[***] Jomini, Le Baron de. Translated from the French by George H. Mendell and William P. Craighill. *The Art of War.* Philadelphia: Lippincott, 1862.

[****] Chambers, John Whiteclay, and Fred Anderson. *The Oxford Companion to American Military History.* Oxford: Oxford University Press, 1999, pp. 720–1.

This long-planned flight had its genesis many years earlier, during another war fought thousands of kilometers away and between not countries but within one: the American Civil War. Then, as now, new technology was brought to bear, whether the telegraph, railroads, and balloons then as today radio, automobiles, and airships were being used. Balloon technology in particular was intriguing to the armies in the field, as it allowed commanders to gain an overview of the lay of the land and the opposing forces without sending soldiers out on risky reconnaissance missions. This new technology attracted the interest of foreign observers who were embedded more or less closely with the US Army. One of these visitors was young Count Zeppelin.

Born the scion of an ancient line stretching back hundreds of years to the small town of Zepelin in northern Germany, the family had become rich after Zeppelin's grandfather and great-uncle had been hired by the king of Württemberg and thus come south. His father Friedrich had been born in 1807; his mother Amalie Macaire d'Hogguer was from a French refugee family that had settled in Germany before the French Revolution.[1]

Friedrich von Zeppelin was lord steward of the Prince of Hohenzollern-Sigmaringen until his marriage in 1834; thereafter he worked his own estate. It was into this family that Ferdinand Adolf Heinrich August von Zeppelin was born on July 8, 1838. He was born and raised in Constance, on the shores of the Lake of Constance, which lies on the border between Germany and Switzerland. His youth would end in 1852 with the death of his mother, whose sweetness, intelligence, and lively interest in those around her made her a favorite of all who knew her.[2] The following year, young Count Zeppelin entered the polytechnic school in Stuttgart. However, he spent only two years here before switching to the military school in Ludwigsburg, some 10 kilometers north of Stuttgart. Two years later, he left this school with the rank of lieutenant and entered the army. Just one year later, however, he was granted leave to go to the University of Tübingen, where he studied government, mechanical engineering, and chemistry. Unfortunately, he had to break off his studies to take part in the Second Italian War of Independence, where he served as an engineer.[3]

It was in 1863, while still an officer in the army of Württemberg, that he would take another leave to observe the American Civil War. He traveled to New York and then managed to talk himself onto a French military ship departing for Baltimore. On the way, he unpacked a dozen bottles of excellent German white wine that he had brought along, and proceeded to empty these with the officers. One by one, the officers left to take care of their duties, eventually leaving only Zeppelin and a young cadet. Once they had finished the last bottle, they decided to go for a tour of the ship, ending up high in the rigging of the ship, a place that Zeppelin, as a cavalry officer, had never been before. He fortunately did not lose his balance during this late-night adventure.[4]

Once in Washington, he received permission to embed himself in the Union army. Wearing his uniform of Württemberg, he traveled from one army to the next, and even found himself helping out during an attack on General J. E. B. Stuart. Only his skill as a rider saved him when the flanking maneuver went awry.[5]

During this time, he heard of Thaddeus S. C. Lowe's work and was interested in trying out the balloons for himself. Lowe was a self-taught balloonist whose first ascent had been circa 1858.[6] He had made a name for himself in April 1861, when he flew 350 miles from Ohio to South Carolina and less than two months later, he took the same balloon to Washington to sell his services to the Union. After filling his balloon from city gas mains, he made several ascensions from both the grounds of the Smithsonian and the White House. He even sent message down from the balloon via telegraph. It was enough to convince President Lincoln to use Lowe's technology in battle. While the first ascent, later that June, went well—Confederate scouts believed Lowe's balloon meant that there large numbers of troops nearby and retreated—the second ended poorly when, after a successful mission, he was fired upon by Union troops and ended up landing behind enemy lines, necessitating a rescue by other troops. Nonetheless, Lincoln had had General Winfield Scott create a balloon corps with Lowe at its helm. Since then, Lowe's services had proven useful in numerous battles.[7]

Lowe wanted to help the young German officer, but had explicit instructions from General McClellan not to allow any passengers on his missions. Zeppelin, whose brief during this time seems to have been vague at best, visited other regiments and eventually began traveling through the north, starting at Niagara Falls and heading west. In St. Paul, Minnesota, Zeppelin found himself in a hotel that overlooked an open lot that housed, at the time, a balloonist: John H. Steiner. Steiner had served in the balloon corps with Lowe for about a year, but had quit the previous year when there were continual problems with being paid, as well as differences of opinion with General Pope, under whom he was serving, about the role of balloons in war. That Zeppelin and Steiner, who was also German, would meet was almost foreordained, and when Steiner began to give balloon flights, the young count was one of his passengers. Zeppelin would write to his parents that evening, "Just now I ascended with Prof. Steiner, the famous aeronaut, to an altitude of two or three hundred meters. The ground is exceptionally fitted for demonstrating the importance of the balloon in military reconnaissance."[8]

Zeppelin had some idea of being allowed to take a nontethered flight, but the source of lifting gas that Steiner had was unable to supply sufficient amounts for this—or any other flights—to happen, and so both Zeppelin and Steiner moved on. Zeppelin, however, never forgot about that day, and though it would take some time, he would eventually return to the dream of flight and make it practicable.[9]

Back in Germany, Zeppelin would return to the army, get married, and serve during the Franco-Prussian War, where he took part in the very first action of the war: leading a twelve-man team through Alsace to determine the location of French troops. At first, their tactics of simply galloping through the towns, grabbing what information they could, worked, but after a day of this, they were surrounded by French troops at an estate. Zeppelin was the only one able to flee, stealing a French horse along the way. He managed to elude his pursuers, spending a night at another farm, before returning to German lines with important information as the disposition of French troops.[10]

Later in the war, he noted the use of balloons by those in Paris to escape the city. When the wind was right, Parisians would send up balloons that would drift toward their compatriots outside the German encirclement. Zeppelin understood implicitly that this worked only in one direction: out of the city. Any attempt to get anything into the city would require a dirigible balloon, which did not yet exist, but Zeppelin filed it away as an idea to work on in the future.[11] It was not until 1874 that he would write for the first time his idea of building a rigid airship. And he would not begin turning this into reality until his retirement from the military in 1891.

Zeppelin knew enough about flight that simply trying to build a balloon or an airship with no careful planning was bound to fail. He thus hired Theodor Kober, who had studied at the same school as Zeppelin in Stuttgart and had since graduation worked for the Riedinger balloon factory in Augsburg, not far from Stuttgart in the kingdom of Bavaria.[12] Kober had the right engineering background to attempt what Zeppelin wanted to do. He would spend the next year making calculations and adjusting the plans. Most importantly, he realized that there was no way that a single gondola could be made that was light enough to be able to be lifted, so he had the airship designed with two gondolas below, front and rear.

With this new drawing in hand, Zeppelin went to the Prussian War Ministry, who rejected out of hand the opportunity to pay to build it. In spite of this setback, Zeppelin applied for and received a patent for a "dirigible airtrain" on August 31, 1895.[13] In 1898, he founded a stock corporation to build an airship using his system. He raised one million marks for this purpose.

It would take two years to build the airship, which he gave the hull number LZ 1, for Luftschiff (airship) Zeppelin 1. He first had to find a suitable location for the effort, and chose Manzell, on the shores of the Lake of Constance, with the shed for the airship to be built on the water itself, allowing for easier entrance of the airship. He had calculated the wind resistance of this huge craft and realized that side winds would be hugely problematical. As work proceeded in the shop, on land, and the shed, curiosity among those nearby rose, and newspapers all around the globe published articles based more on fantasy than fact, but all testifying to the hold that Zeppelin had on people's imagination.

Finally, on June 30, 1900, it was time. A huge crowd assembled and waited. And waited. In the end, the Zeppelin people had to admit that they had been unable to fill the airship with enough lifting gas and that the flight would have to be postponed.[14]

Two days later, the reassembled crowd would be rewarded by the sight of the airship being towed out of its hangar on a raft. At three minutes to eight, the ropes were cut and it rose into the air. While there was some difficulty in untangling the ropes, the airship did eventually fly, traveling some 5 kilometers to Immenstaad, just west on the shore of the lake.[15]

Further trials proved even more successful, with Zeppelin flying 27 kilometers per hour, much faster than the previous record. Unfortunately, after two such flights, the money Zeppelin had raised was gone and he was forced to scrap the ship, though Zeppelin did feel that he had learned much from the flights.

It would be five and a half years before Zeppelin would take to the sky again in LZ 2. Unfortunately, the results were similarly mixed as with LZ 1. On its first flight, the height rudder got stuck and the airship had to make an emergency landing. While it was tied down on the ground, a thunderstorm destroyed the ship. In spite of this setback, *Scientific American* opined "that this trip was undertaken merely as a tentative trial. Count von Zeppelin never intended to immediately travel back and forth over the Bodensee [the German name of the Lake of Constance] for hours, but all the details were thoroughly to be tested, first in shorter and then in longer flights."[16]

Scientific American's opinion was endorsed ten months later when LZ 3 flew. It would be far more successful than either of its predecessors and would be eventually turned over to the army, who gave it the name *Z I*.

With this success under his belt, Zeppelin built a newer and better version. Given the hull number LZ 4, it was to be flown for a twenty-four-hour endurance flight before being turned over to the army. Halfway through the flight, an engine broke, which meant that they had to land. The landing, which took place near Echterdingen, Württemberg, was unproblematic, but while the repairs were proceeding, a gust of wind pulled the airship from its moorings and drove it into the trees surrounding the landing site.

This was almost the end of Zeppelin. Out of money, and with none forthcoming from the army for a wrecked ship, it looked like his dream was dead. But then, the people of Germany started sending him money—people who believed as much as he in the future of airships and who wanted him to continue his experiments. The money allowed Zeppelin to found the Zeppelin airship factory corporation.[17]

It would take some time. The first three airships that he built for DELAG, the German Airship Travel Corporation that the business manager of the Zeppelin corporation, Alfred Colsman, founded to provide passenger service, all failed to live up to expectations. The first, hull number LZ 6 but never really given a name, was turned over to DELAG after completing almost forty successful flights. DELAG then flew excursion flights from several cities, completing thirty-four revenue flights. However, it was mishandled while being parked in its hangar after less than six months in service. The second airship destined for DELAG, the *Deutschland* managed only two successful flights for paying passengers. Sources vary as to how many passengers were on board for these two flights, but those that did traveled in style:

> The airship is equipped with a restaurant which will supply the passengers with a buffet service such as afforded on railroad trains. The passengers sit in a carpeted and mahogany walled cabin from the windows of which they can view the scenery as they sweep along.[18]

On its third flight, on which DELAG had invited numerous journalists, the motor failed and the airship crashed into the Teutoburg Forest in Prussia. Fortunately, no passengers were injured; only one crew member was slightly injured during the exit from the airship.

The next airship, LZ 7, which reused as many parts of LZ 7 as it could and was given the name *Deutschland II*, made twenty-four flights over a month and a half before being caught in a gust of air while leaving its shed and ending up bent and lying with its bow up on the roof of the hangar. Once again, no passengers were injured, even though they were already on board and had to be helped by the local fire brigade to reach the safety of the ground.[19]

Finally, LZ 10 was launched in June 1911. Once the usual test flights had been completed and it had been christened *Schwaben*, DELAG began taking paying passengers. Over the next year, it would fly 218 flights and take 1,553 passengers.[20] While it, too, eventually succumbed to fire after being pulled loose by winds, it had shown that it was possible to make money with airships, leading to the building of *Viktoria Luise*, *Hansa*, and *Sachsen* over the next two years.[21]

The *Viktoria Luise* would complete more than four hundred flights ferrying passengers by the end of 1913,[22] while the *Hansa* would make almost four hundred passenger flights, including one flight from Hamburg to Copenhagen and back on September 19, 1912—the first commercial, international flight for a Zeppelin.[23] The *Sachsen* would complete 419 flights, including one that featured the first parachute jump from an airship.[24]

However, even as the civilian flights were making a name for him, Zeppelin continued to pursue military ventures—in fact, he wanted nothing to do with the commercialization of his invention, one of the reasons why DELAG was an entirely separate corporation from the Zeppelin Company. Between the delivery of the *Sachsen* and the beginning of the war a little over a year later, Zeppelin finished eight airships for the military—six for the army and two for the navy. At the outbreak of war, the three remaining DELAG airships were also impressed into service.

In spite of this, the military had only ten airships at the beginning of the war, two of which were immediately decommissioned as being obsolete.

The army airships were given names that consist of a Z followed by a number, while the navy used the letter L to distinguish their airships. All Zeppelins also had a hull number, essentially a serial number that would help keep track of which airship was which, even after being renamed. The army, later in the war, would use the hull number as the airship name, then for reasons of confusion, began adding 30 to the number. Thus the airship with hull number LZ 90 was given the name *LZ 120*.

All participants had begun the new war with great hopes for a quick victory. The Germans attacked Belgium on August 4, in order to sweep through this country and into northern France. They soon found themselves slowed by the series of fortresses surrounding the city of Liège, just inside the border. It was time to try out a new weapon that Germany had been integrating into its armed forces since 1908: the Zeppelin. The army's *Z VI*, which had been delivered in November of the previous year, took off from its base near Cologne two days later and flew about 100 kilometers southwest and over the embattled city. In 1916, a German author described the flight:

> The airship Z VI delivered an exceptional performance in the fight around Liège and was successful in its attack. The first bomb was dropped from a height of six hundred meters. It was a dud. The airship then dropped down to three hundred meters and dropped a further twelve bombs, which all immediately exploded. The city of Liège was thus soon burning in several places. All bombs were dropped out of the rear gondola by a sergeant of the crew. On their return to Cologne, he was honored by thousands of spectators. He was the first Zeppelin crewman to receive the Iron Cross.[25]

However, in this description, the author was taking some liberties with the truth. Since they did not have bombs, they threw out the explosives they had: artillery shells. In order to drop these, they had had to reduce altitude, and found themselves fired upon by small arms, making it prudent that the airship turn around and begin its return trip. As they reached German lines, it became clear that the airship had been hit numerous times, and that they were losing lift rapidly. While they managed to stay in the air for almost 100 kilometers, they had been pushed farther south, and finally had to land in a town halfway between Cologne and Bonn, about 20 kilometers due south of their destination. While the airship was lost, none of the crew were killed.[26] It was, in short, not an auspicious beginning to the war in the air for Count Zeppelin's creations.

The navy began the war with only one airship: *L 3*, hull number LZ 24. While they would also receive the DELAG airships *Viktoria Luise* and *Hansa*, both of those were immediately relegated to training status. In spite of its lonely status, *L 3* went to work. About a week after the attack on Liège, *L 3* while on patrol successfully spotted a Dutch warship. It would continue to fly reconnaissance flights over the North Sea, though often without any great success, either due to the weather or the fact that there were no allied ships to be found.[27]

On August 21, the army airship *Z IX* was sent to bomb Dunkirk, Antwerp, Zeebrügge, Calais, and Lille.[28] This was quite a tall order, as the ship could carry all of ten bombs. The divergence between the airship's capabilities and the missions set for it would continue to be a major problem for this new technology in the early going of the war.

Two days later, Zeppelins were once again brought into play, this time for a reconnaissance mission. All across the Vosges Mountains in the Alsace region of Germany that France had invaded at the start of the war, French troops were retreating. The German high command wanted to know where, exactly, these troops were fleeing to—once again, a possible mission for these new weapons. Two army airships, *Z VII* and *Z VIII*, both of a newer class than that *Z VI*, whose flight had ended so ignominiously two weeks earlier, were sent out to observe the French retreat.

Unfortunately, the airships were shot up on their way over the troops—most likely by their own men as well—and both crashed. While *Z VII* managed to land behind German lines, *Z VIII* landed in between the fronts, and the crew had to make their way back to German lines on foot.[29]

On the eastern front, with its more open field, airships were increasingly brought into action, often with the same results as in the west. For instance, while *Z V* managed to bomb Mława on August 28, it was badly hit and had to land. The crew was captured by Russians and sent to Siberia.[30]

August ended on a high note for airships: the *SL II*, an airship built by the Schütte-Lanz Company and used by the Austro-Hungarian army, completed a reconnaissance flight on August 30. Schütte-Lanz, founded by engineer Johann Schütte and industrialist Karl Lanz, was Zeppelin's biggest competitor. Starting in 1911, they had built rigid airships. From the start, they had the hulls with a streamlined form that Zeppelins would only acquire in the R class like *LZ 120*. Otherwise, they were far behind the Zeppelins, with only two models built before the outbreak of war—and the only *SL II* still in service, as the first had been destroyed during a storm. The biggest difference between the two types of airships was that the Schütte-Lanz airships used plywood for their skeletons, rather than aluminum.[31]

In spite of *SL II*'s success, the final tally for the first month of the war for the airships used by the German military was not great. Of the airships the German military started the war with, four had been lost—and only one, a new navy Zeppelin *L 4*, had been built. However, the production in Friedrichshafen was gearing up, and seven airships were scheduled for completion before the end of the year.

On the ground, the German advance through Belgium and France that had preceded inexorably throughout August was stopped on the Marne River in the middle of September. Troops from both sides now began shifting ever farther northwest and toward the English Channel in a series of flanking maneuvers. The sea was reached on October 19, and major movement on the western front ceased. On the eastern front, while the distances covered attacking and retreating were greater, the overall result was the same—no party could gain the upper hand.

Attack flights continued, however. On the eastern front, *Z IV*, which had been in Königsberg in East Prussia at the beginning of the war, and then flown reconnaissance missions on the western front for two months before being sent to the east again, flew over the Prussian city of Insterburg, which had been captured by Russian troops in August. Dropping bombs on Russian soldiers, the airship did little in the way of damage but did raise the morale of the Germans in the town. It continued to fly against targets, most frequently Warsaw, though by the beginning of the following year, after taking considerable damage in an attack on Lyck in East Prussia, another German city captured by Russia in the early days of the war, the airship was retired from active service and turned into a training ship.[32]

On October 19, the navy airship *L 5* became the first to get over the English Channel.[33] There has been great interest in attacking England, but so far the airships had been entirely focused on the battles raging on the ground. Furthermore, the Kaiser was concerned about bombing his own family, so there was some reluctance here. Instead of following up on this, the flights continued over the continent. On October 26, Paris was attacked for the first time by *Z X*. One of the newest airships, it had flown for the first time less than two weeks earlier.[34]

In the new year, the order finally came to attack England. The first attack, mounted by four navy Zeppelins, failed due to the weather. On January 19, three airships started, two from outside Hamburg, one from the airship base in Nordholz in the very north of Germany, destination England. While one of the airships had to turn back before reaching the English channel due to a broken crankshaft, the other two, *L 3* and *L 4*, continued on. Shortly before 9:00 p.m., *L 3* would become the first German airship over Britain. After ascertaining his location, Captain Fritz would point his airship at Yarmouth, a British naval base, on which it then dropped six explosive and seven incendiary bombs. *L 4* also made it to the coast and dropped several bombs on locations that the captain, Magnus Count von Platen-Hallermund, thought either had fired on him or were somehow militarily important. That he only managed to bomb a few small insignificant villages was something that the British press made much of and, indeed, did concern the German higher-ups as well. Nonetheless, the two airships had made it over England and pointed the way to further attacks.[35]

An order of February 12 of the Kaiser gave more explicit instructions as to what could and could not be attacked. He remained worried about his family across the English Channel and urged that only military targets be pursued.[36] It would be several months before these attacks would be carried out, however.

The first attempt under these new orders occurred on April 14. A single navy airship, *L 9*, took off from Hage, on the North Sea coast in northeastern Germany. Its brief was to scout the area to the west, but when the weather continued to be good, the commander, Heinrich Mathy, decided that he would continue on to England. While he was aiming for Tyne and its shipyards, he actually arrived at Blyth, a mining town well away from the shipyards. He dropped bombs nonetheless, with only slight effect. They arrived safely at their base early the following morning.[37]

In spite of its fairly poor result, Major Peter Strasser, who had become head of airships when the first head, Friedrich Metzing, had died when the first navy Zeppelin *L 1* had crashed in 1913, decided to follow up with another raid that very same day. While three navy Zeppelins made it over England this time, none of them dropped bombs where they thought they would—one dropped none at all, as they did not even realize they had made landfall.[38]

Over the next month, the only flights over England were done by Erich Linnarz in *LZ 38*. Starting with their flight on April 29, when they become the first army airship to reach England, the crew made five successful flights, with the one May 31 being the first to actually reach London—in spite of having one of their gas bags badly damaged as they crossed over Ramsgate. They spent less than twenty minutes over the capital but started a number of fires throughout it. They were the first enemy airship to manage an attack here.[39]

After this, more and more attacks were launched against England in general and London in particular. Starting on August 8, 1915, Zeppelins were sent over England every few days, though no more than three at a time. On August 17, two navy airships repeated *LZ 38*'s feat, to be followed in early September by a three army airship attack. This phase ended in the middle of September with a single airship, *L 13*, attacking England. Until late March of the following year, airships flew against England only rarely, though a late January 1916 raid was the biggest of the war with nine naval Zeppelins attacking. April of 1916 is a busy time again, with multiple airships, both army and navy, flying.

This burst of activity died down on May 2, and it was not until July 28, 1916, almost exactly one year before *LZ 120* would take off, that another attack was started. From then until early September, there were continual raids, with up to nine airships flying at once.

On September 2, 1916, a combined army and navy attack sent fourteen airships, including two built by the Schütte-Lanz company, over London. One of these, *SL 11*, was shot down by William Leefe Robinson flying a B.E.2c plane and firing incendiary bullets. It was the first German airship shot down over England.[40]

It would hardly be the last, and from then until the end of the year, five further Zeppelins would be destroyed by British fighters.

In this time, another front would open, in the southeast of Europe against Romania after that country joined the war on the allied side on August 27, 1916. Four army airships—*LZ 101*, *LZ 81*, *LZ 97*, and *LZ 86*—were sent there and had decent success in dropping bombs on Bucharest. One author purporting to be the first officer of an airship even published a book later that year extolling the successes on this front earlier that year.[41]

LZ 101 was the first to attack, managing to drop bombs on Bucharest the day after Romania had declared war. However, even in this backwater, life was not easy. *LZ 81* with captain Felix Jacobi—Lehmann's brother-in-law—at the helm was shot up enough that it has to do an emergency landing that the airship did not survive. *LZ 86* had a more successful flight on September 4, but crashed on landing, an accident that killed not only the captain but eight of his crew. So, within a week of the new front opening, half of the airships had gone out of action.[42]

It was probably this last blow that made the army reconsider its airship bet. While they would still accept four new airships, including *LZ 120*, the bulk of the Zeppelin production now went to the navy.

Count Zeppelin himself would not see this ignominious end of the army airships, since he had died on March 8, 1917. While he had been involved in the day-to-day operations of his various companies to the end, he had also ensured that there were sufficient people working beneath him who could continue his work, including Hugo Eckener and Alfred Colsman—and, beginning shortly, Ernst Lehmann.

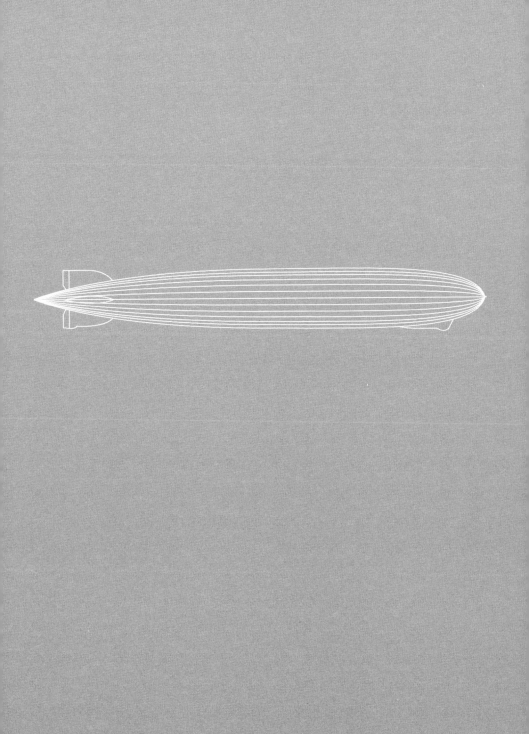

CHAPTER 3
JULY 27, 6:00 A.M.–JULY 27, 12:00 NOON

German torpedo boat photographed from a Zeppelin. These small and maneuverable ships were used to get close to the opposing ships before they could be fired upon to then shoot torpedoes. They were built low to the water to make spotting them even more difficult.

Robert Pohl wakes up early the next morning, well before 7:00 a.m., and still, thankfully, in his hammock. He had slept well, in spite of the engine noise, and the continuous back and forth of the crew on the gangway next to his resting place. Climbing gingerly out of his hammock, he regains the relative security of the catwalk, makes his way to the ladder leading to the front car, and swings onto it.

The ladder, as he knows from long experience, lurches down a few centimeters, which gives power, via a few wires and pulleys, to open the hatches both in the ship's keel and below in the gondola. Bracing himself against the rush of air that greets him as he emerges from the keel, Pohl carefully climbs down the ladder. As always, he gives thanks for the way the ladder is situated—in such a way that he is pressed against the ladder as he descends the 2.5 meters to the cabin. The cool morning air blows away any residual tiredness, and he emerges into the gondola fully awake and hungry.

His first stop, however, is the navigator's desk, situated directly next to the ladder. The navigator shows him their location on a map: just a bit past Kolberg, on the south shore of the Baltic Sea. Pohl makes a quick calculation of the distance traveled: they have managed only about 300 kilometers in the seven-plus hours since departure, or about half of what *LZ 120* is capable of. This in spite of the fact that the airship has been running on all six engines throughout the night. Only now does the crew shut down three of the engines, in accordance with Lehmann's plans to conserve fuel and thereby increase the length of time aloft.

Pohl peers out of the window, where he can just make out Kolberg, the spa town and port located on the banks of the Persante River. Today mainly known as a resort, well used by Berliners, it had, over one hundred years earlier, seared itself into German consciousness when it had held out for over two months against Napoleon's overwhelming force during his conquest of Germany.[1] In the intervening years, it has become a symbol of German military prowess, and has spawned plays[2] and books[3] celebrating the siege. As Pohl's eyes sweep the landscape, he wonders which battles of the current war will be famous one hundred years from now. The battle of Tannenberg, where his friend Rudolf Hörnigk had fought. Maybe the Galician breakthrough he had celebrated just a few days earlier. He reflects that it all depends on the outcome of the war whether German victories will be celebrated or decried. Pohl sighs. Time for breakfast.

Fortunately, he is well provisioned. In spite of the increasing desperation of the civilian population for food, even as Pohl has assisted his mother in undermining the rationing in many small ways over the last year, the army is still well stocked, and the food on board, while not gourmet by any description, is quite plentiful: one double pan bread (the basic ration for German armies for centuries), rye with bran (though by now probably stretched with substances Pohl tried not to think about), two boxes of cookies, three slabs of chocolate, a piece of cheese, a half kilogram of potted meat, three smoked sausages weighing a total of 2 kilograms, and a quarter kilogram of lard. To drink, he has six liters of coffee and three bottles of seltzer water. Settling down on a creaking wicker chair, he gets to work.

Pohl had learned early on in the war to eat when food was available. In the very first letter to his mother after the beginning of the war, he wrote of a food shortage, one he believed was due to the trains being used for the war effort. Pohl had assured his mother that this was just temporary, but as the war stretched on, and rationing became more prevalent, he had often assisted his mother in circumventing the rules put into place. She, for her part, sent him a continuous supply of food boxes, allowing him to supplement his meager rations. The Allied blockade of Germany, coupled with the conscription of farmworkers into the army, along with a general focus on industrial production, had exacerbated food shortages. The situation had worsened the previous fall, when weather killed the potato crop and turnips, rather than being animal feed, became a staple of Germans' diet. This indignity had caused food riots. Just five days before liftoff, Pohl had sent his sister a letter requesting she buy 12 kilograms of oranges for 50 marks and hide them in such a way that even if house searches become reality, they would not be found. In the same letter, he requested she not eat the Kriegsmus, an ersatz jam made of rutabagas and sugar, which "smelled of boot polish and tasted of wood shavings,"[4] but instead to use it as sweetener for other things. In short, food insecurity has become an everyday topic, and the knowledge that his food was assured for at least the time aboard the Zeppelin gives Pohl a certain satisfaction.

As he eats, Pohl looks around the cabin. In contrast to other Zeppelins he had been in, it is simply one large open space. Lehmann had requested the removal of internal walls in order to increase the size.[5] Only the small, separate, soundproofed room for the wireless operator has been kept. While the officers busy themselves at the front of the cabin, the rear is taken up by a table and a number of armchairs in which to eat, or read or talk or do pretty much anything except smoke.

The only minus of this otherwise comfortable spot is the continual and overwhelming noise of the engine, which is separated from the radio room by just a thin wall. Only when this motor is turned off as part of Lehmann's attempt to conserve fuel for the long trip is normal conversation possible. Pohl is reminded of an attempt Lehmann had made of playing his guitar in the quietest part of the Zeppelin—the radio room. It had not been a success, while the sound dampening was sufficient for normal radio work, it made listening to music an entirely unpleasant experience, and Pohl had soon asked him to desist.

After breakfast, Pohl approaches the front of the car where the second watch is now in charge of the airship. He has a look at the barograph, a simple barometer connected to a stylus that draws a line showing the current altitude on a cylinder of paper. The cylinder is in turn connected to a clockwork, and so their altitude can be read out for any moment since takeoff. The whole apparatus is connected to the struts making up the gondola via a series of rubber bands that holds it at a comfortable position to read. In spite of the previous evening's weather, the elevator control operator had managed to keep to 200 meters throughout that time. The perfect height, Pohl feels, to examine the landscape below.

Now over the water, and with no further land to look at, Pohl asks whether he can try his hand at steering the airship. The pilots, who have just set course for a small island in the middle of the Baltic Sea and with the weather, while still somewhat hazy, no longer any danger to the vessel, acquiesce. They have Pohl step up to the waist-high wheel and have him look around. Surrounding him is a 50-centimeter-deep ledge that stretches around him, behind that the windows, which were, as he has ascertained, not made of glass, but the far lighter cellulose acetate. From this vantage point, he can see 270 degrees around, all of which shows equally empty sea. To his left stands the elevator control operator, to his right the navigator at a small table.

Pohl turns the wheel. The wires, which he had seen snaking through the keel of the ship, transmit this movement all the way back to the 26 square meter flaps at the stern, and they tilt slightly. *LZ 120* reacts smoothly to this, veering slightly out of its path. Pohl turns the steering wheel the other way, once again the giant airship follows his command. The officers then have Pohl return to the original bearing. While he enjoys the responsiveness of the airship, Pohl is also fully aware of the many others—particularly the elevator control operator, responsible for keeping the airship at the altitude Lehmann has ordered—in flying *LZ 120*, and he is happy to turn over the controls back to the professionals. He remains near the pilot, however, who points out the island of Usedom, which separates the Baltic Sea from the Stettiner Haff at the mouth of the Oder River, to their left.

For this section of the trip, the weather allows for more swift progress, and they arrive at the Greifswalder Oie at 8:00 a.m. Situated just north of the western tip of Usedom, it is a small island notable mainly for the large lighthouse that has guarded the island since the 1850s.[6] Today, with the weather still cloudy and hazy, it makes for a clear target to aim for. From there, the airship continues to follow the coastline at a healthy distance, turning sharply southeast and into the Bay of Greifswald and toward the city of the same name at its end. Greifswald is actually 5 kilometers up the river Wyk from the bay itself, well protected from the winter storms that mark the Baltic Sea.

Pohl knows Greifswald because of its university, which had been founded in 1456,[7] making it the fourth-oldest in Germany. He mainly knows it as the location of Professor Johannes Stark, a physicist with whom he has had several, generally unpleasant, interactions. Nonetheless, Stark is well known for having asked Albert Einstein for a paper on relativity in 1907, and it was working on this paper that had given Einstein the impetus to think about the problem in a new way, which had resulted in his 1915 paper on general relativity.

Previously at the university was Günther Falckenberg, who had been with Pohl in the physics department in the Berlin University before the war. Today, Falckenberg is assisting in wireless telegraphy in the navy.

The university is also the where Johann Mannhardt had received his doctorate in law. Mannhardt had been at high school with Pohl, and he had played in important role in the early days of the war in spiriting their mutual friend Otto Michahelles out of the United States. Michahelles had been working in Colombia for the Hamburg America Line, and with the outbreak of war had wanted to return to Germany. He had gotten as far as New York when further travel was forbidden. Mannhardt had then helped get both of them onto a Danish steamer, with papers that claimed that they were able seamen. They had worked their way across the ocean, steering the ship, cleaning, and operating the engines. They had completed the voyage in spite of being stopped by an English ship whose captain demanded to see the papers of all of those on board. Pohl had written the whole story to his mother in a letter on September 25, 1914.

The airship continues to follow the shoreline, which takes it to the southwest corner of Rügen, Germany's largest island.[8] Pohl had last seen this island the previous year, when he had flown over it on a Zeppelin being transferred from Wildeshausen in the north of Germany near Bremen to Kovno in German occupied Russia. In a letter he wrote to his mother on November 17, 1916, he had referred to the island as "adventurously shaped" and had seen a seagoing steamer near the Stubbenkammer chalk cliffs located on the northeast corner of the island. The ship had been stranded there, but with mysterious cables running into the water. Lehmann had actually flown circles around it in a failed effort to determine what was going on. This time, the plan is to circumnavigate the island, but the weather does not allow it. With rain on the western horizon, the decision is made to head northeast, toward the island of Bornholm.

It is time to go exploring. In spite of the sheer size of the airship, there are not that many places to go to, but Pohl has yet to visit one of them—the platform on the very top of the vessel. Getting there requires returning to the walkway in the keel of the ship and then climbing the ladder that leads straight up just aft of the ladder down to the main gondola. It is not an ascent for the faint of heart.

Immediately upon leaving the familiar triangular walkway, Pohl finds himself within a narrow tube made of duralumin slats that stretches up 25 meters. Surrounding the tube on the left and right are the giant bags that hold the lifting gas. Pohl tries not to think of the immense amount of highly flammable gas that is just a few layers of goldbeater's skin and cotton away from him.

After several minutes climbing, he exits the square hatchway just aft of the gunner's platform. To the front of the ship stretches a trapezoidal platform of corrugated aluminum, about 10 meters deep and 6 at its widest. Directly next to the hatch, left and right of the center of the ship, are two mounts for machine guns with semicircular platforms surrounding them, while farther forward there is a single mount with a circular platform around it.

While it would be a most uncomfortable place to visit with no protection, what with wind streaming past him at about 50 kilometers per hour, there is a U-shaped small canvas windscreen that surrounds the front of the platform. While the windscreen is a little less than a meter high, it redirects the air as to pass some three meters over the heads of the people standing behind it, allowing them to stand comfortably and—when called upon—fire the machine guns.

Below the wind screen, and extending back another couple of meters, is the railing, a simple arrangement of duralumin pipes that Pohl always felt was more for show than an actual safety feature. Nonetheless, they give him something to hold onto as he walks around the perimeter of the platform.

Finding himself alone on the top of the airship, Pohl gets into his favorite position: stretched out on his stomach, which allows him to look down around the side of the airship and to the water far below. Visible from there was the island of Bornholm. A good-sized island that guards the narrows between Sweden and Germany, it actually belongs to Denmark, although it had been owned to all of the above in its turbulent history, finally choosing Denmark in 1660.[9] With 600 square kilometers and under 45,000 people, it consists almost entirely of granite, and it is dotted with farms that attempt to grow food on the thin soil.[10]

Lehmann steers the *LZ 120* along the southern shore, then turned north to proceed along the western side of the island to the northernmost tip of the island. From here, he flies a few circles so that all could see the Helligdomklipper, granite cliffs that stretch along the northern side of the island and are the principle attraction on the island.[11] Having completed this tour, Lehmann then sets course for the Danish island of Falster, 160 kilometers due west of Bornholm. The real destination is beyond this island, however: Flensburg, more exactly the town of Glücksburg just northwest of it, which is where Pohl's mother lives.

CHAPTER 4
ROBERT WICHARD POHL

Robert Wichard Pohl and his sister, Margot Eleanor Pohl, in 1908

The path taken by *LZ 120* over the past twelve hours mirrored the path taken by Pohl's father fifty years earlier. While Pohl had done it without stopping or even touching the ground, his father had done so in slow, deliberate steps. Eugen Robert Pohl was born in Insterburg in 1846, the son of Robert Pohl, circuit judge, and Louise Marie Pohl, *née* Schmidt. He grew up in Gumbinnen, a small town of less than 10,000 inhabitants 125 kilometers east of Seerappen. Gumbinnen was at the time almost literally the end of the line. Only the towns of Stallupöhnen and Eydtkuhnen separated it from the border of the Russian Empire 35 kilometers to the east. This became particularly relevant five years after his birth when a train track was laid through town, connecting St. Petersburg with Königsberg.

Pohl's family had been in the area for many generations. His great-great-great-grandfather Gottfried Pohl had been in charge of the church school in Bilderweitschen, just 5 kilometers northwest of Eydtkuhnen, in the early eighteenth century. Gottfried Pohl's descendants all lived in this northeastern-most corner of Prussia for the next century, moving to Tilsit and Königsberg before Eugen Robert Pohl's father had moved to Gumbinnen.

While Gumbinnen was all that young Pohl needed at first, it was soon clear that he would need to move farther west to gain an education. His first stop was 90 kilometers north to Tilsit, but then he moved west to Königsberg, his father's birthplace, then on to Danzig and finally Berlin, where he first worked in the F. Wöhlert factory, then studied engineering at the Royal Technical University in Charlottenburg. His studies were interrupted by the Franco-Prussian War, in which he served in the German Navy. He was unable to finish his studies thereafter, so instead moved to Scotland, where, after a brief time working on locomotives, he found work in several of the many shipyards on the Clyde. After seven years of absorbing the knowledge there, he returned to Germany. Sadly, he first suffered a major injury, which cost him ten months in a hospital.[1]

When he had recovered, he began working for the Woermann Linie, a company responsible for the German West Africa trade. His longtime connection here ensured that his house was full of African souvenirs. Over the years, he also added posts at the Bureau Veritas, who ensured compliance with generally accepted standards in shipbuilding, as well as for the Hamburg-Amerikanische Packetfahrt-Aktien-Gesellschaft—better known as the Hamburg America Line—and was responsible for ensuring that ships that they had built at shipyards across Europe (and particularly in Scotland) were built correctly.[2]

In Hamburg, he also met Martha Lange, the daughter of Wichard Lange, who had opened and was running a school. They married in 1882 and their first child was born on March 25, 1883. She was given the name Julie Eleanor. Sadly, Julie would die less than five months later.

A little over a year later, on August 10, 1884, they had another child. He was named Robert after his father (and grandfather) and Wichard after his mother's father. He was baptized on October 22 of that same year. Three and a half years later, his sister Margot Eleanor was born.

In 1892, a cholera epidemic swept through Hamburg. It would have a profound impact on the city, which made enormous efforts to clean up the water as well as improve drainage in response.[3] Pohl's reaction was a bit different: from then on, he refused to drink anything but bottled water.

Young Robert soon showed talent in academics. While he first attended his grandfather's school, he soon switched to the Hamburger Academic School of the Johanneum, the oldest and most prestigious high school in the city. It had been founded in 1529, and since had educated many of Germany's scientists, intellectuals, and leaders. Among them were Heinrich Hertz, who had proved the theory of electromagnetic waves proposed by James Clerk Maxwell. A nephew of Hertz's, Gustav Hertz was a few years behind Pohl at the school, and they had remained friendly. One of his teachers was Hermann Schubert, who had been at the school since 1876. Pohl, in a letter to his mother written May 15, 1903, admitted that he did not fully understand how much Schubert had taught him until he was studying more abstruse mathematics in college.

Even as a high school student, he showed an interest in physics, convincing his father to buy not only cast-off telegraph equipment from the imperial postal service, but also an x-ray tube, then a brand-new invention. He used this tube to peer inside not just his own hands and feet, but those of friends and family as well.

He received his Abitur in the spring of 1903 and immediately thereafter moved to Heidelberg to study physics. He also began his writing weekly letters to his mother that described not only his successes in school but his life in general.

The very first letter, written April 21, describes the house in which he found a room and how it was perfect for him: extremely clean not only in his rooms, but all the rooms of the house, and a wonderful view up and down the Neckar River, from the Bismarck tower to the northwest, all the way around to the Heidelberg castle to the east. Pohl's first days at the university were busy, not just in his studies, but in determining what sort of student he wanted to be, as a letter he wrote on April 26 to his father describes. A number of his colleagues from the Johanneum were there as well, and together they explored the town and what it had to offer. The biggest hurdle Pohl had to face was the question of beer. An integral part of German universities, he had never really acquired the taste for it. Even worse for him, it tended to be the cheapest item on a menu, and he worried that if he did not begin drinking it, he would soon be broke. The question of money was one that concerned him deeply in the early going, he had no interest in wasting his father's hard-earned cash.

Pohl was heavily recruited by a number of fraternities, but he soon decided that this lifestyle was not for him, that going to bed at 1:00 a.m. twice a week, even without having been drinking, would keep him from learning his differential equations. He was also entirely turned off when he heard from others that one of the fraternities was already mentioning him as a new member. He was therefore perfectly happy when lectures started and he could concentrate on actually learning something instead of spending the day idling about, as much as he had enjoyed that for the first few days.

Studying turned out to be a good decision for Pohl. His first physics professor was Georg Hermann Quincke, who had been a teacher for some forty years, as well as researching broad areas of the subject. Mathematics he learned from Leo Königsberger, who had been in the business as long as Quincke. Pohl particularly appreciated the latter's ability to make clear even the most abstruse topics. Of his teachers, probably the best-known was his philosophy teacher, Kuno Fischer, whose analysis of the different schools of philosophy would impact his many students over the years.

The only fly in the ointment in regards to his study of physics were the other students in his lecture, in particular the medical students, who were required to pass a physics exam later in their studies. The exam was of far lower level than what they were learning here, so many did not bother to attend the lectures and, when they did, they were there only in body, spending their time in class writing letters and working on other non-physics-related topics. Pohl, in the same letter in which he written about Schubert, wrote that he wished that they were in their own lectures, and let the actual physics students get on with it—with "it" being repeating experiments endlessly until they worked.

Pohl would also become somewhat politically active in this time, the eleventh election to the German parliament took place on June 16, 1903. Pohl went to a meeting of the social democrats and was quite taken by it at first, when they threw out the Russian students. However, the candidate that they had speak did not appeal to him at all as he gave a speech full of platitudes and lacking in grammar, as he wrote in a letter four days after the election.

In the end, Pohl only spent a semester in Heidelberg, transferring to Berlin in October of that year. He there became one of Professor Emil Warburg's students at the Friedrich-Wilhelm University. Warburg had been in Berlin for some ten years at this point, and had recently become the head of the new German Physical Society, of which Pohl became a member that year. It was in their proceedings that Pohl would publish his very first paper less than two years later: "About the Illumination of Ionized Gases."[4] It elaborated and extended work done by another physicist, Bernhard Walter, who lived and worked in Hamburg, having taught at the Johanneum many years earlier. Two weeks later, the same journal would publish Albert Einstein's paper on Brownian motion,[5] the second of three papers that made that year such an extraordinary one for him.

That same year, in spite of not having yet finished his doctoral thesis, Pohl was made an assistant in the physics department. He was, however, already deep into the research for his thesis, and had surprised himself in January of that year when he had given a talk on the subject and found himself able to formulate his thoughts on the fly. That same year he also moved to a new apartment just north of the famous victory column in the middle of Berlin's Tiergarten, a few minutes walk along the river to the physics institute.

Early in 1906, he turned in the first draft of his thesis to his adviser, Paul Drude. Unfortunately, in spite of the fact that Drude and others had read it, Drude forgot entirely about this, and it was not until being reminded of this fact in late April that a date was set to test Pohl on the subject, a crucial step in receiving his doctorate. On May 6 of that year, Drude took him through the wringer, then four days later he and two other colleagues repeated the procedure. On June 30, 1906, Pohl received his doctorate of philosophy with a thesis titled, "Über die Einwirkung stiller elektrischer Entladung auf Ammoniak und Sauerstoff" ("About the action of static electrical discharge on ammonia and oxygen").[6]

Five days later, Drude was dead. Pohl was one of the first to enter the room where he had shot himself, he found Drude's wife desperately trying to stanch the blood. Pohl did all he could to help, but it was too late.

A month later, Pohl went on vacation. Together with a fellow physics student, James Franck, they traveled to the Baltic Sea and the island of Hiddensee. They spent the days walking on the beach, swimming through the waves, climbing around the cliffs and napping. It was just the change that they needed.

Franck would complete his dissertation later that year, and the two of them would find themselves embroiled in a full-on scientific dispute the following year, when they discovered what they believed were mistakes in a book by Erich Marx, a professor of physics at the Leipzig university.[7] Marx had been attempting to determine the speed of propagation of x-rays. Franck and Pohl were certain that he was measuring something completely different.[8] For the next few months, rebuttals and re-rebuttals flew back and forth, and the two young scientists soon began to tire of the work. However, they were bolstered by remarks from their higher-ups in the physics department and, in particular, a short but devastating review of the original paper by Max von Laue,[9] another colleague who would soon thereafter win a Nobel Prize.

Between this and Pohl's actual work, he was stretched to the limit but still had the opportunity to go to parties at various colleagues as well as at friends of his parents from Hamburg, theater visits, and on one memorable occasion, an ice hockey game.

One other nonuniversity activity he participated was in elections. In 1907, a physicist and social democrat named Martin Arons was running for parliament. Unfortunately, he was doing so as a social democrat and had been kicked out of the university for being a member of that party. Pohl, Franck, and other students worked hard to ensure that Arons would not be elected, as Pohl wrote to his mother on January 26. While Arons lost the initial election by one thousand votes, his opponent would have to run again in a runoff, again, however, his opponent, Johannes Kaempf, won. Kaempf was the only member of parliament that year from Berlin who was not a Social Democrat. In 1912, he would be elected president of the German Parliament, a position he still held in 1917.

Even as Pohl's research moved forward, he found that his main work at the university was getting the experimental lectures going. When he had first been assigned to this, he had been appalled at the state of the apparatus used to demonstrate physical laws, and so set about getting proper devices built, ones that would simply and clearly show even those in the back row the principles of physics. He was rewarded with ever-increasing numbers of students in his lectures, though of course then he complained to his mother in a letter written October 31, 1908, about how many people were stuffed into the room, rendering the air quality poor.

In between all this work, he found the time to publish his first book. Published as a monograph in the series with the grandiose title "Science," Pohl looked at the state of the art in transmitting pictures over great distances using electricity.[10] In a slim, forty-five-page pamphlet, he examined all the technologies that had been invented for this purpose up until then. While some where entirely mechanical, requiring the use of a picture printed in three dimensions, others used the property of Selenium that its electrical properties changed when exposed to light to break down a picture into discrete elements whose brightness could be transmitted by electricity.

Whenever he could, however, he went back to his research, and continued to make good progress, although there were setbacks, as when he made what he thought was a new discovery, only to find out that Ernest Rutherford had beaten him to the punch. In his letters to his mother, he described all the setbacks as simply part of the whole process of science, that you just had to keep moving and something would work out.

In spite of his later fascination by flight, he did not spend much time dealing with this new technology. Only once, when there was a flying week at the Johannisthal Airport in October 1910, did he have the opportunity to see airplanes in action. He was utterly taken. At times, eight planes were in the air at once. He was particularly impressed by the monoplanes, which he compared to dragonflies. Their ability to take off, circle twice, and be so far up that they looked like birds also left him speechless. His primary takeaway, however, was that the shape of the wing was not so important. What really mattered was the quality of the engines. Those with well-tried engines could stay up for hours—while others were back on the ground in half an hour. The truth of this was proven by the German airplane pioneer Otto Lindpaintner, who managed to stay aloft for over eleven and a half hours, winning the War Minister's Grand Prize for his efforts. Pohl wrote to his mother immediately that afternoon, in order to give her the full understanding of the experience.

In 1911, Pohl gave his habilitation lecture, whose acceptance would also open the door to become a professor at a German university. For a subject, he returned to something that had intrigued him since he was a schoolboy: x-rays. As a topic he chose an overview of the current state of understanding of their properties. He did not sweat the details; he wrote to his mother, setting out the evening before he was to give the lecture to enjoy a spring evening with a friend on the water. The main work was done in a half-hour walk he took in the Tiergarten, between his apartment and the institute, directly before he started speaking. He was mainly worried about going on too long.

Shortly after this, and before he could be given his diploma, his father passed away while in their summer house in Glücksburg near Flensburg. When Pohl searched through his papers to find what his father had written him over the years, the last item was a letter congratulating him to his successful exam. A month later, on May 13, 1911, Pohl would become an official member of the Berlin University physics faculty. He held a lecture that day to mark the occasion, and when he received his habilitation diploma, it was this date that was printed on it.

Later that year, he traveled to England to attend the meeting of the British Association for the Advancement of Science in Portsmouth. While the trip was mainly a success, especially that he traveled with his colleague at the university, Frederick Lindemann, whose father was a well-known London businessman, whom Pohl had the opportunity to meet. The only negative of the meeting was that Pohl was denied the opportunity to visit the Royal shipyards because he was German.

The following year, Vieweg publishers, who had previously published his work on transmission of pictures, asked him produce a book on x-rays. He spent that spring working on it, on and off, then the summer with his family in their summer house finishing it up. It was published later that year.[11] Pohl was also made secretary of the German Physical Society, he had been vice-secretary for the previous two years. He would continue to hold this position into the war, while his friend James Franck would be vice-secretary.

In May 1914, a momentous change happen in the Berlin physics institute: Albert Einstein, probably the most famous physicist in the world, was made its head. His first lecture, held on May 19, was a crowded affair. Everyone at the institute wanted to hear what the great man was working on. Pohl attended and understood that Einstein was working on a new theory of gravitation. Unfortunately, once it got into the mathematical details, he was completely unable to understand any of it, though he bucked himself up with the thought that, of his colleagues, only Max Planck had any chance of following Einstein's train of thought. In spite of this, Pohl was pleased about Einstein's new job, as Einstein understood and supported the experimental work that Pohl and his younger colleagues were doing.

That evening, Pohl threw himself into the tails that he had received for his Abitur and went to his colleague Emil Warburg's house for a dinner in honor of their new chef. It was a warm evening, and once the dinner was over, Pohl and others were happy to make their way into the garden. At the French doors leading outside, Einstein spotted Pohl and requested that he join him in the darkest corner of the yard, to talk physics, away from the masses of people. Pohl happily obliged, and they remained there for the rest of the evening, except for one time when Pohl convinced Einstein that this party was, in fact, in his honor, and that he should thus be part of it. However, as they reached the house, Einstein saw the huge crowds around the punch bowl and fled to the darkest corner with Pohl again. Pohl complained to his mother that the upshot was that he had not been able to speak with anyone else at the party. The evening, however, was not quite over: after the party broke up, Einstein and Pohl were joined by Franck and they set off for a nearby cafe, partially to continue the physics talk, but mainly to celebrate the fact that this was the first time ever that Einstein had worn a coat and tails. Pohl and Franck consoled him with the assurance that his new article of clothing was unlikely to get worn out in his current position. The following day, Pohl sent a long letter to his mother describing the evening in great detail.

The real news of the year was, of course, the beginning of the war. Pohl was by no means prowar, on the day before German mobilization, he still held out hope that the war would not happen at all, writing to his mother only that the war "might" happen. However, once the shooting started, he was immediately greatly in favor of it and attempted to join up. But as an almost thirty-year-old with no military background, he found that nobody at the War Ministry had any interest in him. Instead, the Pohl that was taken on immediately was his sister, who had studied to be a nurse, a job that was now in great demand.

On August 4, 1914, England declared war on Germany. Pohl was utterly shocked by this turn of events, figuring that there was no way that they would come to the defense of France and that, instead, they would be happy that Germany was fighting Russia. On that day, the British ambassador retrieved his passport from the German foreign office and was therefore out on the street when Pohl found himself face to face with him. Pohl was so overcome with anger and revulsion at the man before him that he prepared to punch him in the face, and was stopped from doing this only by a police officer with a drawn weapon. After due consideration, however, he was happy that neither he nor the rest of the mob that had had the same reaction to the ambassador had been able to act on their impulses, as it would simply have given the English another reason to hate the Germans.

The rest of August was an exercise in frustration for Pohl. He spent his days trying to be accepted at any of the many military divisions that were being set up, and his evenings venting his frustration in not being taken in letters to his mother. Even his thirtieth birthday on August 10 did little to raise his mood. By the middle of August he was so frustrated that he considered actually turning back to his physics work.

And then, on the first of September, finally a call to action. It was hardly what he had expected, or from whom, because it was his sister that called. Apparently the nurse at her hospital who was in charge of the x-ray equipment had been called away on a family emergency, they needed someone who knew their way around an x-ray machine. Pohl was off like a shot and, together with a nurse from another hospital, got to work. They took pictures of twenty injured soldiers, and Pohl proudly stated that he had found the source of the damage in all but one instance. One case intrigued him particularly: a piece of shrapnel had struck a soldier in the finger but had continued under the skin into the hand itself. Neither the soldier nor the doctors who had been treating him were aware of its true location; only the x-ray machine made it immediately clear what had happened. He wrote a letter to his mother the following day to tell her the good news, but had to keep it short as he was due back at the hospital.

Pohl would return to this hospital over the next few days, and was happy to do so. Most intriguing to him was the number of times that the soldiers had broken metatarsal bones in their feet—not because of any external damage, but simply because they had walked too far too fast. Pohl saw these injuries as simply an acceptable by-product of the extreme speed with which Germany was winning the war.

A week later, his work was done at his sister's hospital. New nurses had been brought in that could do the work. However, Pohl had heard that the reserve hospitals did not have any x-ray equipment whatsoever, and given the steady stream of patients coming in from both the east and west, they were in dire need of these. Pohl pooled his talents with a petroleum engineer named Barth and a former colleague Erich Regener and devised a plan to help. Since trying to go through channels had thus far not worked, they simply showed up at one of the larger hospitals and announced that they could help. After the head of the hospital had determined that these three did not want to have uniforms or medals, but simply a room in which to do their work, they were greeted with great enthusiasm. Pohl was appalled at the one hospital that he visited. While the beds and night tables were all the best one could hope for, there was literally no place to wash your hands in the barracks.

Pohl went to work organizing the x-ray tubes, while Regener had his mechanic put together the electrical equipment needed. Barth, in turn, was responsible for supplying the plates needed to make the pictures.

Three days later, Pohl could report that they were in business. The hospital that had been installed in an old milk factory just a few steps away from Pohl's apartment had their x-ray equipment and they could take pictures as needed. Pohl was a bit astounded that he had to explain to the doctors what, exactly, they were seeing on the pictures, that many of the doctors were not at all experienced in orthopedics, and that, apparently, many of those who had been trained in this regard were sitting around waiting to hear whether they would be pulled into the national guard. It was the amount of waste and mismanagement that Pohl saw that drove him to distraction. He was happy that he had not given money to the German Red Cross at the beginning of the war, but instead was now spending it directly for items that he knew were actually needed.

On September 17, he ate lunch, as was his wont, at the Trarbach restaurant. They had not yet raised their prices and remained good value. But what really struck him that day was a young soldier sitting at the next table, surrounded by friends and family. While his left arm, right hand, and chin were all heavily bandaged, the real point of interest was the Iron Cross medal that was pinned to his chest. Pohl was deeply impressed by this, writing immediately about what he had seen to his mother that evening.

Otherwise, the news was mixed about his colleagues. He was happy when he did not hear anything from them, figuring that no news was good news. They were spread across all fields of battle, some in positions that took advantage of their knowledge, others as simple infantry soldiers.

One of those, a good friend from Hamburg named Otto Carl Kiep, he knew to be entirely indefatigable. But even he had sent a letter to his mother in which he expressed the hopes that he would receive a minor wound, just so that he could spend a few days with his family, days in which he could get out of his clothes, wash, and finally cure himself of the sore throat that has been plaguing him. This in spite of the fact that he had been awarded the Iron Cross for his actions in France.

Pohl still managed to keep up the round of visits that he had enjoyed before the war. In late September he took the train to Malchow, northwest of Berlin and well on the way to the Baltic Sea. The train took three and a half hours, instead of the two it would have taken prewar. The Kosmack family greeted him warmly.

They, like Pohl's father, split their time between Germany and Scotland, though they were in the import-export business, and the sons were still running the Scottish end, which led the parents to fear the worst. They had, in fact, not received any messages from abroad. While Pohl was there, he had the opportunity to see Encke's Comet, which had first been seen again a few days earlier. Pohl had been unable to see it in Berlin, due to the overpowering light pollution. Out here in the deep darkness of the country even a faint comet such as Encke could be seen, as he wrote to his mother on his return to Berlin on September 29.

Shortly after his return from Malchow, Pohl took several x-rays to staff officer Frik, who helped him understand what was going on in the pictures. At this point, things got quiet for Pohl. The initial burst of installations in the new hospitals was done, and the more he heard from this friends at the front, the less he wanted to join them. If something that was of interest, where he could actually do some good came along, that would be fine. But just to carry a rifle around, that no longer interested him.

Slowly, news trickled in from the front—mainly good news, that his friends were safe and bored. Occasionally worrisome tidings, like when he heard that the son of Max Planck, Erwin, had been badly wounded and left behind during a German retreat in France, and had been taken captive by the French. However, even here there was some good news, in that the father had already received letters from his son, and he appeared safe and recovering from a wound to the foot.

In late October, Margot Pohl made a disturbing find in the list of the injured: Ewald Lüders, with whom she knew her brother had finished school back in 1903.[12] He had become a lawyer, specializing in Oriental law, and had been at the Oriental Institute in Hamburg before being called up. He had been badly injured in the leg a month or two earlier, and died of his wounds on the twenty-second of October, just after he had been given the Iron Cross and two days before his injuries were published.[13]

As October wound down and the university semester started up again, Pohl decided that he was quite happy where he was, he spent more time worrying about what was going on with the people around his mother and complaining about the actions of those arrayed against Germany than actively trying to find war work to do.

The semester began slowly, with Pohl noting that there were only forty students in the introductory lab instead of the usual two hundred. Nonetheless, he felt that he should begin his own work again, and soon found himself drawn back to it. On November 6 at 7:30 p.m., Pohl put pen to paper to write his mother about this, but after fifteen minutes, had to cut his writing short as there was a meeting of the German Physical Society to go to, a meeting that was to have a lasting impact on his work for the rest of the war.

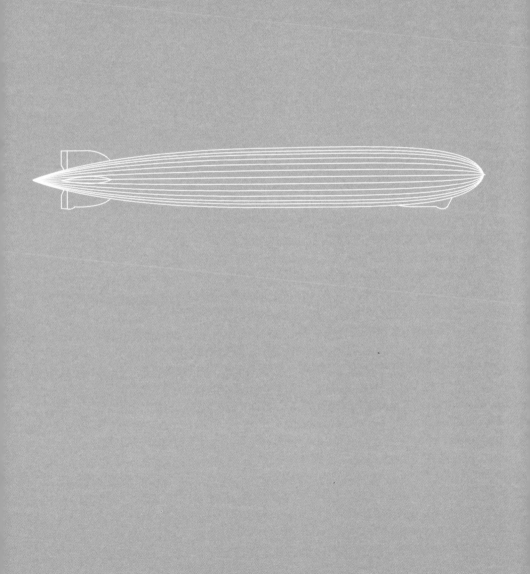

CHAPTER 5
JULY 27, 12:00 NOON–JULY 28, 6:00 A.M.

Blick vom Luftschiff auf Ostseebad Glücksburg

Postcard titled "Blick vom Luftschiff auf Ostseebad Glücksburg" (View from an airship of the Baltic seaside resort Glücksburg) The picture was most likely taken during the Zeppelin *Hansa*'s flight of August 11, 1912, in which it took off from Hamburg-Fuhlsbüttel, flew to Kiel, then to Glücksburg and Flensburg before returning to Hamburg. In the picture, the Glücksburg castle can be seen at the center, the house in which Pohl's mother lives is one of those on the right side. The postcard was printed by Friedrich Peters, who produced many postcards of the area in the early twentieth century. This particular card was sent by Pohl's daughter Ottilie to her grandmother, ca. 1930.

The next stretch of flight takes *LZ 120* across the channel separating Germany from Sweden, so at 2:15 p.m. they find themselves directly south of Trelleborg, the southernmost town in Sweden, and located just a few kilometers from the southernmost point in that country. Pohl knows it best as the endpoint of ferries leaving from Sassnitz on the German island of Rügen when traveling to Scandinavia.[1]

As the airship passes by Trelleborg, the airship is running on three engines at not quite 40 km/h under clear skies and heading toward Falster, in southern Denmark, and thus on a direct path to Glücksburg, which they hope to reach by 8:00 p.m. Known mainly for Glücksburg Castle, its sixteenth-century stronghold rising out of the middle of a man-made lake, this town is located some 10 kilometers northeast of the city of Flensburg, and was a minor tourist destination, rating only a single sentence in the latest Baedeker travel guide: "The 1582–87 built palace, picturesquely situated on a beech tree encircled pond, belongs to Duke Friedrich Ferdinand of Glücksburg."[2] It is, however, far more to Pohl, whose father had bought a house in the town many years earlier as a summer cottage. With Flensburg just three hours from Hamburg and then another ten minutes from there to Glücksburg, it was the perfect distance for a weekend getaway, and had been mother Pohl's main habitation since the death of her husband six years earlier. In his mind's eye, Pohl could already see the landscape: flat fields surrounded by hedgerows, in the distance the bright white castle with its red roof, surrounded by water, with the town itself stretched along a single road running north-south just to the east of it, while beyond the castle the waters of the Flensburg Firth glowed in the sunlight. Flying over this well-loved landscape, with the opportunity to wave to his mother from on high, is the fondest wish of Professor Pohl.

It is not to be. To the west, Lehmann spots rain, and decides that prudence is dictated. He orders the ship to turn ever farther to the left until they find themselves heading straight back to the island of Rügen again. They arrive there around 5:00 p.m., then continue along its western shore until they arrive at the top of Hiddensee, whose western coast they are now following south. Pohl is a bit worried by this delay but is certain that they still have multiple chances to fly over Glücksburg. In the meantime, he takes the opportunity to look over the island on which he had spent several enjoyable days celebrating his twenty-second birthday with his friend and colleague James Franck. This island, which stretches 17 kilometers along the west coast of the island of Rügen, is reachable only via boat from the seaport of Stralsund. While it had recently become more popular, it still rates no more than a paragraph in the current *Baedeker* guide.[3]

They had spent the mornings wandering up and down the beaches with their pants rolled up to their knees, and then swimming and enjoying the fact that the beaches were almost entirely empty in spite of it being a warm August. For lunch, they would walk from Kloster, the major town on the island to Vitte, 2 kilometers south, and located on one of the narrow stretches of the island. The lunches had been simple, healthy, and what seems most important at this point, generous, and had ensured that they could take a solid nap thereafter. Really, the only fly in the ointment had been the enormous number of artists of both sexes who infested the place, which were to be seen "painting eagerly in front every fisherman's house, every mud wall." After lunch, they would tackle the most difficult part of their schedule, that of finding a proper place to take their nap, a place that was sunny but protected, whether on the beach, the fields, or among the sand dunes. After their nap and a coffee break, it was time to explore the island by foot, and in particular the steep hills that made up the northwestern edge of the island, below the Dornbusch lighthouse that had been protecting shipping since 1888 and remained a striking white column capped by a red dome today. Finally, the day's expedition complete, they would head back across the top of the island, to the tiny town of Grieben, which consisted of a stretch of road with about a dozen houses on it. Here, a dinner of eggs, butter, and bread would be consumed before a ten-hour night's sleep could be had. It was idyllic and almost completely the opposite of what he is currently experiencing. Pohl thinks back fondly to those days, when the only real schedule was that of the local ferryboat, his only worry being whether he would finish the letter in which he described his experiences in time for the ferry to transport it to his mother.

At the southern tip of Hiddensee, the airship turns west to fly along the north coast of the Zingst Peninsula. Zingst is a wide V-shaped peninsula connected at the very western end to the German mainland. Between the peninsula and the coast lie two lagoons, and where these lagoons meet are a series of islands that have been used to create a railroad bridge across to the longer east-western leg of the V. It is an extremely quiet corner of the country. The whole peninsula rates only a paragraph in the current *Baedeker*, and the town of Zingst itself, midway along the longer leg exactly one sentence: "Fishing village and bath on the peninsula of the same name; 4,000 guests per year."[4]

However, there is a reason for Pohl to look at it more closely: Here, too, Pohl knows someone—Erna Frik, the wife of Dr. Karl Frik, the x-ray specialist who had helped Pohl in the early days of the war to interpret images that Pohl had made of wounded troops. Only a few years older than Pohl, he had spent five years as chief doctor with the German troops in East Africa before returning to Berlin and the Kaiser-Wilhelm academy.[5] While Frik himself had gone to war on the western front, Pohl had continued to spend time with Frau Frik and so the opportunity to wave to her as they pass over the island on which she was summering was not to be missed. The airship slows down and drops to 250 meters, giving those below—including hopefully Frau Frik—the opportunity to see the flags being waved to them.

LZ 120 continues slowly along the coast passing the northwest corner of the Zingst Peninsula just before 7:00 p.m. From the air, this headland jutting out into the sea looks like a wave crashing on a shore. It is named Darßer Ort, and it consists mainly of sand, flat beaches nearer the ocean, and higher sand dunes farther south. On the west coast, not far from the tip, is a red brick lighthouse, built in the 1840s, and one of the oldest on the German Baltic coast. The airship then turns south to follow the narrow white sand beach. Below pass a series of seaside resort towns: Ahrenshoop and Wustrow on the Zingst Peninsula; then Müritz, Warnemünde, and Heiligendamm on the mainland. Each of which is greeted in turn, though not as fully as Zingst had been earlier.

Just before the airship turns southeast into the great Bay of Lübeck, it passes Fulgen, Brunshaupten, and Arendsee. Fulgen had been a seaside town since 1857, when the first tourist hotel had been built there. Since then, a train station had been built, connecting the three towns, which were in competition as often as not, with the tracks that already connected Heiligendamm with Doberan to the southeast. This new mode of transport assured that the three towns attracted about 30,000 visitors per year before the war. The most noticeable feature of the towns is the state forest that is surrounded left and right by Arendsee and Brunshaupten.[6]

As they are passing over these three seaside towns, Pohl retires to the rear of the airship. He climbs up the ladder into the keel of the ship and walks aft along the gangway that spans the rump of the airship. He goes past the ladder that leads down to the rear motor room, a place he is happy to avoid. The air inside, he knows, is heavy with oil and gasoline fumes, and the mood tense. Each engine is closely watched by the machinists for any deviation from their normal operation, each opening and closing of the valves, every move of every lever observed. The machinists bend over their work like priests over an altar, not just so they will miss nothing, but because the low ceiling of the gondola does not allow them to stand fully erect. The heat, only somewhat mitigated by the stream of fresh air rolling by the open windows, is intense. And above all, the noise, a steady rattle of the engines and the loud swish of the propellers that makes any conversation impossible. The machinists have long since learned to communicate via an improvised set of hand signals. It is, Pohl feels, not too different from his vision of hell, and he is happy that he does not have to spend any time in it.[7]

Instead, he continues along the walkway, following it as it curves slowly upward and, finally, crawling the last section on his hands and knees, he reaches a short narrow ladder that leads up. Emerging on the outside of the ship, he finds himself in the stern machine gun platform. Set into the stern of the ship, it is about a meter deep, and has a corrugated aluminum floor that is trapezoidal in shape, widening from less than a meter toward the front to the back. It is just long enough to stretch out in, especially as the gun that would have been set up here is safely stowed below. From here, he has a spectacular view of not only the rudders of the airship but of the scenery below and behind the ship.

The view, however, is not what Pohl has come here for. Rather, it is peace and quiet—or as close as you were to get that on this airship with only the "soft and soothing murmur of the wind and a very faint, almost imperceptible hum from the engines"[8] to indicate that you were underway, as Lehmann put it. Almost as importantly, there is no danger of him falling out, as the platform is sunk into the body of the airship. It is just large enough to stretch out in, and that is exactly what he does, after wrapping himself in his fur coat and blankets. Sinking below the level of the walls surrounding him, Pohl feels not the least breath of air and is soon asleep, happy in the thought that he will see his mother in the morrow—even if only from the air.

The giant airship continues its slow way west into the setting sun. Running on just three engines, it is doing just 30 kilometers per hour through the misty air. Lehmann is in no rush. They are less than 200 kilometers southeast from Flensburg and could cover that distance in under two hours under ordinary circumstances. However, there is no point in being there before daybreak, and so Lehmann flies instead due north to the island of Fehmarn, a small island separated from the mainland by a one-half-kilometer strait and known for the many cattle that are raised on it. Dotted throughout by small farming villages, it has been entirely spared from those seeking a rest in the seaside towns that otherwise marked the Baltic coast, the only mention in tourist publications was that there was, indeed, a ten-minute ferry from to the island.[9]

From Fehmarn, Lehmann turns south and across the water to the island of Poel, at the head of the Bay of Wismar. As they enter this bay under clear skies, Pohl sleeps deeply and misses the sight of the stars above and the deep black sea below. The airship is as quiet as it will get, the off-duty crew fast asleep, those on the watch quietly going about their business.

Lehmann then orders them to turn due west, toward the Jutland Peninsula that contains, at its tip, the southern reaches of Denmark. It is around here that Pohl briefly wakes up and finds himself looking down on a sight utterly different from the bucolic beaches that they have seen thus far.

They are over Lübeck, another of the major Baltic Sea ports, and for many years, the most important cities of the Hanseatic League that had controlled trade in that area of the world for so long. Founded in 1143, a few kilometers up the Trave River, it had immediately been an extremely important harbor, as even large ships could make it all the way into the city. Less than a hundred years after being founded, Lübeck had, along with Hamburg, Rostock, Wismar, Greifswald, and Stralsund, founded the Hanseatic League, which according to the latest Baedeker was "an alliance of the great commercial towns of N. Germany, which formed a peace-loving but powerful bond of union between Western and Eastern Europe."[10] Lübeck had prospered, especially after the League had managed to defeat the Danes in their attempt in the fourteenth century to monopolize Baltic trade. Its current streetscape reflects this long-abiding power, medieval architecture marking the city, with bricks being the main building material.[11]

Pohl can see none of this, as he is over a very different area of town. Below, and looking like a good-sized town with railroad tracks replacing roads, are the giant iron works of Lübeck. Built in 1906 by the city of Lübeck in an attempt to break out of the city's long-standing mono economy as a trading city, it was soon joined by further heavy industry, which continued to expand, especially after the outbreak of war.[12] Pohl sees it bathed in the red and green light from huge arc lamps that allow production to go around the clock, these factories and hundreds of men—and, increasingly, women—churn out some of the vast amount of iron and steel necessary for the German war effort. Pohl goes back to sleep in the assumption that when he next awakes, he will be above Glücksburg and his mother.

CHAPTER 6
ERNST AUGUST LEHMANN

Ernst August Lehmann, *on far right*, with, *from left*, Hans Luther, President Franklin Delano Roosevelt, and Hugo Eckener in the White House, Washington, DC, in 1936. *Harris & Ewing Collection / Library of Congress*

Ernst August Lehmann was born on March 12, 1886, in Ludwigshafen. This city on the Rhine, opposite Mannheim, was at the time that Lehmann was born growing rapidly mainly because it was the seat of the chemical concern Badische Anilin und Soda Fabrik—better known by its initials BASF— where his father, a chemistry PhD, was a manager. Ludwig Lehmann had been born in Speyer, just a few kilometers farther up the Rhine. His mother, the former Luise Friederike Schafer, came from a the town of Diez, about 100 kilometers north. Her father was mayor of the town when she was born.[1]

Over the next years, three siblings were born. The first was Otto Albert in 1887, then Maria Elisabetha in 1889. Sadly, the latter would die in 1893. Two years later, however, there arrived a further daughter and a final child: Louise Mathilde Anna.

Lehmann would graduate in 1904 from the local preparatory high school, a school that had been founded in 1873, but only recently expanded to offer the full qualifications for university study. Lehmann, however, did not immediately take advantage of this opportunity, but instead moved all the way north to the city of Kiel. While the population of Ludwigshafen had almost tripled in the years that he lived there, Kiel was still almost twice that of Ludwigshafen. In Kiel, Lehmann worked in the shipyard and joined the German navy. During his time in the navy, he served on the school ship SMS *Stosch*, a ship some twenty-four years old at this time, and one that had been used for training for most of its life.[2] Over the following two years he rose to the rank of Ensign of the naval reserves. Around this time, his brother would join the German army, rising to the rank of noncommissioned officer over the next year.

In 1906, Lehmann moved to Berlin, the capital of the German Reich and a city of two million inhabitants—an enormous difference to Kiel—and began studying engineering and, in particular, ship and shipbuilding engineering at the Royal Technical University, where Pohl's father had studied many years earlier. He would graduate six years later.[3]

Immediately after graduation, he began working as a naval architect, but shortly thereafter moved to Friedrichshafen to work for Count Zeppelin. That same year—1912—his younger brother Otto would switch careers and begin studying to be a painter at the Munich Academy of Art.

Early the following year, Lehmann would begin to learn how to fly a Zeppelin. His teacher was Dr. Hugo Eckener. Eckener, who had originally studied—and received his doctorate in—psychology, had then become a newspaper reporter. As a correspondent of the *Frankfurter Zeitung*, he had watched the flights of Zeppelin's first two airships. While impressed with Zeppelin himself, he had been critical of the performance of the airships. Count Zeppelin sought out Eckener to ask further questions about how he could improve the airships, and was so impressed by the young man that he had hired him as a publicist, a job that soon turned full-time. It was soon noticed that Eckener had a real knack for flying, and within a short time had become their number-one flight instructor.[4]

Eckener saw a kindred spirit in Lehmann, and took the young engineer under his wing. While Lehmann was undergoing flight training, the Zeppelin company finished building its seventeenth Zeppelin. The fourth of the new H class of Zeppelins, it was the first of these to be built for civilian use, and so was given not an incomprehensible letter/number combination, but an actual name: *Sachsen*, in honor of that southeast German state.[5]

Sachsen was the sixth airship built for DELAG, the first for them in almost a year, and one of only three in service at the time. Its first flight came on May 4, 1913; the following day, Lehmann flew its first revenue flight. However, he was not always in command of the airship. For instance, when the Zeppelin hangar in Leipzig—the largest in the world at the time—was opened late the following month, it was Count Zeppelin himself who flew the *Sachsen* there as part of the ceremonies.

The new airship was an immediate success. In an article noting the number of flights and passengers flown by DELAG airships *Flight* magazine mentions that by June, the *Sachsen* had already flown fifty-eight times and carried 1,336 passengers.[6]

Lehmann spent the fall flying cruises all around Germany. As winter approached, however, demand slackened and, simultaneously, the *L 2*, the navy's only airship, crashed. Major Strasser requested the use of the *Sachsen* to train navy airmen. The flights were quite different from the tea cruises that they had been doing up to then; Lehmann would set the airship down on the Elbe River that snakes through Hamburg, and would even land in the inner harbor of that city for practice. Mainly, however, the *Sachsen* was engaged in flights across Germany, including into the North and Baltic Seas: Heligoland, Fehmarn, Gjedser. On January 10, he resumed his civilian flights, completing more than a hundred of them over the next seven months.

On July 31, 1914, Lehmann received an ominous telegram: Both he and *Sachsen* were to stay within 50 kilometers of their hangar. It meant, as Lehmann knew, war. He immediately went and dug his naval lieutenant's uniform out of the bottom of his trunk.[7] The first orders he received thereafter did not portend immediate danger. While other Zeppelins were sent to the front, his civilian airship needed refitting first, and so he was sent to Potsdam, near Berlin.[8]

An old garrison town, Potsdam was remarkably quiet, in spite of the more numerous uniforms to be seen there. While he waited for the bomb racks, a bombardier's station, better radio equipment as well as machine guns to be added to his airship, Lehmann took it easy, including long lunches at the Hotel Stadt Königsberg. Known for its terrace overlooking the Havel River,[9] this was where Lehmann was finishing a leisurely lunch one day when he was approached by two men in uniform. The older was Baron Max Ferdinand Ludwig von Gemmingen-Guttenberg, the younger, Lieutenant Kurt Ackermann. While they had wildly different backgrounds, they had bonded over their love of Zeppelins. Gemmingen, whose mother was the sister of Count Zeppelin, had been involved in their development for some time, while Ackermann, the son of a wealthy Berlin businessman, simply loved to fly and had recently acquired a private pilot's license.[10]

Both officers had been assigned to serve with Lehmann on the *Sachsen*. While Gemmingen was the general staff officer, and thus nominally in charge of the military activities aboard the airship, Ackermann was there as their bombing officer. Fortunately for Lehmann, Gemmingen understood only too well the nature of Zeppelins, and thus did not attempt—as some staff officers had—to make it attempt missions that were dangerous or downright suicidal. In fact, Lehmann and he became close friends over the following years.

Gemmingen, who was by this time fifty-two years old, was in principle too old to serve but had volunteered to continue to serve on his uncle's airships.

With the ship now prepared for battle, Lehmann was ordered to Cologne, where they took over the hangar of the ill-fated *Z VI*, which, after having carried out the first bombing attack of the war, had been badly damaged in flying over Liège in the opening week of the war. While it had managed to limp back into Germany, it came down near Bonn and been destroyed.[11]

Whether the army high command became leery of using Zeppelins after having lost three in the first week of the war, or was simply distracted by other aspects of the war, Lehmann could not determine. He felt forgotten, but decided to make the best of the situation and train his men. This meant getting up every morning at 3:00 a.m., and taking off an hour later, and then drop bombs onto targets. In particular, Lehmann made sure that the men understood the use of the bomb sight, as well as ensuring that the helmsman and bombing officers understood how to communicate.[12]

Eventually, Gemmingen grew tired of waiting and drove the 100-plus kilometers to Coblenz to find out whether they had indeed been forgotten. The upshot was that Gemmingen and Lehmann were ordered to show up for a conference, in which the two airshipmen would help figure out how, exactly, the airships in general and the *Sachsen* in particular were to be used—a request that Lehmann and Gemmingen jumped at.[13]

In this time, the German army was rolling through Belgium and had almost surrounded Antwerp. Only one route led out, a route that contained a railway line. Lehmann and Gemmingen suggested that they bomb a strategic railway junction, which would have greatly reduced the number of soldiers who could flee. This would have required packing the *Sachsen* to the gills with bombs, but the two airshipmen felt that this was exactly what they had trained for. The higher-ups did not agree, and a significant number of Belgian troops were able to flee along this route.

Lehmann and company did have the opportunity to help in the attack on Antwerp. Late in the evening on August 24, they took off from Cologne and headed west. They first flew over Aachen, the German city located where Germany, Holland, and Belgium come together. Rising up, they passed over the Belgian border to reach the city of Liège, which had been in German hands for less than a week at this point. Past Liège, they flew into a cloud bank that covered their progress across German lines and toward Antwerp. As they reached this city, the clouds dispersed, leaving the airship easily noticeable in the bright moonlight. It was thus necessary to wait until the moon had set to continue on with the mission. Once darkness settled in, a further issue made itself known—warm air meant that the airship wanted to sink closer to the defensive weaponry of the city. Lehmann had to point the nose upward and call for full engines, which left the crew sliding around helplessly in the gondola, and far from able to drop bombs as they had during their training. Lehmann pressed on in the knowledge that dropping the bombs would lighten the ship enough to make her manageable. The noise of the engine was enough to alert the defenders, and soon guns started to ring out, and spotlights began searching the sky for the invader. A few bombs dropped on the city silenced the guns, although it was not clear to the crew if this was because they had hit their target, or that the explosions had simply caused the defenders to seek cover. After shutting down the main searchlight with a well-placed bomb, the rest of the attack went smoothly, dropping incendiary bombs on the forts ringing the city and saving the explosives for the main train station in the center of the city. After only twenty minutes, the attack was over. The first intimations of dawn were also rising. It was time to head home, which they reached at 11:00 a.m. on the twenty-fifth, exactly twelve hours after liftoff.[14]

About a week later, the crew repeated the attack. A *New York Times* reporter wrote of the attack:

One of the cigar-shaped creations of Count Zeppelin reappeared over the sleeping city in the early hours of this morning. At 3:45 a.m. I was awakened by a terrific noise, a rattling musketry fire alternating with a cannonade and the bursting of shells. It was apparent that were were having a second and a long-threatened visit from Count Zeppelin. The first visit terrified us on Tuesday morning, Aug. 25, and Zeppelin No. 2 was long overdue. The cannonade which I heard was the welcome given to the visitor by the Belgian troops.[15]

The reporter then went on to describe the damage: "Five bombs were dropped on one group of houses, but only destroyed three of them, slightly injuring some of the inhabitants." It was thus significantly less damage than was done the first time around, which he judged was due to the Belgian artillery being better prepared.

A little less than three weeks later, a further attempt to attack the city failed entirely, and in general, the attacks made by *Sachsen* and *Z IX*, which had been built just before the war and was the only other army airship on the western front, proved to be less and less important as the Germans pushed into France. Until the end of the year, the Zeppelins were mainly used for reconnaissance and no further bombing attacks were attempted.[16]

The rest of the year passed quietly for Lehmann and his crew. After the fall of the French city of Maubeuge, he and Gemmingen were called to inspect a French airship hangar there. They were not impressed by the state of French lighter-than-air technology, one of the men commented that the French airships were "just good enough for target practice."[17]

In personal news, on October 14, Lehmann's brother, Otto, joined the army air corps, and was stationed in Johannisthal for training.[18]

The new year was to bring large changes, as Lehmann and his men were transferred to *Z XII*.[19] The twenty-sixth Zeppelin built, it first flew on December 14, 1914. While in its dimensions only slightly larger than that of *Sachsen*, the airship was built with war in mind, and was in fact the first Zeppelin built during the war, as well as the first built using Duralumin, a new, harder, aluminum alloy. The most important change was that this was the first airship with a corridor within the hull, a forerunner of the gangway that Pohl has been using to move around *LZ 120* during this trip.

The first step for Lehmann and company was to add a new technology to the airship—the spy basket. The idea was simple—lower a crewman on a rope well below the Zeppelin, so that the airship could remain in or above the clouds, but the basket was in clear air and could direct the airship without it being seen from the ground. Lehmann joined forces with a local civil engineer named Hagen to produce the first prototype. It used available materials—including a butter cask—to make a proof of concept. The first experiment involved flying in clear weather, but with a blindfolded helmsman. Lehmann had himself lowered below the airship and then, via a field telephone that he had installed in the observation car, gave orders to the helmsman, who was able to easily guide the airship exactly as requested by Lehmann.[20]

The next step was to build a proper cable and winch that was driven by the engines of the Zeppelin, as well as a purpose-built basket. It was, indeed, a basket—made of wicker—that looked like a small airplane. Inside were everything the lookout would need: compass, telephone, light, chart table, and, most importantly, a comfortable chair.

While the work on the spy basket went well, the *Z XII* was, in general, less successful. This was mainly due to the extremely cold weather that plagued Europe in the first months of 1915. One attempt to bomb the French city of Nancy was foiled by the bitter cold, with it becoming necessary for the crew to break up frozen hunks of oil by hand in order to restart one of the engines.[21] However, changes to the engines were made to avoid issues of this sort, and on March 8, *Z XII* was moved to the hangar in Maubeuge that Lehmann had inspected the previous year. This meant that they were that much closer to the action, and, in fact, almost immediately afterward they were given instructions that allowed them to raid military targets in England—with a preference for London—at any time they felt that conditions were right. This was a considerable relief to Lehmann, who felt that the vagaries of the weather made it difficult to have any central planning involved in these attacks. Lehmann was particularly keen to be the first to attack London itself. While navy airships had managed to drop bombs on England's east coast on January 19, the heart of the empire had yet to experience a Zeppelin attack, and Lehmann felt that he and his crew were best equipped for this sort of expedition.

On March 11, they had their first chance. The message "Fetwa Eins"—"Fatwa One"—indicated that the decision had been made on high that bombing raids on London had been authorized. This was by no means a straightforward decision. The Kaiser, whose close family was reigning in England, had given strict instructions as to what could and could not be bombed there.[22] Lehmann and Gemmingen had gone through these instructions, and felt that they could carry them out to the Kaiser's satisfaction.

Except that they could not. While they had lifted off immediately on receiving authorization, they had soon found themselves thwarted by the weather. Lehmann managed to drop some bombs on Dunkirk, which gave the expedition some meaning, but the real target had been left unscathed.

Five days later, they tried again. This time, they made it over the British capital, only to find it utterly covered in impenetrable fog. Not even the Thames, where Lehmann hoped that there would be patches to see through, was visible. They tried both rising to 3,000 meters and down as low as they could go—nothing. In the end, they had to turn around. Over Calais, the conditions improved to the point where they felt that they could use the observation car. After much wrangling, Gemmingen was given precedence over Lehmann in using this for the first time in combat. They spent twenty-three minutes over the city, dropping bombs precisely on the railways station, storehouses, the arsenal, and other places. While the defenders of the city could hear the Zeppelin and see the destruction wrought by it, they had no chance of defending against it.[23]

The return to Maubeuge was uneventful, but the landing was not: changes in the air pressure had made the altimeter read the wrong height, and Lehmann brought his airship down hard on a railway line, with the tail catching in a telegraph pole. It would take two weeks to repair the damage.[24]

In early April, with his ship now repaired, Lehmann attempted an attack on Boulogne. Headwinds stymied the flight, and Lehmann decided that it was time for *Z XII* to be overhauled.[25] While work was proceeding, he was ordered east and to support General Paul von Hindenburg, who had been recalled from retirement to lead the German forces on the eastern front. Once the repairs had been completed, Lehmann and his men were posted to Allenstein,[26] a garrison town near the Russian border in East Prussia.[27]

While in Allenstein, Lehmann met with Hindenburg who put Lehmann and his crew to work supporting German troops. The first mission was an attack on Pułtusk, just south of Allenstein in Poland, just 50 kilometers from Warsaw. While the Zeppelin was kept from attacking the defending troops to give the German troops cover while they approached, the fog that had hindered the airship also provided the cover needed by the attackers.[28]

Other attacks were more successful. In particular, raids on railway lines kept the Russians from resupplying troops at the front. In August, Lehmann and *Z XII* dropped 9 tons of explosives on the line between Warsaw and Dunaburg, an important transportation hub connected with the rest of the Russian Empire.[29]

Another attack on Białystok started well—by the time the Zeppelin was done with its attack, the railway yard there was in flames—but on the way back the airship ran out of lift and fuel and had to land on a lake 16 kilometers from their base. Fortunately, the rising sun warmed the hydrogen gas to the point where they could take off again and return to their hangar in Allenstein.[30] After *Z XII* was repaired, the ship was moved to Königsberg, from where the airship was sent to attack railway lines around Vilna.[31]

As summer turned to fall, and the weather began to cool, Lehmann and his ship were ordered back west. The final flight to Darmstadt was miserable, as it rained the whole way. Furthermore, there was no radio on board, nor any way of determining their location. In the end, sheer luck prevailed, when Lehmann finally found a break in the clouds, he was within an hour's flight of his destination.[32] While *Z XII* was turned into a training ship, Lehmann was given a new airship, *LZ 90.*

Lehmann's new command was still being built in Potsdam, and while he waited he received the worst of news: his brother Otto had been killed. Otto had originally been an artist, and had even made paintings exhorting the Germans to buy war bonds, but had become a pilot. He had been flying over Colmar, just behind German lines, when he had crashed and was killed.[33]

As 1915 ended, Lehmann could look over a mixed record. While he had finally made it over England, he had failed to make it over London itself. His brother had been killed. But he had also married Susanne Dienemann,[34] and looked forward to a time when the war would not keep him from her permanently.

It was not until the new year that he could take command of his new ship, as issues with the airship, and particularly its motors, kept it from flying. Meanwhile, the German naval airships had begun their attacks on England in earnest. Lehmann could only hear about these secondhand.

While waiting for the airship to be finished, Lehmann met someone with whom he would spend considerable amounts of time over the next year and a half: Professor Pohl. Pohl had been installing navigation devices in other airships and wanted to do the same for *LZ 90*. Unfortunately, every time that a flight was scheduled, it had to be canceled. If it was not the fault of the engines, the weather interfered. Pohl's letters to his mother from December 27, 1915, until February 6 the following year are a litany of failed flights—until the last letter, which describes a two-and-a-half-hour flight in beautiful sunshine over Magdeburg and Braunschweig to Hanover, whose only problem was an issue with a motor that required them to land immediately instead of going for a cruise of several hours.

Thereafter, Lehmann and *LZ 90* were ordered to Spich, halfway between Cologne and Bonn, from where it would be able to attack across enemy lines. On February 28, they set off for a long test flight. They flew south along the Moselle River, then along the Rhine to Bingen and then back to Frankfurt am Main—from there to Darmstadt and Heidelberg. It was around here that one of the motors died on them. Flying on the other motors, he headed west toward Saarlouis and Saarbrücken. Around here the weather turned bad and so Lehmann turned back east and ended up spending the night flying back and forth between Mannheim and Frankfurt am Main, as there were three free airship hangars in that general vicinity and none other open in all of Germany. Lehmann did not want to be too far from a safe harbor in case the weather turned further. Pohl was not happy about this, as he wrote to his mother the following day, he felt that he could have made better experiments elsewhere in Germany, but Lehmann insisted. The safety of his men and his ship came first. In the end, they landed in Trier, having spent twenty hours in the air, and while much of the flight was done only on three engines, there was some satisfaction that *LZ 90* was finally ready for action.

That first night, they started for Verdun, but had to return due to two engines failing. Two days and two new engines later, they tried again. This time, it was the weather that kept them from completing their mission. Three days after this, however, they finally made it. Once again, the target was a railway yard, this one in Bar-le-Duc, and part of the defenses of Verdun. While the attack initially succeeded, they soon found themselves fired on by a new anti-Zeppelin weapon: truck-mounted incendiary shells. Lehmann called for full speed ahead, and ascended as quickly as he could to get out of range of the shells. Before one could reach them, they had found a cloud bank and safety.[35]

At the end of that month came the next big attempt—another attack on England. At first, all was well. Patches of rain were easily dodged. As they were reaching England, already able to recognize some of the features of the coast, two engines went out. Lehmann made the decision to delay the attack on London until they had been repaired. When one engine could not be fixed due to missing parts, Lehmann turned home. Over Norwich they were shot at, and he dropped his bombs there before returning safely home.[36]

Two days later, along with two other army Zeppelins, he tried again. After waiting for darkness over Ghent, they headed for the British coast. Over England, they were fired at, but once the moon set, they found themselves hidden behind a layer of cloud which rendered the British searchlights useless. Unfortunately, the haze also made it difficult to make out the land below. As they were searching, two things happened almost simultaneously: a new, more powerful searchlight cut through the cloud and picked them out in the sky, and new incendiary shells were fired at them. It was a nervous few minutes as they searched for a welcoming cloud to hide inside. Emerging from it, now with no searchlights pointed at them, they were able to pick out the docks that had been their target all along. They released their bombs there and elsewhere on the eastern end of London, the loss of which also caused the airship to rise to 4,000 meters. The trip home was punctuated by a number of attempts to fire at them, all of which failed due to the defenders underestimating the height at which they were.[37]

Shortly after this attack, the decision was made to revamp *LZ 90*, and thus Lehmann found himself, once again, assigned to a new ship: *LZ 98*. It would, however, not be ready until the end of the month. In the meantime, Lehmann went to Friedrichshafen, where the ship was being built. While he waited, he had the opportunity to look over the new R-class Zeppelins that were being built. *LZ 98* was a Q class, and thus about 15 meters longer than his previous airship; the new ones were another 20 meters longer. Lehmann spent the time waiting visiting with Count Zeppelin, who would often invite him and Baron von Gemmingen to his house. They would discuss the possibilities for civilian flight after the war. Zeppelin mentioned that, before the war, he had been designing an airship that would be able to make the Atlantic crossing. It had not been that much bigger than the current R-class Zeppelins.[38]

When *LZ 98* was completed, Lehmann flew it to Hanover. As a special guest, he had Count Zeppelin along. On their way, they flew over the town of Zepelin, located just south of Rostock near the Baltic Sea, where the Zeppelin clan had originated.[39]

After a brief flight to Nordholz, the main Navy airship station, Lehmann was ready for the next mission: to attack England. The first attempt almost ended in disaster. The weather had been threatening all day, but Lehmann went up in the hope that improvement was on the horizon. It was not. In the end, even as they had England in sight, the rain forced them to turn around, and then on their way back, they were hit multiple times by lightning. Fortunately, while the strikes did create small holes in the Zeppelin, they did not ignite any of the hydrogen, and Lehmann and his crew arrived in their hangar in Hanover safely.[40]

The next major attack was also one of the biggest of the war, and one of the few done by a combined army and navy flotilla. Sixteen total airships, a dozen navy and four army, took off on the afternoon of September 2, 1916. This time, *LZ 98* made it over England, but Lehmann discovered that the British had vastly improved their defenses. While the newer airships could reach altitudes that airplanes could not, the older ones had to rely on cloud banks and the luck and skill of their commanders to avoid being shot down. Nonetheless, Lehmann managed to drop bombs on Gravesend, though not London itself.[41]

Shortly after their return to their hangar in northwestern Germany, Lehmann and his wife went to Berlin for a few days. In the train on the way back, Mrs. Lehmann discovered Professor Pohl elsewhere in the train and invited him to join them. It was a sprightly party that made its way across northwestern Germany, as Pohl's letter to his mother the following day indicated.

In Wildeshausen, Pohl set to work on a new targeting telescope that he hoped to develop for the airships. Once again, the weather made for trouble. While they were able to fly a few times, the work Pohl was to do was slowed down considerably by the frequency of crosswinds and rain. In the end, he had to depart without having completed his work, but promised to return as soon as the weather allowed for the two further flights he needed to complete his work, as he wrote in a letter on September 19.

Finally, in late September, work was finished and another attack on England was planned. This time, it was not the weather but the lack thereof that stymied the airship. It was simply too bright out, and Lehmann turned back to avoid turning his airship into a target.

It was shortly thereafter that Lehmann, in consultation with other airship pilots, agreed that they would refuse to attack England unless directly ordered to do so. It was simply too likely that they would be shot down in such an effort. While this decision was not widely publicized, Pohl did hear of it and passed it on to his mother in a letter he wrote on September 28.

A little over a week later, Pohl showed his concern for Lehmann's situation, asking his mother to pass on a message to his sister to send three bottles of whisky to Wildeshausen. "Who knows," he added, "how much longer one can do anything for him?"

Lehmann himself was, when not drinking Margot's whiskey, busy perfecting the observation car. While the weather was reducing the amount he could fly, he hoped to have a few good days on which he could fly, days where low-hanging clouds over clear air made for the right conditions to use the car.[42] Early in November, Lehmann and his ship were, once again, transferred east, this time to Kovno. From there, the idea was to attack Russian targets, particularly Petrograd, as the Russian city of Saint Petersburg had been renamed in 1914 after the German attack—the Russian name of this city was Sankt Peterburg, both the "Sankt" and "burg" were taken from the German and thus no longer acceptable. Whatever its name, the city had been the capital of Russia since 1712. Petrograd was 640 kilometers from Kovno, and almost due north. The main reason for bombing this city was to continue to foment the internal unrest that had been roiling Russia since the war had begun or, as Lehmann put it, "stir up the masses" and convince them to continue their revolution against the Tsar. As so often, the weather interfered. The conditions necessary to cross the vast space that was the Russian Empire were exactly those that would make the flights difficult. Lehmann and Gemmingen worked on these issues as the flew east, and were able to give it a try in early December.[43]

While they were able to get over the Russian lines with no problem, hiding in the clouds as they went, a storm brewing behind them necessitated their return to the hangar, where they spend the next few days protected from the ice and snow that the storm brought. Since the biggest issues facing them was the delay in getting the weather reports, they moved the Zeppelin to Wainoden, which had, like Kovno, been part of the Russian empire until it had been captured by the Germans earlier in the war, but was closer to their target. Nonetheless, the weather kept interfering. In the end, the weather succeeded in foiling them every time through the winter. [44]

Around the end of the year, Lehmann was, once again, given command of a new ship. He turned over *LZ 98* to Joachim von Gemmingen, a nephew of Max von Gemmingen's, who had previously as first officer on *LZ 98*, and who had proven himself, and was, Lehmann felt, an excellent replacement for him. Lehmann traveled southeast to the shores of the Lake of Constance and the Zeppelin factory, where the Zeppelin with hull number LZ 90, soon to be army airship *LZ 120*, awaited.[45]

CHAPTER 7
JULY 28, 6:00 A.M.–JULY 28, 10:30 A.M.

Hamburg from the air. In the center is the outer Alster; the main train station can be seen in the lower center. The tracks leading to the left separate the inner and the outer Alster.

Pohl wakes briefly before sunrise and looks out over a sea of fog, which he assumes means that they are near the island of Fehmarn and thus a bit over a hundred kilometers from Flensburg, which, given the slow speed that they are currently flying, means that he has plenty of time to catch up on his sleep before seeing his mother.

He wakes again before 7:00 a.m. Below him are fields surrounded by hedgerows—exactly what he knows to be in the area around Glücksburg. There are, however, no landmarks that allow him to determine their exact current location. It is thus necessary to make his way to the front gondola to find the answer to this question. The response from the navigator is disappointing: They are nowhere near Flensburg and, in fact, no longer on their way to Glücksburg. Instead, they had had to turn around around at the island of Schleimünde, only about 40 kilometers from their goal, and are now headed due south, toward Hamburg. Disappointed, Pohl returns to the stern. Fortunately, as they head south, the weather clears and as they have dropped to about 400 meters, he has a magnificent view of the city of his birth.

Hamburg had lost a significant portion of its population since the outbreak of war, but is still about three times as big as it had been when he was born almost exactly thirty-three years earlier. It is considered, behind London and New York, the third most important trading—"commercial"—city in the world,[1] and evidence of this can be seen from above, with multiple canals threading through every part of the city, each stacked with ships of all shapes and sizes, in between packed with industrial buildings, of which only the broad roofs can be seen from here.

Situated upstream from the North Sea on the Elbe River, it was an early member of the Hanseatic League and remains its most important member.[2] Its most prominent landmark is the Binnen-Alster, a man-made lake in the center that was created by damming the Alster River, which flows into the Elbe in Hamburg. Around it are situated numerous landmarks, including the headquarters of the Hamburg-Amerikanische Packetfahrt-Aktien-Gesellschaft, for whom his father had worked at the time of his birth, and which had merged with the Woermann Linie, for whom he had worked for most of his career.

From the machine gun nest in the stern, Pohl can see it all—the whole city and its harbor, with its labyrinth of water, the shipyards and the quays that he had visited with his father to see the ships with their exotic African cargo. Beyond that stretch the houses of the citizens, interspersed with the spires of the thirty-five churches that they attended.[3] Outstanding among these is the bright copper dome of the St. Michael's Church, the largest in Hamburg and the tower of the Nikolai Church, the third-tallest in the world.[4] Among the houses, Pohl can even make out his old home in the Ritterstrasse 112 and, just down the street, that of his old friend Gerhard Bubendey, whose father and grandfather had both been professors at the Johanneum.

Bubendey, in spite of being only a little younger than Pohl, has been in the war since almost the beginning. He had been in the middle of the Second Battle of Ypres, a series of engagements in April and May 1915 that had seen the first use of poison gas on the western front. During this time, he survived two attacks. Pohl would try repeatedly to find a spot of Bubendey in the radio corps, a position that would keep his good friend that much safer. They would see each other occasionally, but mainly would keep in touch by letters. Bubendey once again found himself in the middle of the fighting during the Battle of the Somme in September 1916 and, after a brief visit home, would return to the western front only to be in the thick of the fighting around Arras. Pohl had actually visited him there just a month and a half earlier, and had been pleased to see that he was somewhat protected as the adjutant for his battalion, though still responsible for the trenches that made up the Hindenburg Line. Bubendey had been on Pohl's mind for much of the war; when he heard of the conditions that the soldiers were exposed to, it was Bubendey that would personify these dangers.

LZ 120 continues on over Hamburg, and Pohl watches the city roll by below. He passes over the oil factory owned in part by his uncle Friedrich Wilhelm Stuewer, near the central market, just east of the old city, and surrounded by the canals that made Hamburg such a commercial center. Finally, as they head east out of the city, he sees the garden center run by the famous Lund family, whose son Ernst had been a classmate at the Johanneum. It was, in short, a brief but intense visit to his old home.

The next stop is the lake of Ratzeburg. A 1-kilometer-long and 2-kilometer-wide lake just south of Lübeck and west-north-west of Hamburg, it stretches north-south, with the town of Ratzeburg in the southern tip, with three other lakes surrounding this triangular island. Easily visible from above is the town's cathedral, completed in the thirteenth century. Not visible from above, but to be read in any travel guide, was that the land on which the cathedral sits belongs to the state of Mecklenburg-Strelitz, while the southern part, in other words the town itself, belongs to Prussia.[5] However, Lehmann is not here to marvel at the oddities of German states, but to take a picture of a friend's house. He brings the airship down and takes the pictures, which gave Pohl the opportunity to observe that the town is significantly more attractive under the bright sun than it had been when he raced through it on the train from Berlin to Kiel.

Pohl looks over the shoulder of the navigator and realizes that the flight to their next destination, Wismar, will take them almost over Rastorf, a small estate 10 kilometers south of that city. While Rastorf itself is barely a flyspeck on the map, he knows it well, as he has family there. His mother's mother had been born a Middendorf, and although his grandmother had passed away two years before

Pohl's birth, he continues to have contact with his cousins. Arthur Middendorf had bought a 5.5-square-kilometer freehold there that included a nearby sub-freehold plus smithy and a windmill,[6] and Pohl had often heard of the quality and quantity of their harvests. Pohl had been close to the manor in the past, when he had been on the Bobitz to Kleinen section of the Hamburg-Stettin railway line:[7] just before reaching Kleinen, about a kilometer of open fields to the north, was the ancillary estate Glashagen, which was itself some 2 kilometers from the main holdings in Rastorf.[8] This is, however, the first time that he will have had the opportunity to actually see the farm, even if from the air.

He asks, and receives permission, to make this slight deviation from their route. Once in the area, it takes a little time to locate their estate, and the sight—and sound—of a giant airship directly above their heads causes the inhabitants to race outside to gawk, in spite of the fact that it is only about 8:00 a.m. Lehmann brings the airship down as far as he can—which was not that far, as the 200-meter antennas are trailing off the front and the captain avoids having them brush the ground at all costs. Nonetheless, the bright yellow flag that Pohl waves from the gondola does the trick—his relatives far below understand that this greeting is, indeed, for them.

From Rastorf, it is a short flight north to Wismar. Located at the southern end of the Bay of Wismar, which is, in turn, protected from the rough Baltic Sea waters by the Poel Island, Wismar has a long history as a port. It had been founded as a city in the thirteenth century, and had joined other towns in the Hanseatic League later that century. For most of the seventeenth century and until 1803, Wismar had belonged to Sweden but had been sold for 1,250,000 thalers to Mecklenburg, with the caveat that they could buy back the city for the same sum, plus 3 percent interest, in one hundred years. In 1903, on realizing this meant that buying the city back would cost a hundred million marks, Sweden formally renounced its claim to the city, and thus it remained a part of the grand-duchy of Mecklenburg-Schwerin.[9] It is generally considered to have one of the best harbors on the Baltic Sea. Unfortunately Pohl can see none of this, the churches there, nor the broad and straight streets that were a testament to the town's long-standing wealth. The weather had slowly changed from mist to lowlying, impenetrable fog, and given the difficulty he has in seeing anything of the landscape, Pohl decides it is time for another nap. He makes his way to the stern and the box he now considers his own bedroom, wraps himself up, and goes to sleep.

Below the clouds continue to hide the flat land that defines northern Germany, and thus the fact that they are passing within some 20 kilometers of Zepelin, the ancestral home of Count Zeppelin, goes unnoticed by all. Much like Rastorf, it is a small village in the middle of nowhere, and, were it not for its Count Zeppelin, would be entirely without note. It contains some thirty houses clustered at a crossroads around a church, and is situated just east of the Zepeliner Forest, on the other side of which is the nearest train station, that of Bützow. In the forest was erected in 1910 a monument to its favorite son. It consists of a roughly shaped piece of granite, inset on which is a bronze tablet with the inscription "To Count Ferdinand von Zeppelin, at the origin of his dynasty. 1286–1910." This stone is flanked left and right by two walls of smaller stones, and framed by two majestic oaks.[10]

Twenty-five kilometers almost due north of this small town, *LZ 120* approaches Rostock, another Baltic port, this one located 12 kilometers up the Warnow River. Like Wismar, it had been an early member of the Hanseatic League, and had been one of its most important members through the fifteenth century. With more than sixty thousand inhabitants, it is about three times the size of Wismar.[11] It also had been a university town since 1418, a university that Pohl mainly knew as the one that employed his colleague from his early days in Berlin and now one of the radiotelegraph specialists in the navy, Günther Falckenberg, as a professor before the war.

While the weather clears over Rostock, allowing for a good view of the city and its harbor, Pohl sleeps. He is not sad to miss this town, which he had overflown the previous year, at which time he commented only that the gigantic villas that dotted the Baltic coast in the area of Rostock were enough to generate feelings of envy in him. Better to sleep than to repeat that experience.

LZ 120 continues to fly over land, well south of the lagoons that separated the Zingst Peninsula from the mainland. They leave the grand-duchy of Mecklenburg-Schwerin and reenter Prussia. At 9:55, they reach Stralsund and the Baltic coast again, for the first time since the middle of the previous night. Once again, this is a town that was not new to Pohl. He had flown over it the previous year with Lehmann on their way to Kovno. By now, the weather has cleared and he could have seen the triangular town below, bounded on two sides by two lagoons and the Strela Sound, which separates the island of Rügen from the German mainland, on the third. Along the waterfront, too, can be seen the train track via which Pohl had arrived in Rügen eleven years earlier. The tracks curl around the old city, and then arrive at the harbor where passengers load straight onto the ship for the 2.5-kilometer ride across to Rügen. While Pohl had gotten off there, a mail ship from Sassnitz, in the northeastern corner of the island, would have taken him to Trelleborg, Sweden.[12]

The city of Stralsund itself Pohl had deemed "old-fashioned" the previous year—an opinion echoed in the 1911 *Encyclopaedia Britannica*, which elaborates: "The quaint architecture of the houses, many of which present their curious and handsome gables to the street, gives Stralsund an interesting and oldfashioned appearance."[13] It was, like so many other cities they had passed recently, an old Hanseatic town that could trace its origins to the thirteenth century. While it had now grown to have some 30,000 inhabitants, it had reached close to that number as early as the 1860s, and had thus barely grown in some fifty years. It, too, had been part of Sweden as of the Thirty Years' War, then was taken by France in 1807 and only become part of Prussia in 1815.[14]

At this point, Lehmann turns south, passing on the left the island of Dänholm in middle of the Strela Sound. On it can be seen the fortifications that had for so many years protected Stralsund. The great airship continues east, once again following the coast. Pohl, up in his nest, sleeps on.

Below, the Sound widens into the Bay of Greifswald. Lehmann hugs the coast, so that they pass close to the city of Greifswald once again. It is here that Pohl wakes up. He recognizes the city from above, looks at his watch, and calculates that they have now been in the air for about thirty-nine hours, and thus longer than any other airship that he knew of. Assuming that they land safely, the record is theirs. And there is absolutely no sign that Lehmann has any interest in landing yet.

CHAPTER 8
AIRSHIP DISTANCE RECORDS

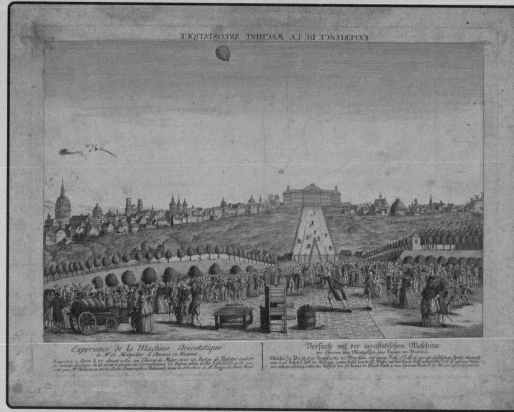

The scene on the Champs de Mars in Paris on August 27, 1783, as Jacques Charles and the Robert brothers launched the first hydrogen-filled balloon. *Library of Congress*

On the afternoon of August 27, 1783, a huge crowd of curious Parisians descended on the venerable Champs de Mars. They were drawn by the opportunity to see for themselves nothing less than the overcoming of gravity.

At the center of attention was Jacques Charles, a physicist, as well as the Robert brothers Anne-Jean and Nicolas-Louis, who were engineers. All three had been galvanized by the work of the Montgolfier brothers, who had made a public demonstration of a hot air balloon on June 4 of that year. However, Charles, working off the research of Henry Cavendish, decided to use hydrogen as a lifting agent, while the Robert brothers built the balloon of rubberized silk, in contrast to the Montgolfier brothers' paper.

Four days earlier in the Place des Victoires, the three inventors had begun filling their balloon with hydrogen, a slow procedure, and as the days passed and more and more people heard about the coming experiment, they were forced to move to the Champs de Mars—where the Eiffel Tower would be built one hundred years later—as the only place in Paris with the space available to handle the crowds. At 5:00 p.m., two cannon blasts alerted the crowd that liftoff was imminent; in a steady rain, the balloon finally had filled out properly and was released.

It immediately rose to 1,000 meters and flew to the village of Gonesse, some 20 kilometers away—where it was attacked by local peasants who had no idea what this strange contraption that had fallen out of the sky heralded.

Back at the Champs de Mars, one spectator asked another: "What good is it?" to which the other replied, "What good is a newborn baby?"[1]

The man with the answer was none other than Benjamin Franklin, since December 1776 the ambassador to France. Three days later, he had a less flippant answer as to the use of this new invention. In a letter to Sir Joseph Banks, the head of the British Royal Society, he wrote: "Among the Pleasantries Conversation produces on this Subject, some suppose Flying to be now invented, and that since Men may be supported in the Air, nothing is wanted but some light handy Instruments to give and direct Motion."[2]

Franklin's comment was both prescient and premature. After all, no one had yet been up in a balloon—though that was soon to change—and of the three technologies needed to build an airship, only one was now even close to being viable. In fact, it would be almost sixty years until the first true airship would take flight.

The biggest obstacle to airships was that all the current sources of power—human, animal, water, wind—were not usable in an airship, and steam engines, which had been in operation since the early eighteenth century, remained far too heavy for use in an airship. Not only that, the means of transferring energy from the source into actual propulsion was simply unknown. Though Leonardo da Vinci had sketched an idea for a helicopter with a rotor very much like the propellers that would be needed to push a ship, no working model had been built.

In fact, it would be fifty years before someone actually tried to build a steerable balloon. In 1834, the Comte de Lennox, a Philadelphia-born former soldier who had become enamored with flight in 1832, when he had taken his first flight, decided that he would build a dirigible. Building on the work of Dr. Le Berrier, his dirigible, dubbed *L'Aigle* (The Eagle), was 50 meters long and had 2,800 cubic meters of hydrogen to lift it. The car suspended below had room for sixteen crew members, who were equipped with oars to direct the airship.[3] Whether this would have actually worked is unclear. Oars are generally useful when used to maneuver a vessel between two differing media (e.g., a boat floating on water).

In spite of the many unanswered—and apparently untested—questions around his airship, Lennox was so sure that he would succeed that he announced that his first trip would be from Paris to London, and that he would soon be flying this route for paying passengers. In any case, since the airship never actually took off, the questions were all moot. The large number of Parisians who assembled on the Champs de Mars on August 17, 1834, were displeased when the airship's envelope burst while being filled, and proceeded to thoroughly demolish Lennox's creation.[4]

While Le Berrier died soon after, "of grief," as an account of the story would put it fifty years later,[5] Lennox would move to London, where he continued his research, coming up with a design the following year that was, if possible, even less airworthy than *L'Aigle*, and would die suddenly two years later.

It would be almost another twenty years before there would be a successful airship. This was Henri Giffard's 1852 creation. Giffard solved two problems at once. The first was indeed a "light handy Instrument" to produce power: a steam engine that produced 3 or 4 horsepower, while weighing only 48 kilograms, a fairly reasonable 16 kg/hp,[6] or about a tenth of the power to weight ratio of *LZ 120*'s HSLu motors, and far better than the usual 500 kg/hp that characterized the state of the 1852 art.

Furthermore, Giffard had invented a propeller, a simple arrangement of two paddles on either end of a stick that was connected at its middle to the drive shaft of the engine. The two paddles were at slight angles to the air through which they cut, thus forcing air backward—and the airship (which Giffard never named) forward. On September 24, 1852, Giffard launched his airship from the Hippodrom in Paris and flew to Elancourt, a distance of 27 kilometers. Since his airship's top speed was, at best, 2–3 meters/second (some 8 kilometers per hour), even the lightest wind would be insurmountable. In fact, Giffard found from the start that he could, at best, steer against the wind; the location of his landing was given not by his wish but where the wind took him. Returning to his takeoff point was out of the question, so Giffard had to find alternative means of getting home.[7]

In spite of all of these caveats, this was the first time that an aircraft had managed to create and apply energy to guide its route—a historic success. In particular, the ability of the airship to remain horizontal and the fact that the coal-powered engine did not ignite the flammable coal gas that gave the airship its buoyancy were mentioned as proof that lighter-than-air travel was a real possibility. Sadly, Giffard not only did not replicate his flight but never managed to get another airship into the air. Instead, he devoted himself to balloons and, in the late 1870s, sold tethered balloon flights to the citizens of Paris.

Over the next fifty years, huge strides were made in motors, both steam as well as the new invention of gas-powered engines. They remained, however, either too heavy or too finicky to work in airships, and thus inventors tried to create airships that would be steerable even without engines. One of the more clever dirigibles was made by a US inventor named Solomon Andrews. Andrews had first made a name for himself a few years earlier, during the Civil War, when he had suggested to Abraham Lincoln that he had a dirigible airship. And, indeed, in contrast to other inventors, Andrews had shown off his *Aereon*, flying multiple times over Perth Amboy, New Jersey. Eventually, Andrews managed to get as far as showing off models of his airships to members of Congress—who were duly impressed—but by the time any further decision could be reached, it was already March 1865, and with the war almost over, no further money would flow for new technologies such as this.

Andrews's idea was based on the fact that a board held under water can be made to go either forward or backward, depending on which end is allowed to go up first. The airship was built of three tubes tied together, with a weight below that could be swung fore and aft. By moving this weight, either the bow or stern of the airship could be raised—and the craft would move in that direction.

His second airship, named *Aereon 2*, used a system of levers to compress and release the gas, going between being positively and negatively buoyant. As the airship rose and fell, in each case moving forward as well as up or down, it could then be steered using the rudder.

On June 5, 1865, Andrews took off from lower Manhattan and flew for 43 kilometers, steering the airship over New York City in a way that enthralled crowds below. After landing in Oyster Bay, Andrews announced plans for a bigger and better airship, but a financial panic a few years later destroyed both Andrews's income and his dreams of a new class of airship.

Even before Andrews had taken off, a new propulsion technology that would revolutionize not only the airship but all other industries had been invented: that of the internal combustion engine. A far cry from the engines powering *LZ 120*, the first examples as built by the Belgian Étienne Lenoir, burned uncompressed coal gas,[8] making them far less efficient than those built by Maybach fifty years later—but remained a distinct improvement over steam engines. In 1872, Paul Haenlein, a German engineer, built the first airship powered by this new invention. Haenlein, in contrast to many of his predecessors, took care in building his airship, starting by building a model airship, which he successfully tested multiple times in both Mainz and Vienna. The latter tests generated sufficient interest for money to be raised to build a full-scale variant. Built in Brno, in Austria-Hungary, it was relatively small, with space for only two aeronauts. In 1872, tests were made on the new airship, dubbed *Aeolus* after the ruler of the wind in Greek mythology. The tests were quite successful, other than that they never actually let the airship loose. Instead, it was held by crew members on the ground throughout. In spite of this, *Aeolus* managed upward of 11 miles per hour and showed itself to be easily steered, especially when the motors were on full.[9] On May 9, 1873, however, the Viennese stock market crashed[10] and took with it Haenlein's company—and any hope of building on his successes.

Earlier that year, however, there had been another record-breaking flight, undertaken by the Frenchman Dupuy de Lome, who had gained fame as a steamship engineer, and then had become intrigued by balloons, and especially dirigible balloons, during the 1871 siege of Paris by the Prussians. He began building the airship during the siege, but building a giant balloon while surrounded by the enemy is not the easiest of tasks, and so the first flight would not take place until the following year. In February 1872, the airship, now named *Dupuy de Lome*, would fly almost three times as far as Solomon Andrews had flown. There were, however, significant issues with the flight. De Lome's airship used humans to power it; thus the flight could be called—at best—steered. Most of the trip from Fort Neuf de Vincennes in southeast Paris to Montescourt, due south of Saint Quentin and northeast of Paris, was done at the whim of the wind; at best, the four men who were plying the shaft that turned the propeller could affect the direction, not direct it. In spite of this, De Lome announced himself satisfied and announced that he would be inaugurating flight service between Paris and other European cities, with flights to happen whenever the wind was correct or correct enough that the sailors could ensure that the airship arrived at the proper destination. Needless to say, this never quite worked out and de Lome—who was one of France's most celebrated engineers—went back to his main project, that of building a tunnel to England.[11]

All of the previously described airships shared one significant problem: they were incapable of returning to their starting point, since they simply lacked the power to counteract any but the mildest winds. It would be twelve years after de Lome's flight that this would change, with the August 9, 1884, flight of an airship built by Charles Renard and Arthur Constantin Krebs. Their airship, modestly named *La France*, managed to fly about 8 kilometers in twenty minutes, but—most importantly—returned to its takeoff spot. With an average speed of about 18 kph, it was not that much more capable than its predecessors. However, and more importantly, Renard and Krebs managed to repeat their triumph numerous times over the next year. While they were kept from a proper return in two cases, once because of an accident and once because of high winds, four times they were able to make a successful flight. On their flight of September 23, 1885, they managed an average speed of 24 kilometers per hour and were observed by the French military, who had begun to take an interest in this new technology.[12] The main problem with *La France*—as well as the brothers Tissandier's airship, which had also successfully flown in 1883 and 1884[13]—was that they were powered by an electrical engine, which sharply limited their radius of action. Nonetheless, the lessons gleaned from these two new airships showed the way to new possibilities.

It would be another fifteen years before there was someone who could capitalize on these opportunities, someone who had both the interest and the money to buy one of the newer, lightweight, internal combustion motors. This man was Alberto Santos-Dumont, and in his home country of Brazil, he is revered as the father of flight.

Santos-Dumont had been born on a ranch in Brazil, into a rich family, and could well have spent his time in the life of leisure. Instead, he found himself drawn to the mechanical, spending his time working on the engines that powered the plantation. He found an outlet for his passion after seeing his first balloon, when he was about fifteen. Over the next few years, he spent time in Paris, where he was saddened to see that there were no airships, but fortunately a lively ballooning scene, of which he was soon a part. His first balloon, named *Brazil*, was a small, one-man balloon. In 1897, he decided to build on the work of Henri Giffard, and—after examining all engines available—settled on a small petroleum-powered one that had been built to power a tricycle. He tested it out in a road race and found it to work well, but dropped out for fear of hurting the engine. Instead, he focused on building a small airship built around the motor. In September 1898, it was ready for flight. Dubbed *Santos-Dumont No. 1*, it proved to be only marginally airworthy, but Santos-Dumont was undeterred, and continued to refine his plans—and build new airships.

In 1900, a new target presented itself: the Deutsch Prize. Offered by Henri Deutsch de la Meurthe, it was to be given to the first person to fly a course starting from the Paris Aero Club's Aerostation in St. Cloud, a suburb of Paris, complete one turn around the Eiffel Tower, and returning to its point of origin, all within thirty minutes. All eyes were on Santos-Dumont, whose airships had previously managed just such a trip. The airship builder himself realized immediately that his current airship—*No. 4*—was not capable of a feat such as this. He therefore set out immediately to build one that could win the prize.

Early in the morning of July 13, 1901, he made his first attempt in *No. 5*, a rebuilt version of *No. 4*. Unfortunately, after making the turn around the Eiffel Tower in ten minutes, the return voyage had been hampered by a strong headwind, and—already ten minutes over the time limit—the motor quit, depositing *No. 5* in a chestnut tree gracing the garden of Edmond de Rothschild.

Undaunted, Santos-Dumont commissioned *No. 6* and—after a few minor accidents while testing out his new airship—decided to attempt to win the Deutsch Prize on October 19, 1901. This time, the trip proceeded with no hitch. There was some discussion as to the exact moment of his return, whether he had in fact made it within the time limit, but M. Deutsch himself agreed that the conditions had been met, and Santos-Dumont had not only won the prize but had proven that an airship could, indeed, run on a schedule. It pointed to a new day in the building and flying of airships.[14]

One of the innovations Santos-Dumont had worked out was that of a keel, a rigid section along the bottom of the balloon, which lessened the chance of a simple leaking balloon becoming a tragedy as the airship lost all rigidity along with the loss of some gas. This idea was built upon by a number of inventors, not least by Schwarz, who built the entire gas bag out of aluminum, making an entirely rigid envelope.[15] Schwarz's airship failed spectacularly, but his ideas—particularly the use of aluminum—were picked up by Count Zeppelin, who began a slow and steady work on the airship question in Manzell, resulting in the 1900 flight of LZ 1. This Zeppelin, which took off from the calm waters of Lake Constance, did not break any speed, distance, or time aloft records. While many of his predecessors had greeted every success, be it ever so humble, with immediate plans for a globe-spanning airship line, Zeppelin preferred to test everything thoroughly before proceeding.

It would be 1907 before Zeppelin's third craft, hull number LZ 3, would break the distance and time aloft record. In the meantime, only the Lebaudy brothers's airship *Le Jaune*, had shown that any progress was being made. While the distance flown was actually less than de Lome's 1872 record, *Le Jaune* was actually powered by an internal combustion engine. Furthermore, Lebaudy managed numerous flights of similar length, a replicability unmatched by previous airships.[16]

The magazine *Wiener Luftschiffer-Zeitung* (*Viennese Airshipman's Newspaper*) described the scene, in particular the representatives of the Reich, including Major Hans Georg Friedrich Groß, several members of the airship battalion, and Georg von Arco of the Telefunken corporation, whose main business lay in the relatively new question of wireless telegraphy.

> The failures of the official attempts on September 28 were made up for in triumphant style by a record-breaking flight, which left behind all previous distance attempts in balloon airships. Graf Zeppelin managed to complete a s e v e n h o u r flight in his balloon! [Odd spacing as in the original; this method of emphasis appears to be uniquely German][17]

Further dispatches within the main article described the flight: at about 11:30 a.m. on September 28, the Zeppelin took off from the surface of Lake Constance near Friedrichshafen, then traveling northeast over the towns of Ravensburg and Weingarten, where they thousands cheered them on. From there, they returned to their beginning spot and then flew a long circle around the perimeter of the lake. When they arrived again, after a flight distance estimated to be 350 kilometers, the aircraft was still fully functional, and so Count Zeppelin dropped off two of his passengers, took on two more, and completed another one hour flight.

This record flight kicked off a whole series of further attempts to improve either the time aloft or distance traveled records. Zeppelin's time aloft record lasted exactly one month: it was beaten on October 28 of the same year by Major Groß, who together with Nikolaus Basenach had built a semirigid airship that they were interested in selling to the German army. Their airship, named *M-a*, took off from Tegel, in Berlin, and returned there after a flight of some 200 kilometers and eight hours and ten minutes in the air.[18]

Unsurprisingly, Zeppelin did not allow this to stand, and he was ready for a new attempt on July 1 of the following year, now in his newest airship, with hull number LZ 4. It was intended for the army, but the army required a twenty-four-hour flight before paying for it and thus had not yet been given a name. Once again, the airship took off from Lake Constance at 8:30 a.m., then flying west to Constance and Schaffhausen, then south to Lucerne before returning via Zürich and Winterthur. Landing was at 8:30 p.m., for a solid twelve-hour flight. Furthermore, the distance traveled was some 350 kilometers, for an average speed of 30 kilometers per hour.[19]

Before Zeppelin could return to the air and any attempt at record-breaking, Groß and Basenach would fly their new airship *M I* for thirteen hours, leaving again from

Tegel, flying west to Magdeburg, and back. Once again, while not increasing the record for distance flown, they were in the air about an hour longer than Zeppelin had been.[20]

Obviously, this required an answer, and so Count Zeppelin returned to the hunt in *Z I*, the same airship he had used in his 1907 attempt. Since then, the airship had been rebuilt after an accident, and been turned over to the army, who had also given it a proper name. The British magazine *Flight* reported ten days later:

> What is reported as a secret military flight was successfully carried out by the Zeppelin airship early last week, when it remained in the air all night, and complete a return voyage of thirteen hours' duration. Exactly what happened is, of course, unknown, but the movement was evidently attended with considerable success. The start took place at 10 o'clock from Friedrichshafen on Tuesday evening, April 6th, and the airship did not return to its shed until eleven o'clock the next morning, an altogether creditable performance for "His Majesty's Airship 'Zeppelin I.'"[21]

The article furthermore added that the flight had been eleven minutes longer than that of *M I* the previous year and that, once again, a twenty-four-hour flight had been envisioned, but that "some slight mishap" had was responsible for cutting short the attempt.

Late the following month, Count Zeppelin finally managed his twenty-four-hour flight, this time in *Z II* (hull number LZ 5). In fact, he managed a flight of almost thirty-eight hours, but unfortunately, the airship crashed in landing, so this would not, in fact, count as a record. Instead, it would be Major Groß who would set the next marker, both for distance and time.[22] On August 4, 1909, his *M II* took off from Tegel and, after flying southeast through Thuringia and Saxony, returned sixteen hours later to Tegel, having covered some 460 kilometers.[23] A little less than a year later, Zeppelin *Deutschland* (hull number LZ 7) would improve on the distance record, flying 540 kilometers at a stretch. More impressively, this feat was accomplished in only nine hours.

For the last six years, it had thus been only German airships vying for the records. This would change the following year when the French Clement-Bayard airship *Adjutant Vincenot* would fly over sixteen hours, and cover 650 kilometers, taking off on July 7, 1911, from its hangar in Compiègne and flying between there and Soissons.[24]

Another Clement-Bayard airship, the *Clement Bayard II a*, had established another record the previous year, flying some 290 kilometers in six hours—but did this between Paris and London, becoming the first airship to cross the English Channel,[25] a little over a year since Louis Blériot had managed the feat in his airplane—and 125 years since the crossing had been made in a balloon, by Jean Pierre François Blanchard and John Jeffries, who had managed the feat just a year and a half after the experiment witnessed by Benjamin Franklin in 1783.[26]

The *Adjutant Vincenot*'s record would only stand briefly. On September 18, another French airship, the *Adjutant Reau*, took off from Issy, just southwest of Paris, and flying southeast all the way to Belfort, almost on the Swiss border, before returning home. They landed the following day, twenty-one hours and twenty minutes after takeoff. The round-trip distance to Belfort was 740 kilometers, but deviations from this route—including to Verdun—had brought the total distance traveled to about 1,000 kilometers.[27]

While all these flights were written up in the press of the time, they were not, in general, recognized records. In order to be official, they had to be monitored by the Fédération Aéronautique Internationale (FAI—World Air Sports Federation), which has monitored air records since its founding in 1905. Just before the outbreak of the World War, they listed as records two flights by an Italian airship, the *Piccolo 5*, as longest time aloft—fifteen hours, set on June 25, 1913, and on July 30, the longest distance, 810 kilometers.[28]

The French and Germans, however, continued to vie for the records, without, however, getting any sort of certification for their efforts. So, for instance, Zeppelin *Z I* (hull number LZ 19, and, in fact, the third airship named *Z I*) took off on July 3, 1913, from Frankfurt, and landed nineteen hours later in Königsberg, having flown 950 kilometers.[29] This record would be beaten in October of the same year by the *Citta di Ferrara*, an Italian airship,[30] only to lose the record to the Schütte-Lanz airship *SL II* the following April.[31] All three of these records, however, referred only to the distance traveled—the time aloft record remained the *Adjutant Reau*'s 21:20.

This would change on May 22, 1914, when Count Zeppelin would take back both records. On May 22, 1914, the newest Zeppelin, with hull number LZ 24, took off from Friedrichshafen. Built for the navy, it had been named *L 3*, and was the first of the M-class Zeppelins that would be the mainstay of the German Zeppelin fleet for the opening months of the war.

The first hours were spent over the Lake of Constance, making sure that all systems were working, then they headed south to Basel, before turning north to Frankfurt and then Metz and Bingen. The latter leg was of particular interest in that it was reported that the airship managed to complete the 150-kilometer stretch in an hour. This was, in truth, unlikely, in that the top speed of the airship was about one half that. Unless they were blown along by a strong gale (or had managed to get up into the jet stream), there was no way that this airship could have achieved such speed. From Bingen, the airship headed north to the island of Heligoland in the North Sea, then back down via Hamburg to Berlin. A final detour to Stettin and back completed a 2,000-kilometer trip that finally ended in the Berlin suburb of Johannisthal. The airship had been in the air for almost thirty-five hours, and had thus beaten not only the distance but time aloft records by almost 50 percent. It was a triumph of engineering for Count Zeppelin and the Zeppelin corporation—and a short-lived one.[32] A month later, the Clement-Bayard airship *Adjutant Vincenot*, which had held both records three years earlier for about two months but had since been thoroughly rebuilt, flew for thirty-five hours and twenty minutes, taking off on June 28—the very same day Gavrilo Princip had assassinated Archduke Franz Ferdinand of Austria—from Toul and flying a large circuit that included Paris before returning to Toul.[33] It had been in constant contact with the ground via a radio transceiver in the Eiffel Tower, the newspapers of the time reported.[34]

A month later, the war broke out, and there were no further attempts at any record keeping on the continent. Across the English Channel, however, a new record had been set. The British, who had never been players in the airship record hunt, had been investigating airships for patrol duty since the beginning of the war, with the Sea Scout class entering service in March 1915, followed by the Coastal class the following year. In January of the same year, approval was given for the building of six new, larger, airships at the Royal Naval Airship Station in Kingsnorth, southeast of London and not far from the English Channel. The first airship produced, *North Sea 1*, would take to the air a little over a year later. While only a fifth of the size of *LZ 120*, it had been built for one purpose—to stay aloft for long stretches of time. And thus, at 6:00 a.m. June 26, 1917, the airship took off from its station in Pulham, Norfolk, and did not return to earth until 7:22 on the twenty-eighth, having been in the air for forty-nine hours and twenty-two minutes, and traveling almost 2,500 kilometers in that time—both records well above what any other airship had managed, prewar. However, the North Sea class was, on the whole, not yet ready for introduction to the war effort. Even while *North Sea 1* was completing its record-breaking flight, its sister ship *North Sea 2*, also on an endurance mission, lost gas and wrecked.[35] While Lehmann and his crew were floating over the Baltic Sea, the engineers in RNAS Kingsnorth were desperately trying to reengineer their fleet.

Either way, 49:22 hours and 2,500 kilometers were the records that Lehmann was attempting to better at this moment.

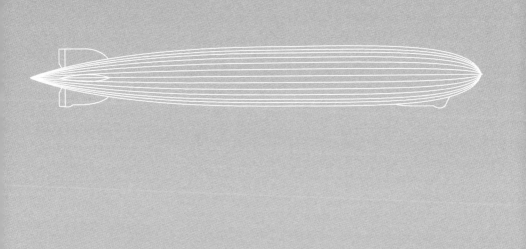

CHAPTER 9
JULY 28, 10:30 A.M.–JULY 28, 11:30 P.M.

Frau Susanne Lehmann. Born Susanne Dienemann in 1886 of Pomeranian (i.e., exactly the area of northern Germany that *LZ 120* was flying over for most of the flight) extraction, she married Ernst August Lehmann in 1915. They had no children.

Professor Pohl wakes up around 10:30 as they pass Greifswald once again. He goes forward to the cabin, where there is a general consensus that all aboard should get cleaned up, and—in particular—shave. After all, the next towns they are to fly over are three famous seaside towns on islands that separate the Stettiner Haff from the Baltic Sea at the mouth of the Oder River: Heringsdorf, Swinemünde, and Misdroy. The three resort towns were spread out across two islands, Usedom and Wollin. These islands had been a center of commerce since around 1000 AD, excavations on Wollin had discovered Arabian coins from that era. Unsurprisingly, given their location, they had also been important fishing grounds but also the wide-open lands away from the sea had been farmed since the sixteenth century. More surprising was that there was also considerable mining activity.[1]

However, since 1824, there had been an enormous change in its use. In that year, the town of Swinemünde had opened bathing beaches. It was the second Baltic bathing resort to open, after Heiligendamm, 150 kilometers to the west, which had opened in 1793. It was followed shortly thereafter by Heringsdorf, which had quickly become—and remained—the most fashionable of the Baltic resorts.[2] Misdroy was a comparative latecomer, beginning its change from a fishing village in 1835, when visitors repelled by the citylike atmosphere that reigned in the other two towns arrived there.[3] The towns remained in the public consciousness through regular visits by royalty, including a 1907 visit by Kaiser Wilhelm II and Tsar Nicholas II, a visit that had been arranged to impress the Tsar of the new-found power of the German empire.[4]

The towns were particularly popular among Berliners, as that city was only a three-and-a-half-hour train ride away.[5] Swinemünde attracted by far the most visitors, with some 40,000 prewar, while Misdroy had less than half that amount. As befits the most fashionable of the resorts, Heringsdorf came in third with some 12,000.[6]

Beyond these towns, the whole geography laid out below is quite remarkable. Along the coast are two islands, Usedom and Wollin, separated by the Swine River. While Heringsdorf and Swinemünde are on the former island, Misdroy is on the latter. Swinemünde is, in contrast to the other two towns, also an important port, as goods that could not go down the Swine and across the Stettiner Haff to Stettin, 30 kilometers up the Oder River, had to be transshipped here. Since the widening of the Swine, the town had lost in importance as a port, but gained it as a resort.[7]

The Stettiner Haff had played a small part in airship history, when in November 1908, Major Groß had involuntarily landed there with his airship *M I*. The plan had been to prove that this airship would be able to fly for an extended period of time—possibly even beat the record of thirteen hours that Gross had set just two months ago in the same airship. Unfortunately, everything had gone wrong on takeoff in Berlin, when they had found themselves lost in the fog. They almost immediately gave up on the idea of an extended flight, and instead decided to spend the night in the air and then return to Berlin. After mistaking one train track for another, they suddenly realized that they had drifted very far from their original plan when they saw that they were over the Stettiner Haff. Opting to land on Wollin on the other side of the water, they pulled the release valve—but they did so too early, and thus found themselves on the water, 200 meters from shore. Fortunately, they drifted onto shore at which time they released the rest of their lifting gas. A troop of mechanics was sent to repair the airship, and it was soon thereafter transferred to Cologne.[8] Today, as they fly along under clear skies, with the land stretched out below as on a map, the uncertainty and panic of ten years ago seems quite impossible.

Instead, in honor of the seaside towns below, an electric water heater has been added to the chaos that reigns on the table—and, in fact, all surfaces—in the back of the main cabin. Empty seltzer and coffee bottles, sausage peels, cheese rinds, and breadcrumbs all combine to endanger the interspersed maps and novels with grease spots. The hot water produced by the cooker is combined with a bit of soap to produce some form of shaving cream. Three shaving brushes, one attached to the telephone, one to a thermos bottle, and one that floats around the cabin, are used to spread the resulting foam across the cheeks of the airship crew.

The process goes reasonably smoothly, with the flight engineer Buczilowsky managing to avoid hacking into his pimples as he had done the previous day, so no need to break out the first aid kit again. Only August Grözinger, a machinist who was listed on the manifest as a machine gunner stationed in the gondolas, manages to cut himself, and he masters the situation by pulling a piece of sticking plaster out of his wallet, cutting it down to size, and covering it in dirt from his filthy gloves before using it to staunch the bleeding.

In short, Pohl declares the operation a complete success, even if First Officer Schehl manages to lose the bowl they had used for the hot water overboard when tossing out the leftover soap and water. His fingers were still covered in soap scum and were thus unable to hold on to the precious item.

The next stop is attached with a somewhat more somber note. It is neither the town, Köslin, nor the person that they would be looking for that were at issue, but rather the reason for her attendance there. Lehmann's wife, Susanne, is visiting her sister, who had recently lost her husband in the war.

Köslin, a manufacturing town of some twenty thousand inhabitants, is easy to find—situated on the main road from Stettin to Danzig, its squashed-oval shape makes it stand out among all the other towns that dot this region.[9] Furthermore, Lehmann's wife and sister-in-law are staying in a house directly on the market which was just north of the main road in the very center of town.

Difficulties arise when Lehmann attempts to bring *LZ 120* down for a closer look. The amount of fuel that has been burned in the previous thirty-six hours has markedly lightened the airship, combined with the warming effects of the clear skies which further bolstered the vessel's lift, make it impossible to fly far enough down. Pointing the nose down and turning up the engines allows Lehmann to bring the airship down to about 450 meters, but no closer. Fortunately, even at this height, an airship is not easily overlooked, and soon the crew can see two small figures in the window of the corner house in which Lehmann's wife is staying.

With this visit out of the way, Lehmann orders the airship to head due north. It is time, he decides, to take seriously the reason he had given for this flight: reconnaissance. At about 1:20 p.m., they cross the Baltic coast and head toward Öland, a long thin island just off the east coast of Sweden. It is the second-largest island in Sweden, begins about 100 kilometers north of the southern tip of that country, and stretches some 137 kilometers north. It is, however, no more than 16 kilometers wide at its widest. It is separated from the town of Kalmar by a narrow band of water—named the Kalmar Sound—that is not quite 6 kilometers wide at its most narrow. The island is mainly known for its stone, orthocerene limestone made of prehistoric animals, and well filled with fossils, and therefore in great demand for paving stones. In spite of the island being "arid and exposed to extreme heat in summer," it had a population of just under 30,000.[10]

As they putter up alongside Öland at a steady 80 kilometers per hour, Lehmann decides to motivate his troops and orders that the one warm meal that he had planned for the trip would be served.

This is not an easy task. The first step is to heat the pea soup that had been brought on board. This requires one of the machinists to connect a specially built double-hulled metal pot to the cooling water line from one motor. The radiators are installed between the top of the motor gondolas and the keel, so that they could be refilled from inside the Zeppelin. This means that the water can also be used for other purposes. In this case, water that had been heated by the motor flows through the gap between the two hulls of the pot. The water then heats the soup to the appropriate temperature, and can then be served to the hungry crew, who stand waiting on the catwalk in the keel.

The first to receive his food decides that he would like to eat his meal in the relative peace of the main gondola, and thus steps onto the ladder that would allow him to climb down. As soon as he enters the rush of wind that whistles through the ladder, the contents of the plate are blown away, much to his regret and the amusement of the rest of the crew.

The others getting their food are more cautious, and eat their soup while standing on the gangway in the keel of the airship. It is not the most comfortable place to have a meal, but preferable to the alternative. Knowing that this is their only warm meal for the next two plus days means that the crew—and even Professor Pohl, who is leery of the aftereffects therefrom—choose to crumble into the soup large chunks of the soldier's bread that they have on board, bread whose usual rye flour had been stretched by the use of potato flour.

The results are almost immediate and devastating. The amount of gas produced is beyond even Pohl's most pessimistic projections, and it is not long before everyone has given up on any kind of sense of dignity and is relieving their gastric distress as loudly and malodorously as possible. It is time to seek some peace, quiet, and above all, fresh air.

Pohl thus returns to the stern of the ship, onto the gun platform, sits down cross-legged on the corrugated aluminum sheet that makes up the bottom of it, digs a small graph-paper notebook out of his pocket, as well as the stumpy pencil that is his preferred writing implement, and begins a letter to his mother.

That the overwhelming nature of his current experience is making itself known is immediately apparent from the very first letters he writes: the date, which is off by ten days, stating that it is the eighteenth of July rather than the twenty-eighth. The following address, though somewhat odd, is indeed completely correct. His name he used for his mother was "Murl," his own odd reworking of "mother." He continues:

> I can't imagine that I have ever written to you from a place as strange as the one in which I find myself today. I am sitting about 600 m up in the air on the stern platform of the *LZ 120*, which is proceeding along parallel to the southern coast of Sweden, just outside of its territorial limits. It is sunny and there is a brisk breeze. It is quite gusty, and I am sitting crosslegged on the ground, which accounts for the somewhat poor handwriting. You may wonder why I have chosen a place apparently so unsuited to writing, when there are obviously tables and even comfortable wicker chairs on board. Unfortunately, this . . .

At this point, Pohl has filled a page with his chunky handwriting and he turns over the paper and continues:

> . . . furniture can only be found in the front gondola, where there are invariably 6–8 people bouncing around, creating too much chaos. Back here I have my office all to myself, and you know how important that is to me. Imagine the

stern of the ship, with S the stabilizing [here he adds a picture showing the stern of the airship] fins: R the rudders, F the flag, and K is my box. The floor is about 1.2 × 2.5 meters, and just deep enough in the middle so I can sit down. It is wonderfully quiet; one can hear only the swishing of the flowing air and feel a very mild quiver in the stern. There is no sign of the droning of the motors, which otherwise pervades the ship. If I stand up, all I see of the ship are the four fins and the four rudders, as well as the snarl of guy ropes which hold up these surfaces. I see nothing of the actual hull of the ship, as the body is too strongly curved. Otherwise, I can see 360 degrees around me, as far as the eye can see, and I can even spit over the flag at the stern, as I just demonstrated to myself. Right now, I see only water and blue sky, on the port side I can see the setting sun and a few stony islands, whose main raison d'être seems to be to push out the territorial limits of Sweden. While I have been writing, we have turned around, after meeting a German convoy and a couple of suspicious individuals, who immediately escaped into the neutral zone upon seeing us, we are now flying along the east coast towards north, obviously east of Öland, as there isn't enough water between it and the main land to allow for international travel there.

At this point in his writing, the sun is beginning to set, so Pohl stretches the canvas cover over the gun platform which he has now decided is his. He then goes forward to the main cabin, where he is told that they were moving slowly north just to the east of Öland. For some reason, the crew notes this as being the Kalmar Sound, which is a very narrow band of water separating the island from the Swedish mainland. There is no way that this would not have raised complaints from the Swedish side; it was in Lehmann's best interest to remain just outside Swedish territorial waters.

The airship is now also far enough from its home base that it makes sense for Pohl to attempt some experiments. After all, that was why he had ostensibly signed up for this trip in the first place. He takes over the radioman's office in the back of the main cabin, slips on the headphones, and begins searching for the familiar signals from the antennas that he has had erected all over Germany, in Tondern, Nordholz, near Wangerooge, near Bocholt, and near Ghent.

At this distance, however, the signals are so attenuated that they are hardly distinguishable from the background noise. The distance he is working at is about twice the distance that a Zeppelin radio operator would have to work with if over England. Furthermore, the difference in direction to the five stations he is attempting to listen to are so minute that even a decent signal would not have given enough accuracy for a reliable location.

After an hour or so of fruitless attempts, Pohl gives up and decides to return to his eyrie in the back of the airship. This is, as he realizes as he climbs up into the hull, much more easily said than done. While he was doing his experiments, the sun had set completely and left the Zeppelin in darkness. Particularly the keel of the airship is dark, and the 180-meter passage back to the stern seems interminable. His footsteps are accompanied by the ominous creaking of the duralumin gangway, a noise that that attests to the fact that the walkway was built to be as light as possible.[11]

While the gloom was something Pohl was aware of, and had indeed prepared for by bringing along a flashlight on the flight, he had left this important tool on the gunner's platform earlier. Fortunately, however, each girder, step, and even the fuel barrels are marked with radium paint, delivering just enough light ensure that he does not miss a step, and he arrives safe and sound in his little nest, where he falls asleep wrapped in his blankets.

The time is about 11:30 p.m. The airship continues its course through the night, heading generally north, high above the straits separating the islands of Öland and Gotland.

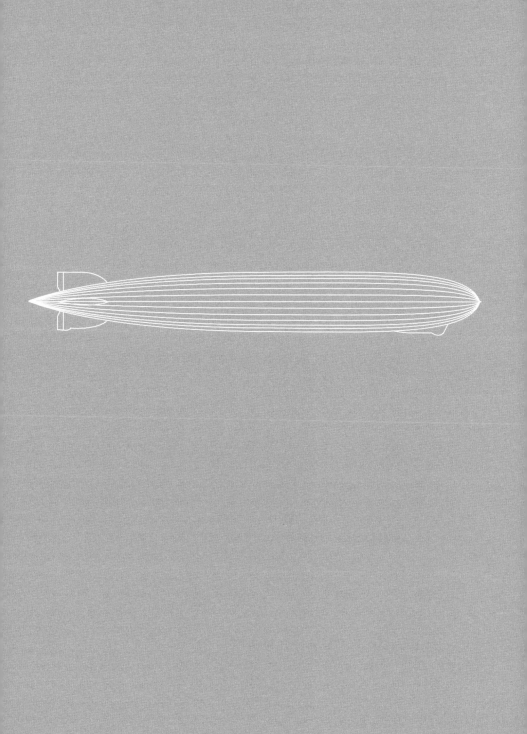

CHAPTER 10
RADIO DIRECTION FINDING

Robert Wichard Pohl, *at right*, in front of an antenna array T547 in 1917. With him are (*from left*) Private Rohrbach, First Lieutenant Viktor Wendelstadt, and Captain Ellister.

Robert Pohl had downed his pen on November 6, 1914, in order to make it on time to the meeting of the German Physical Society. He was under no illusion that the meeting would be of great interest, but as the secretary of the society, and with his deputy, James Franck, away in the army, it was important that he go.

The meeting, which had as its main attraction a lecture by the society's president, Fritz Haber, on the heat of reaction and specific heat of ammonia, was otherwise bereft of the usual demonstrations, introduction of new members or even moments of silence for fallen members. Pohl did his duty in filling out the relevant sections in the minute book.[1]

While the meeting itself may have been uninspiring, the postlecture meeting would make a lasting impact on Pohl, and fundamentally change his role in the war effort. During the postsession get-together, Pohl found himself sitting next to Second Lieutenant von Lepel, of the large and militarily important Lepel family, who was high up in the telegraph troops. Pohl complained to him about not being able to help the Fatherland, and Lepel assured him that he would soon have his chance, as experts who also had military training were rare on the ground, that they would soon look farther afield for this sort of expertise. Pohl described this meeting in a letter to his mother on November 8, adding that he hoped that he would be able to do his small part in the enormous job ahead.

During their talk, Lepel had invited Pohl to Treptow, a suburb of Berlin, where the radio unit had its headquarters. Twelve days later, Pohl took him up on the offer. He was first given a tour of the station, which was built to the most modern standards, and without regard to its cost. After this, they all repaired to the cafeteria, where Pohl was introduced to Hans Georg Friedrich Groß, who was an early airship pioneer and now a part of the airship unit, in spite of being vehemently against the Zeppelin construction. Groß had designed semirigid airships, and a series of four ships, on which he collaborated with with Nikolaus Basenach, were built and flown by him prewar. The last, the *M IV*, managed a flight of thirteen hours and 300 kilometers in 1907.

Groß impressed Pohl immensely, and he left Treptow with the assurance that his talents would be used properly by the radio group. In fact, they even gave him his first assignment: to create a way of determining the location of an enemy radio. Pohl knew this to be theoretically simple, and in fact had been solved by Max Dieckmann, a physicist who had researched wireless telegraphy before the war and had worked with Count Zeppelin in that time.[2] The question was simply whether or not a practical apparatus could be built, one that was simple enough for troops to carry around with them on the front lines. Pohl had also been asked to help build a new radio station, and had received the assurance that he would, eventually, be inducted into the army. His biggest worry as he left that day was that the war would be over before all of this came to fruition, a thought he shared with his mother in a letter he wrote later that day.

As always, it was "hurry up and wait," and while the army slowly made up its mind to use Pohl, he continued to spend two hours a day on his x-ray work, as well as starting that semester's classes. He was teaching an experimental physics class, which required a fair bit of preparation of the instruments beforehand. He only had ten students that year in his class, which sharply reduced his income, a change he accepted philosophically.

By mid-December, however, he had been granted the right to request equipment from the Verkehrstechnische Prüfungskommission (VPK; Transport-Technologies Board of Examiners) and had begun putting together a system to determine the location of radio transmitters. Fortunately, the head of the radio-telegraph department within the VPK, and thus Pohl's boss, was Max Wien, a physicist who had spent much of his career looking at ways to improve radio communication. Along with being a colleague and mentor, Wien became a good friend of Pohl's. The only real problem they had was that, as physicists, they felt the need to discuss every little detail and, in particular, their differences of opinion in these matters. It was, Wien once stated and Pohl passed on to his mother in a letter on July 17, good that the officers for whom they were working were not party to these discussions, as it made it look as if the physicists did not fully understand the issues at hand.

In the meantime, though, Pohl had the first working prototype ready, and was detailed a driver and several radio technicians to help run the experiments outside of a lab. While his work proceeded well, he was continually angered by the way in which the corporations of Germany were overcharging the military for radio equipment, often because the officer in charge of purchasing had worked for this corporation for many years and—to Pohl—seemed to have not the best interests of the German state and military at heart, but that of their previous employer.

Nonetheless, progress continued to be made. In early March 1915, he was officially sent to the telegraph troops and set about improving his ability to work outside by organizing what he referred to as a circus wagon, a small trailer, fully fitted out in the inside as a sleeping quarters and an office. During all this, he was also mustered by the Landsturm, a militia composed of those not capable of being inducted into the army. Fortunately, he only had to spend a few days learning how to march and how to behave—no drinking, no fighting—before he could return full-time to his real work.

In March 1915, the apparatus started to come together. He had the circus wagon brought to Schönfeld, outside of Berlin, as well as the masts and wires needed to build a large antenna. In the middle of this preparation, Pohl was sent to Cuxhaven, to talk to the navy and see what progress they had made in the same direction.

During this visit, he would meet his first Zeppelin pilot: Hans von Schiller, whose sister Henni von Schiller had married Karl Woermann, scion of the Woermann family for whom Pohl's father had worked for so many years. Schiller, who had passed his airship pilot's license test that month under the watchful eye of Hugo Eckener, was serving on board *L 6* under Captain von Buttlar-Brandenfels. Their airship had been part of the first raid that dropped bombs onto England, but had had to turn back early due to a broken crankshaft.[3] Schiller gave a lively account of this adventure and others over breakfast.

After their meal, Pohl was given a tour of the premises, including the rotating airship hangar. Pohl immediately had ideas of how to build them underground, in order to protect the airships from attacks such as one that had happened the previous December, an attack that *L 6* had played an important part in preventing. They then moved on to radio direction finding (RDF). While Pohl was impressed by the quality of the equipment and organization of the naval radio systems, his actual attempts in Nordholz to test their equipment was a bit of a failure.

On the twenty-sixth of March, having returned to Berlin, he began supervising the building of the antenna in Schönfeld. He had been assigned only two soldiers for this work; it was fairly small bore. By the early days of April, it was all set. He spent the next week listening to various stations, including French ones, trying to determine their location, or at least the direction from which they were broadcasting.

By the middle of April, his system was working. While he did not describe in detail how it worked, he did write of his work to his mother while in Schönfeld on April 14:

Incidentally, my physical work is pretty much nil, since everything is up and running, and the actual measurements are in progress. However, these are a bit exhausting, they make high demands on your hearing, but mine is very good and I'm always astounded at how good a sound memory humans possess. It is important for me now to tune two tones that I heard in the telephone receiver a few seconds apart, the error being surprisingly small, provided that no strange sound is heard between the two tones, even writing with a hard pencil on paper disturbs this very considerably and almost unbearable is the frequent crackling and bubbling in the phone due to invisible electrical discharges in the higher atmosphere, which are especially common at this time. The howling of the wind or noises outside of the car are less of a problem to me, and practice helps in this regard, but doing this for more than a few hours a day is impossible, by then you can clearly feel the fatigue and you begin forgetting the original tone. In any case, I am very satisfied with the results and hope to get permission to publish my experiences in the form of a scientific paper when peace reigns again.

A few days later, he presented his results to the VPK. They were impressed and immediately asked him for two versions of his work. One was what he had done already (i.e., locating enemy radios at the front); the other was for Graf Zeppelin himself, in other words, the locating of Zeppelins. Pohl set to work building individual devices that could be used in the field. There was some frustration in getting the local factory to build a prototype.

During this delay, Pohl discovered a mistake in his calculations, which required that he redo a considerable portion thereof. The upshot was, however, that the apparatus that was built based on the new calculations was much better than previously. Finally, and most galling to Pohl, there were patent issues that hindered his work.

While he waited, he was pleased to see James Franck, who was home briefly. Franck told him of his work on poison gases with Fritz Haber, and how it had been successfully used during the current battle in Ypres. In this time, Pohl also came to the decision to stop giving his lectures, that there was no point until peace had returned.

As April turned to May, Pohl became more involved in the actual manufacture of the devices, spending days in the factory where they were being produced. He also spoke with other radio experts, who had made similar measurements in the field, and all pointed to the fact that the new system would work under all circumstance. While waiting for completion, he was sent on another mission: to Friedrichshafen, ostensibly to determine whether that area would be a good one to set up an orientation antenna, but really to show off what he had done. This meant going out to Schönfeld, dismantling his antenna, and transporting it south.

The visit to Friedrichshafen was a complete success. There was no reason to doubt that the Zeppelin works would be an excellent place for an antenna. The visit to the factory also convinced him that the war could have some positive effects: the amount of money spent on airships and their development meant that that the groundwork for transatlantic flight had been laid.

Pohl was all all packed up and set to return to Berlin when he received word that he was invited to dinner with Count Zeppelin himself. There was no way that he would say no to this. Four days later, on May 18, he wrote of the evening to his mother:

He is a lovely old gentleman, short, broad, but not strong, with tiny feet just like my father had. He is very amiable and mentally still very agile, but outwardly one sees his age, especially after spending longer with him. Director Colsman, who was sitting next to me at the dinner table, said afterward that he was worried about the Count, that he had been far too quiet. He is seventy-eight years old.

Back in Berlin, Pohl found a curious letter in his mailbox. It had been written on April 5 by the head of the German Physical Society, Fritz Haber, on the stationary of the Hotel Astoria & Mangelle in Brussels. In it, Haber pointed to the increased work that he had taken on now that he was in the army, and that he must, therefore, resign his position. He had addressed this letter to the board of directors of the society, but lacking any way of copying the letter, had simply sent it to Heinrich Rubens, another board member. Rubens added a note to Max Planck on the back, and sent in on to him, who in turn sent it to Emil Warburg. And so it continued on, passing through the hands of Walther Nernst and Albert Einstein, among others. It eventually reached Karl Scheel, the editor of the journal of the German Physical Society. He made a note as to who had not yet seen it and which members, like James Franck, would not need to see it, as they were at war. Pohl was, of course, on the list as the secretary of the society, but not only had it arrived in his mailbox after he had left for Friedrichshafen, but by the time he returned, the next meeting of the society had come and gone, a meeting in which Max Planck was named chairman. Thus the letter was moot. Pohl kept it, as he knew that the it had been signed by some of the great physicists of the age. He went as far as to note who had signed where, and what their position was.

Pohl spent most of his time trying to get the factory to hurry up with the production, though he took time out to speak with meteorologists about their use of his equipment for weather analysis. By mid-June, the first apparatus was completed and tested in Schönfeld. With his system now ready for implementation, Pohl now began to travel frequently.

The first trip took him to Mława, on the eastern front. While this town had briefly been part of the Kingdom of Prussia, it, and the surrounding district, Plock, had been part of Russian Poland since 1815, though located just east of the German border.[4] It had been captured by the German army earlier in the year.

In Mława, he met one of his colleagues, Gustav Leithäuser, whose father had been a teacher at Pohl's high school, then later received his doctorate from the Berlin University right around when Pohl arrived there. Leithäuser had rigged up a system to do what Pohl now had a more polished version of. He was happy to dismantle his pieces and try out Pohl's. Within two days, they had the new apparatus working: two receivers that could triangulate the location of an enemy transmitter.

In July, Pohl was asked to come to Göttingen, an old university in the middle of Germany. While the ostensible reason was to give a lecture on whatever topic he chose, the real reason is that there was an open professorship there, and they were looking for a replacement. Pohl enjoyed the trip immensely and was especially taken by Professor Peter Debye. Debye, a Dutch physicist, had spent most of his career in Germany.

Back in Berlin, Pohl would have loved to turn to the second part of his original brief, locating Zeppelins, but he was sent to various places on the front, setting up location systems and training soldiers in their use. For the first month, this mainly meant the eastern front, but in August, he was sent to Vienna, where he spoke with local radio engineers, as well as visiting the university.

Finally, he was back in Berlin and ready to begin work. The plan was for him to wait at the Tempelhof Airfield, while a Zeppelin would circle the city and send signals for Pohl to detect. Tempelhof was an old parade ground 5 kilometers due south of the center of Berlin. It had been used as an airport as early as 1909, and had been used by the Wright brothers that year for a flight demonstration. While still used for drills, it was also the perfect place to conduct tests of this nature. Pohl had his circus wagon moved there, to give him a work space. Three times Pohl was ready with his equipment, but a steady rain kept the *Hansa* from flying and thus hindered any further work.

Finally, on August 25, the first sign that success might be in the offing. At 7:00 a.m., Pohl was ready and waiting in Tempelhof, and the weather allowed the *Hansa* to fly. The *Hansa*, an old veteran by now, having been built in 1912 and then serving for two years as a passenger airship before being taken over by the military, had been used solely for training since the beginning of the year. This time, however, her services were not as useful. While Pohl managed to hear a few chirps from her, before he could make any sense of them, they had disappeared, and when he called in to find out what had happened, he was told that the airship had returned to her hangar already, with no reason for this shortened flight given. Fortunately, the following day brought real success, with Pohl able to localize the flying airship.

Early in September, he had to take time off from this work to collect new versions of the enemy triangulation system and deliver them to Brixen, in the Austrian province of Tirol[5] and on the southern front with Italy. The trip did not begin well. Safely ensconced in a modern train leaving Munich, a German officer traveling with him took note of Pohl's baggage, which this officer considered excessive. He thus denounced Pohl to the authorities in their next stop, Innsbruck, and a Austro-Hungarian officer took Pohl into custody. Pohl did not deal well with this sudden turn of events, and lost his temper at the Hungarian. Pohl thus found himself in the local police station for two hours until a German officer showed up and explained that Pohl's orders were all correct, and that there was no need to delay him any further. The upshot was that Pohl ended up in a night train that consisted of old third-class carriages that had been converted to second class by the simple expedient of adding signs indicating their new station in life.

This was not the only delay in the trip, which ended taking almost a week, as teaching people how to set up and use the apparatus took much more time than he would have liked. Thereafter, he had to test out each of the systems as it was delivered by the factory, as far too many of them were defective right from the start and needed repeated trips to the factory for repair.

After that, October was spent traveling through the Balkans, installing systems wherever he went. Toward the end of the month, with another trip to Friedrichshafen in sight, Pohl was introduced to Eduard Grüneisen, who was to help test the systems and, Pohl hoped, eventually take over the job of installing them entirely. Grüneisen, who was a few years older than Pohl, had been working in the Imperial Physical Technical Institute, which was responsible for metrology, the science of measurement. He had been sent to war, but had managed to return safely just as his wife had their third child.

In early November, Pohl returned to Friedrichshafen. He was greeted as an old friend, and spent the first day clambering over their antenna array and the evenings in receptions with the managers of the company and visiting marine officers. After a few days setting up, they had their first attempt at radio location with a Zeppelin. Sadly, the first flight had to be aborted after an hour because of engine trouble. Pohl asked if he might be able to fly on a Zeppelin one of these days, and was told that he could go along on the next one. Three days later, on November 8, he described the flight:

Friday we left at 9 o'clock; at 2 o'clock we arrived back home. We flew to Ulm but continued to carve large loops through the air, flying long stretches parallel to the Alps, which were clearly to be seen in the snow above the clouds; it was wonderful. Our altitude was always between 600 and 1000 m. The "highlight" was the rare and difficult maneuver of a water landing on the Lake of Constance, which worked flawlessly. The whole ride was spectacular; to look down from above on the ground is a beautiful experience.

The Zeppelin in which he flew was the navy airship *L 18*, hull number LZ 52. It had first flown the previous day and would be taken over by Lt. Max Dietrich.

Pohl's trip in *L 18* seems to have been entirely for his own amusement. He gave no indication that any radio direction finding experiments were done during the flight.

On his return to Berlin, this would become his main focus. He spent many days on the field waiting to see if the *Hansa* would fly that day, but at least he did not have to travel well outside of Berlin in order to do so, in contrast to his earlier experiments. Instead, he would often receive an early-morning phone call warning him that no flight was possible that day, obviating the need to leave home for no reason at all.

In between, Pohl would also fly in the Zeppelins, to show the crew how to operate the onboard radio. This required him to travel to Johannisthal, a part of Berlin a bit farther southeast of Tempelhof, but still easily reachable by rail. In mid-November, he climbed aboard the *Hansa* and they took off. Pohl soon realized why he had had difficulties in hearing the signals from the airship before—the crew had no idea how to operate the radio properly. Furthermore, two of the engines broke down almost immediately, necessitating a return to Johannisthal. In the meantime, Pohl amused himself looking down on the well-lit streets below, filled with many busy pedestrians.

In between, there were constant stream of difficulties to endure, whether a request to explain himself at the VPK, or lectures to go to about related topics, or attempts to produce proper maps for his use. He was also sent to Zeppelin and Schütte-Lanz factories, to inspect new airships and test their electrical systems. By late December, however, he had managed to rid himself of the continuing work on the enemy triangulation system, having composed a safety regulation and finding a newly minted engineer to take over from him.

In spite of all his other work, his new system came to fruition, as he would find out. A trip in early December to Straßburg and Metz, two German cities that had been ceded by France after the Franco-Prussian War had him setting up antennas that could be used to guide the ships. His job was, once again, to set up antennas that could be used to guide the ships. And on December 31, Pohl received a phone call that lifted his spirits: *LZ 87*, an army airship flying in Germany, had on the previous day found itself lost in the fog while flying between the German cities of Giessen and Coblenz. They had contacted the Straßburg and Metz stations; within four minutes they knew almost exactly where they were and could complete their flight safely.

This welcome news came as he was waiting for *LZ 90* to complete its first flight, which kept him bouncing between Berlin and Potsdam for a month, almost invariably for no reason at all. The only bright spot in this was that he was frequently accompanied by Lehmann and Gemmingen, two men with whom he saw eye to eye.

In this time Pohl was also finally formally hired by the VPK. This meant a 250 marks salary, plus 90 marks extra because it was wartime, plus 50 marks for being in an airship. Combined with his institute salary—which his boss told him not to mention to the army—this meant that he was actually doing quite well for himself, at least financially. In being hired, he was also to receive a uniform, something that he had been hoping for since the beginning of the war.

By the end of January, the orientation of airships was a done deal. While not every airship was yet fully outfitted, it was just a matter of time until there would be no problem in locating every airship within a few kilometers of its position. The next question was how to guide them all the way back to their hangars, should that become necessary, but this was a problem that others were working on. Pohl considered investing his energies into looking at the finances of the companies that he felt were overcharging the military for their technologies.

On Saturday January 29, 1916, around 9:20 p.m., a Zeppelin arrived over Paris. It was the second attack on the city, and the results were trumpeted in newspapers all around the world. The *New York Times* wrote in a brief article the following day that six were dead, thirty wounded.[6] They would follow up in the next days with more thorough articles that also upped the death toll considerably.[7] The Parisian daily *Le Matin* called it a crime perpetuated by pirates and wrote that twenty-five had been killed and twenty-nine wounded.[8] In Germany, the *Rosenheimer Nachrichten* in Bavaria announced the raid with the banner headline "A Successful Zeppelin Attack on Paris."[9]

In Berlin, Pohl heard of the raid and surmised that the successful attack had been due to his RDF system. After all, the first attempt to bomb Paris had left the three airships that had overflown the French capital in such bad shape that only one survived the return to Germany.[10] In this case, while two airships, *LZ 77* and *LZ 79*, had started the attack, the former had had to drop out because of an issue with its motor; only *LZ 79* had managed to attack the city. Pohl would see the report on this not long after, including the quick sketch its commander, Major Gaissart, had drawn. It showed Paris as a squashed circle with the Seine running through it, the track of *LZ 79* began to the northeast and headed due southwest over the city and on to Versailles before turning to the north again.

The following day, both airships set out again and, this time, both managed to complete their attack. However, *LZ 79* in this case had its rudders damaged, and came down in the Belgian town of Ath, well behind German lines.[11] In spite of this rather mixed result, Pohl immediately sent Count Zeppelin a letter congratulating him on the success of his airships. A few days later, he received a card with the printed message "Many thanks for your friendly praise." It was, however, dated and signed by Zeppelin himself. Pohl sent the card to his mother, that she might be amused by it.

Even as these successes mounted, Pohl saw one major difficulty in them: in order to determine its position, an airship would have to send a radio signal and then receive a message in which it was told its location. While it would have been possible to encode the return message, it would in principle be no problem for the enemy to determine its location just as easily as their own people. Pohl therefore immediately began working on a new system, one which did not require any signals from or directly to an airship. He began work testing this in early February but was, as so often, stymied by the *Hansa's* increasingly fragile engines.

One day in early February, for instance, Pohl traveled out to Johannisthal to test his new system. Due to miscommunication, he arrived after the *Hansa* had already departed, a situation he rued only briefly, as almost immediately after takeoff, all four engines on the old airship broke and it found itself at the mercy of the prevailing winds. While the ground crew climbed into cars to chase after the airship, Pohl and his colleagues congratulated themselves for having failed to arrive on time and returned to the city. Pohl was particularly pleased because he had had the idea of smuggling his friend Hans Geiger, a physicist who was now an artillery officer but in prewar times helped Ernest Rutherford win the 1908 Nobel Prize, on board. In the end, the consequences of being caught doing so outweighed the upside, and now Pohl was happy to spend the evening talking with his old friend in a Berlin restaurant instead of slogging through a muddy field outside Berlin.

In the midst of all of this came a piece of good news: on February 21, he received a telegram from Heinrich Rubens, his boss at the Berlin university, congratulating him on having been offered the job of Professor in Göttingen. Twelve days later, he signed a letter with the cultural ministry that set out the terms of his engagement. Most importantly, they had found someone who could take over his position until the end of the war; Pohl would not have to turn up in Göttingen immediately.

The other issues that Pohl had to deal with at this time was the training of people to use his system as well as getting the factories to produce further radios. Many new airshipmen were recently converted infantry soldiers, for whom airships and radios were entirely new concepts, and had to be brought up to speed in all these matters before they were able to guide the airship properly. While training new operators simply took time, getting the factories to produce what they had promised to do took all manner of phone calls and visits. All of this kept Pohl busy, though he still had time to spend with Captain Lehmann and his wife.

Whenever not dealing with these minor issues, he continued to do radio tests during airship flights. He knew that there were severe security issues with the current system and wanted a new version brought out as soon as possible.

Around the beginning of April, a stack of secret orders from General Joseph Joffre, the commander in chief of the French army, fell into his hands. In reading through them, it became clear that the French had thoroughly mastered the German radio communication and that Pohl's worst fears had come true. It was time for his new system to be brought to fruition.

The problem that Pohl wanted to avoid was that of having the airship signaling the ground in order to determine its location. It was therefore necessary for the radio operators onboard to make the calculations that had previously been done on the ground. Instead of having the airship signal, that signal would be propagated from the earthbound antenna array. Each array consisted of thirty-two antennas, each pointing in a slightly different direction. During operation, each of the antennas would send a signal in turn. It was necessary for the ship to determine which of these signals was the loudest and which would be the antenna pointed at the airship. This would then give a bearing on the antenna array. Repeating the same process with a second antenna array would then allow the airship to triangulate its position. In the meantime, all the enemy would hear were a series of beeps from well-known locations in Germany and occupied territory.

Getting this organized took up much of Pohl's time over the next year. Particularly worrisome was the question of training. While an engineer would have no problem assessing the blips and converting them into a range and thus the location, the untrained soldiers that were more and more becoming a staple of the airship crews needed simpler, more foolproof techniques. It was this that Pohl continued to work on, though. As 1916 dragged on and the Zeppelin attacks dropped off, he found himself dealing with entirely different questions, including that of the dropping of bombs and the targeting thereof.

Fortunately, much of the work for this could be done in Wildeshausen, where Lehmann and his wife were, as well, which meant that any time spent there, even if not in an airship because of the weather, could still be spent in a friendly way. In September of that year, the artillery testing commission published a paper on titled "Release Table for 100-Kilogram Round Bombs, Including the Duration of Their Fall and Wind Correction Angle."[12] It was the result of work done by Pohl earlier that month.

Later that year, he had the opportunity to expand his work on aerial telegraphy when he was taken up in a German airplane to test their system. Thereafter, he was taken up in what was then the newest of German airplanes, a 220 hp biplane capable of flying 180 kilometers per hour. With only a leather helmet and goggles protecting him from the wind, Pohl could feel its full force as the pilot took the airplane through its paces. It was great fun, Pohl wrote his mother on November 1, 1916, as it had taken his mind off his usual radio work.

Shortly after this, he received a message from Lehmann that he and his airship, *LZ 98*, was being transferred from Wildeshausen, to Kovno. Would Pohl like to join him?

Pohl of course would not miss a chance like this. While he had become inured to the usual short flights, an opportunity like this was not one to be missed. Thus, on November 11, 1916, Pohl set out from Berlin with Lehmann and Gemmingen by train, and the three spent the next hours solving the problems facing the German military. On November 16, then, all was prepared. Mrs. Lehmann departed Wildeshausen by train, while Pohl and Lieutenant Lehmann went to the hangar. At around 9:00 a.m., and thereby an hour and a half later than planned, they took off and turned east. They flew over Bremen and Hamburg, where Pohl had a close look at the U-boat shipyard, from there to Lübeck and down the Trave River to the Baltic Sea. From there, they went along the coast: Rostock, Darßer Ort, Hiddensee, across Rügen to Rügenwalde. There was some question if they should pause in the airship hangar in Stolp at this point, but the weather remained good and so they continued through the night—past the Hel Peninsula, across the Bay of Danzig and to Pillau, from where they could see the lights of Königsberg. The weather turned cold and snowy at this point, so Pohl missed seeing his father's home town of Gumbinnen. Instead he wrapped himself up and took a one hour nap in the radio cabin. When he awoke, he could tell from the fact that his ears were popping that they were rising—they had reached their destination and needed to blow off gas in order to reduce their lift so that they could land. This gave Pohl a great view of Kovno and the forts and trenches that had been built to guard it, as well as the hangar they were aiming for. They spiraled down slowly and were in the hangar by 4:15. Pohl completed his night's rest in the barracks, and soon thereafter returned to Berlin to continue his work, which included writing of the flight to his mother. That he had not quite recovered from the night's activities was clear from the date, as he was clearly uncertain what day of the week it was.

The flight would be the last time before the current flight that he would step aboard an airship.

In the meantime, he continued his work, in particular with the location of enemy radio transmitters. It was this that brought him close to the front lines in the middle of 1917. Pohl had been sent to France to check up on their use in the field. He found himself along the front, right where the Nivelle offensive April had pushed slightly into German territory along the Chemins des Dames. Several times, Pohl found himself deep underground in old cellars or canals, where the soldiers had camped out to be safe from allied artillery fire.

On one memorable day, Pohl had traveled to the small town of Saint-Erme, which is located halfway between Laon and Reims. He and his party then by foot headed south and toward the front. While there was some artillery fire that day, there were no directed shots, and while they moved as quickly as possible, they were never targeted. Nonetheless, they were happy to get through the forest and to a divisional headquarter, where they observed the radio setup that had been dug 8 meters underground. While they were still well back from the front lines, the continual gunfire made any further travel in that direction too dangerous, and instead they set off to the rear and the safety of their car again. The rest of the trip, which he described in detail in a letter he wrote on November 17 from the town of Stenay, well behind the front, was not as exciting, though he remained close to the front throughout. This would be the closest Pohl would get to the actual fighting.

CHAPTER 11

JULY 29, 1:00 A.M.–JULY 29, 2:00 P.M.

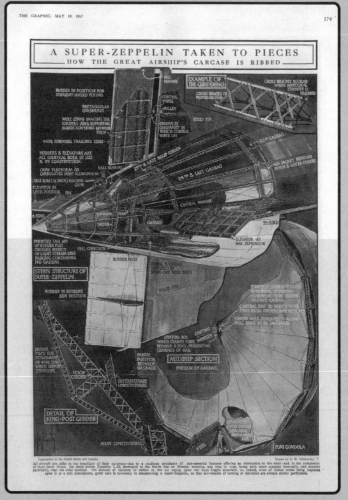

A SUPER-ZEPPELIN TAKEN TO PIECES
HOW THE GREAT AIRSHIP'S CARCASE IS RIBBED

Picture published in the May 19, 1917, edition of British magazine *The Graphic*, showing the tail of of a "Super Zeppelin," as they called the R-class Zeppelins. At the top can be seen the machine gun platform that Pohl spent so much time on. Half a year earlier, *L 33* had been shot down over England, and while the crew had set the airship alight, enough remained to give the British a good idea of how it had been built.

While Pohl was hoping to pass a quiet and peaceful night in his platform in the stern of the ship, it is not to be. It is, however, no external force that causes him to awake at one in the morning. Instead, it is a far more urgent, internal stimulus that has him awake long before he wants to be.

There is no doubt of it. His insides are in revolt and insist that he find a place of relief—and soon. At first, he is not sure that he will be able to move at all, but when the first wave of pain that had awakened him subsides, he divests himself of his fur coat—a not inconsiderable achievement given that the canvas cover ensures that he can not actually stand upright. Once this is completed, he waits for the next wave of pain to subside before tackling the next obstacle: the 5-meter ladder that connects his eyrie with the main keel walkway. For the first time, Pohl is acutely aware of the size—or, rather, the lack thereof—of the treads. All of 15 centimeters wide, they are only marginally wider than his shoes, and given his need to frequently stop and wait for a particularly bad cramp to pass, descending it is truly a feat a circus performer would decline to attempt. Then, on his hands and knees, he creeps through the triangular shaft that is his connection to the main hull of the ship, stopping frequently to let a particularly vicious cramp pass through him. He has to work his way all the way forward in the ship, to find the rudimentary toilets installed for the use of the crew.

Even worse, Pohl realizes as he slowly makes his way farther upright that he does not have the most important tool for the job ahead. It had been left behind in the gondola. In spite of the cramps that seize his intestines, he is forced to lower his way down into the front gondola, where the overnight watch is sailing the airship toward the northern corner of the Gotland. Having left the cabin just two hours before with the stated intention of sleeping through until morning, Pohl has to find some excuse for his quick return, and he covers by feigning interest in English submarines that are supposed to be at large in the area. Once he feels that he had thrown the watch off his true intentions, he digs the toilet paper out of his satchel and reascends into the rump of the ship. With this important gear in hand, the rest of his quest goes smoothly, and in short order, he is once again ensconced in his eyrie.

Only to be awakened by similar internal pressure about an hour later. This time, on descending into the rump of the ship, his sensitive nose immediately tells him that he is no longer alone in his agony. The smell makes it clear that others were afflicted as well. While his trip forward is not as fraught as the first one, this time he finds himself stymied by a groan of "Occupied!" when he reaches the promised land. Finally, the machinist who had beaten him to the punch completes his mission and, having re-encased himself in his flight suit, emerges—only to stop, turn around and disappear into the restroom again. By the time he is finally all finished, two others are waiting with Pohl in the gangway.

Pohl tries to hurry through the process as best as possible, but when he re-emerges, the two who had been waiting have given up: they have each opened one of the hatches that gave access to the keel of the ship through its bottom, and are using these for their relief, a feat that requires considerable agility.

Pohl gives them a commiserating smile and returns to his chamber and its warm blankets, safe in the knowledge that it is unlikely that he would sleep through any further excitement. While he sleeps, the great ship moves steadily north by northeast, heading more or less straight at Stockholm. Around sunrise, it is just south of the island of Torö, which in turn lies due south of the Swedish capital. At 8:00 a.m., they reach the latitude of Stockholm and make a wide turn to the right to begin their long trek south again.

Pohl wakes up early, just as he had assumed he would, makes use of the facilities once more, and then goes to check on their position. Below him the sea is filled with rocky skerries, outcrops in the ocean that he realizes are what his sister had long encouraged him to visit, but had not done so until this moment. He resolves to mention to her that he had finally done so in his next letter.

As it turns out, they are essentially free-ballooning through a somewhat hazy sky. One of the engines is being repaired. The motor had been running irregularly, and the vibration from this had caused the bolts that held one of the flanges that held the drive shaft to shear off. The engine, while only on its second trip, had from the start suffered from oil in one of its cylinders. Multiple efforts had been made to repair it, including the replacement of the entire cylinder, piston, and rings. These repairs had been easy to do—as Lehmann had, since the first night, had the engines operating (like the enlisted men) in eight-hour shifts. There was thus plenty of downtime for such work.

This time, it is more complicated. Repairing the sheared bolts requires slowing even engines currently operating, as the mechanics are forced to open the outer cover in order to access the broken parts, and any speed forward would have caused them to be pushed off the Zeppelin. Thus, for about an hour, the Zeppelin and its crew drift through the skies, while the mechanics Hölzemann and Grözinger do their jobs. While in this case there is plenty of time to drift slowly through the sky, newer Zeppelins actually have extra motors so that in case one breaks down in this manner, the mission can simply be finished on the other engines.

Pohl takes advantage of the quiet to continue writing his letter, this time at the table in the back of the gondola. He calculates that they had been aloft some fifty-seven hours at this point and that it looks like they will continue on for at least another twenty-four hours, much longer than the sixty hours Lehmann had originally planned on. After bringing his mother up to date, Pohl decides that his guts are starting to feel more normal, and that it will be worth testing them out. He starts out with a couple of cookies and some chocolate, since he feels that those are the least likely to upset his stomach again.

The first attempts go down well, so he adds a hunk of Dutch cheese, which also does him no harm. In all, his recovery has gone well, in contrast with those of the pilots, who are hunkered down, freezing, in their fur coats at the controls at the front of the gondola. Their nights had apparently been filled with far more turmoil than Pohl's.

It is time to try out one of the other small luxuries that Lehmann has had installed in the ship—a shower. All the way in the front of the ship, tucked among the mooring gear, is a collapsible rubber tub. Just big enough to stand in, it can be used for quick showers using a bucket full of ballast water connected to a strut above to rinse off. Pohl also takes the opportunity to shave, a far more successful endeavor than on the previous day.

In general he feels good—and the weather reflects his state of being. The navigators make note of the fact that they can, at this point, see a distance of 20 nautical miles. Pohl sits comfortably at the table in the cabin, on a woven rattan chair, across from Baron von Gemmingen. Pohl studies the older man, whose purpose he has never quite divined. In the letter he had written to his mother just before takeoff, he had called him Lehmann's "old patron Lieutenant Commander von Gemmingen, who is the nephew of the old Count, and who has accompanied him on all his flights as 'staff officer' (read: passenger)." And yes, in the crew list, he is given simply as "observer," but he is also, whenever military actions were at hand, in charge of making sure the crew and airship know what they are to achieve. Lehmann's job is simply to do what Gemmingen asks for. Pohl, who has never been along on an actual combat mission, clearly has never understood this important distinction. Either way, right now he is just an older gentleman seated quietly at the table, deeply engrossed in one of the yellow-jacketed books that had been brought aboard.

While Pohl and Gemmingen enjoy the quiet, Lehmann is more active. He has not had much time to rest since takeoff, in spite of having insisted that the men take shifts so as not be be overtired. He had set up two systems: one for officers, one for the men. The enlisted crew were on eight-hour watches, while the officers were on for six hours, then off for six. As far as Lehmann can tell, either of these systems are working fine and would be acceptable if the navy chose to run Zeppelins for days at a time.

Lehmann, on the other hand, has granted himself only the briefest of naps—and those were taken in the hammock that was the closest to the ladder down to the cabin, so as to be available at a moment's notice. Now, as they cruise over the Baltic Sea, he has his men identify each ship that they fly over—in spite of the fact that each one proves to be either Swedish or Danish, and thus utterly harmless. Satisfied that they are gainfully occupied and that the airship is in the best of hands, Lehmann climbs up in the keel and into his hammock in hopes of getting a solid nap in.

Pohl divides his time between the table and his letter, and the windows from which he has a splendid view across the Baltic. Far below he can also see the shadow of the airship as it passes over the waves. Stretched out behind it are extended ghostly tendrils, a kind of vague tail. Whether this is an optical illusion or due to the air disturbed while streaming past the airship, he cannot tell, but it disturbs him enough that he has a picture taken of it, and when he returns to his letter, he adds a small drawing of what he saw, to give his mother a better sense of it.

While Pohl is drawing the sketch of the airship plus tail, he hears that there are dolphins swimming below, but by the time he has rousted himself out of his chair and made it to a window, they are long gone. Instead, Pohl takes the opportunity to look at the coast of the Swedish island Gotland with a telescope.

More interesting was that there was another Zeppelin on the horizon. Via radio, they determine that it is the navy airship *L 37*. This Zeppelin, like *LZ 120*, is an R-class Zeppelin, but one of the first built. It was also the first Zeppelin to be built in the works at Staaken, and has cruised almost exclusively around the Baltic and North Seas.[1] From the radio traffic, Pohl determines that the airship is still quite some distance away, and, in general, the current situation is quiet enough to allow him to go take a nap, so he returns to the gunner's platform, wraps himself up, and goes to sleep.

As he nods off, he looks forward to the next segment of the trip, as a low-pressure system had kept them out of the eastern reaches of the Baltic Sea so far, and there is much he wants to see there, not the least because of family connections going back many years.

As he sleeps, *LZ 120* arrives at the southern end of Gotland, and turns east toward Libau.

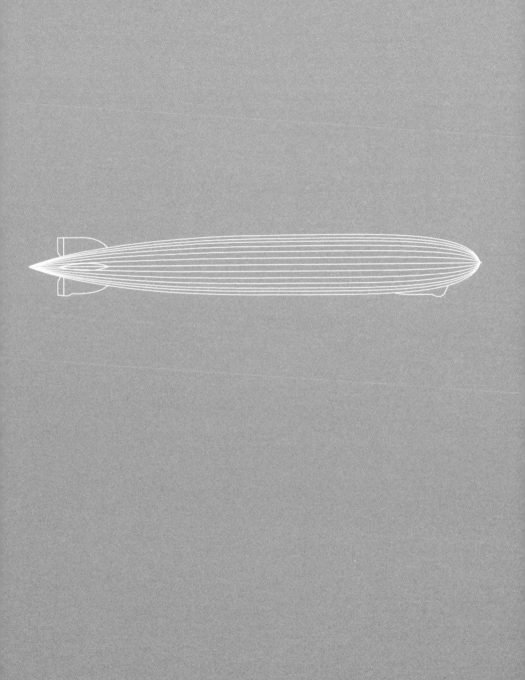

CHAPTER 12
LZ 120

LZ 120 in its hangar in Seerappen. From an album named "Herrn Marine-Obermeister Reetz zur Erinnerung an den Aufbau des Marinearsenals Kiel 1919–1928 und zum 25jährigen Dienst-Jubiläum." *Bundesarchiv, Bild 248-040 / photographer unknown*

On November 22, 1916, the eighty-third airship built by the Zeppelin corporation emerged from the hangar in which had been built, 3 kilometers northeast of the city of Friedrichshafen, the seat of Count Zeppelin's operation since 1900. This new hangar had been constructed to build some of the many airships that the German army and navy had requested in response to the war. The first airship had flown from there on June 7, 1915, and since then they produced eight further airships, mainly for the navy but also one for the army.

This new airship had hull number 84, and was turned over to the navy, who named it *L 38*, thus the direct successor to *L 37* that was currently flying toward *LZ 120*. *L 38* was sent first to Ahlhorn in the northeast of Germany, then on eastward via Seddin to Wainoden, from where it was to attack Petrograd, Russia. On December 2, it took off on an ill-fated attack on Reval and other targets in Estonia. In the course of this flight, and due to the extreme cold that reigned at higher altitudes, the ship crash-landed near Seerappen.

By this time, work was progressing rapidly on a new airship; the workers had begun assembling the parts necessary for the next project even as the previous one was in its final stages. Like *L 38*, it was an R-class Zeppelin, but it was being built not for the navy but for the army.

The first ship of the R class had taken flight on May 28, 1916. The new class was the seventeenth step in the evolution of the Zeppelin, stretching back to A class LZ 1 back in 1900. While prewar classes had somewhere between one and six examples built, the war—and the greater use of the Zeppelins—meant that far more were built of some classes, including twenty-two of the P class. The R class was the first that was designed after the beginning of the war, and used the knowledge gained in the opening months of the war to refine its parameters. Its only limit was its length—the new Zeppelins had to be accommodated in the airship hangars that had been previously built.

LZ 120 was just shy of 200 meters long and 24 meters wide. By way of comparison, this made it 70 meters shorter than the ill-fated RMS *Titanic* and only 4 meters narrower, or about the size of the largest battleships currently patrolling the world's oceans.

The biggest difference between the previous models and this class was how the motors were distributed. The Q class had only four engines, and they were located in the two gondolas, one in front and three in the back. While the front gondola had one engine that drove a propeller immediately behind it, the rear gondola had three, one of which powered a propeller in the same way as the front one, while the other two drove propellers that were mounted left and right of the hull, well clear of the outside of the airship. *LZ 120*, and the rest of the R class had four gondolas with engines, one in front, one in back, both directly under the center of the airship, and two amidship, mounted left and right of the hull. While the setup for the engines was otherwise the same as in the Q class, the two gondolas amidship turned propellers directly behind them.

The six engines that drove *LZ 120* through the air were Maybach HSLu motors, each of which produced 237 horsepower. These straight six-cylinder engines were variants of the Maybach HS engines and were built by the Maybach-Motorenbau GmbH of Friedrichshafen. This company, founded less than ten years earlier by Wilhelm Maybach as Luftfahrzeug-Motorenbau GmbH (Aircraft Motor Manufacturing Corporation), had—as the name suggested—concentrated on developing and building aircraft engines. In 1912, Maybach had changed the name to the one it currently used. From the start, their main customer had been the Zeppelin corporation, and they, like Zeppelin, had developed rapidly during the war.[1] The HS at the beginning of the name came from a method by which aircraft motors were named using the alphabet from the beginning and the end: first AZ, then CX, DW, IR, and finally HS. Why some of the letter combinations was skipped is uncertain. The Lu at the end simply indicated that this was a variant of the last of these. The naming system was changed around 1916, and the HS became the Mb IV, with Zeppelins as of hull number LZ 105 receiving the MB.IVa variant. The engines could push the enormous airship through the air at almost 100 kilometers per hour.

Along with the Maybach corporation, Count Zeppelin had also founded another company to produce parts for his airships: the Zahnradfabrik GmbH (Gear Factory Corporation). He had been unable to find gears that would withstand the strain put on them by an airship, and had therefore decided to produce his own. The company, headquartered in Tettnang just outside of Friedrichshafen, was quietly founded in 1915, with news of its incorporation consisting of a short paragraph in the back of trade papers announcing that they planned to make gears and transmissions for aircraft, automobiles, and motor boats.[2] While they originally concentrated on airship gears, they had—along with the Zeppelin corporation itself—diversified into the airplane market.

The biggest change over the Q class came in the shape of the airship. While early airships had been simple cylinders with caps at the front in rear which tapered rapidly to the bow or stern, later ships had longer noses in the interest of improving their aerodynamics. Over the years, the length of the bow that was tapered had increased, but the bulk of the ship was still a cylinder, a decision that eased the building thereof, as the building of equal-sized rings that this requires is much easier than having to build a different size, depending on where on the airship it was to be installed. The R class, borrowing from earlier Schütte-Lanz airships, now was almost completely streamlined. While some of the middle rings were still the same size, the ship tapered about a third of its length to the front and back. The greater work necessary to build the airship was repaid by increased speed. It was calculated that a streamlined ship needed only 40 percent of the power to fly the same speed as an airship of the same volume but with a blunt nose.[3]

There were thirty-eight rings in all, each with twenty-five sides (or twelve plus the keel depending on how you count them). Every other ring was heavily interconnected with wires. Between each set of wired ones was one without wires, and it was these open space that were filled with nineteen giant gas bags, which were built to fill out the space entirely. Only in the very stern, below Pohl's sleeping quarters, was the Zeppelin empty.

The rings, as well as all other metal parts of the airship, were made of Duralumin. This new invention had radically improved the quality of airships since its invention. Aluminum had been used for twenty years in airships, starting with the ill-fated Schwarz airship of 1897. Previous to that, the cost of aluminum, which, in spite of being the third-most-common element in the earth, had been kept high by the difficulty of refining it. Only when Hall and Héroult independently discovered a way of creating aluminum from alumina in 1886, followed by Bayer's invention of a process to create alumina from common bauxite had the use of aluminum become feasible. Two years before Hall and Héroult, the new Washington Monument in the center of Washington, DC, had been capped with an almost 3-kilogram piece of cast aluminum, the largest thus far created.

David Schwarz was the first to attempt to use this newly available substance for flight. His first attempt took place in Russia, and significant sums were expended, including in the building of a hangar, with no results and Schwarz had to leave the country rapidly.

Back in Germany, Schwarz teamed up with the industrialist Carl Berg, who had experience with aluminum. Their project began in Tempelhof in 1895. In 1896, the airship was first filled with gas, though the quality was insufficient to achieve takeoff. While waiting for gas of sufficient purity to produced, Schwarz collapsed and died. His wife continued with the project.

The airship was 24 meters long and 8 meters wide, and consisted of an aluminum frame over which 0.2 mm thick aluminum sheets were laid, the sheets were then folded and riveted to make them airtight. On November 3, 1897, the airship took off for the first time. It was the first time a rigid airship had flown, and while the hull worked flawlessly, the motor decidedly did not, and they had to make an emergency landing, during which the airship was damaged beyond repair.[4]

Among those who watched this flight—which reached 400 meters—was Count Zeppelin, who would apply the lessons learned that day to his successful airships three years later, using aluminum from Carl Berg to do so.

The greatest problem with aluminum was that it was did not have the structural integrity to handle the needs of an airship. Berg would attempt a number of alloys that would solve this problem. Unfortunately, his lack of scientific background meant that metals produced were not of the quality that Zeppelin needed, in particular since there was a new product that was exactly what he was looking for: Duralumin.

Initially invented by the German metallurgist Alfred Wilm in 1903, it had been refined over the years and put into production in 1909 by the Dürener Metallwerke, who had also given it the new name. It had spread as far as England in 1910, with Vickers, Sons & Maxim being in charge of production and sales there.[5] As of 1914, Zeppelin started to use this new metal,[6] though he would not switch over immediately due to personal reasons: Berg had been an early Zeppelin supporter and Zeppelin corporation general manager Alfred Colsman was married to Berg's daughter. When *LZ 72* began having multiple issues with metal parts bursting, the blame was put entirely on Berg alloy by both the Royal Commission for Investigation of Materials (Königliches Material-Prüfungsamt) and the VPK. Berg began producing a version of Duralumin called Bergmetall. Zeppelin began using only Duralumin for the structural parts of the airships, leaving Berg's metals for non-load-bearing parts like the gondola. The R class was the first that used Duralumin throughout the airship.

Duralumin in itself was also not enough to make the Zeppelins viable; there was also the question of how the girders constructed from the alloy were designed. The key was always maximum strength combined with minimum weight. Each girder was thus made up of multiple thinner segments, each of which was shaped along its long axis to give it more rigidity. Only at the ends of the segment was the metal flat, to allow it to be fastened to the longer girders. The cross braces would be added as necessary; in some places, the numbers would be doubled to increase strength. The long girders produced in this way would then be combined into one or more triangles to make a three-dimensional rigid girder. While the girders used for the rings were smaller and triangular, the longitudinal girders that ran the length of the airship were larger and partly five-sided, made of three triangular constructions. The rings were also created of multiple girders, ten kite-shaped structures, considerable longer than wide, with two additional cross braces in the middle. The eleventh element of the ring was the one through which the keel ran; it was almost three times larger than the others, consisting of three segments with multiple cross-bracing throughout. The keel ran through an A-shaped segment in the bottom, and as you proceeded along the keel, you had to be aware of the height of the cross-piece of the A as you went.

In between the Duralumin rings were the gas bags that contained the hydrogen that gave lift to the airship. About two years earlier, Pohl had written of the composition of these constructions:

> The actual gas cells consist of several layers of goldbeater's skin and fine cotton weave. Goldbeater's skin is the caecum of cattle, each piece smaller than this sheet of paper; you can imagine how many cows had to contribute to the cause of producing these many-layered gasbags, and that the cost of the finished shell approaches 100,000.

The paper on which he had written this letter was all of 42 by 25 centimeters. In one respect, he was not quite correct: it was not the caecum per se, but rather the outside membrane of it that was used. He was completely correct in assuming that a huge number of cattle were needed to produce the gas bags.

The use of this method for keeping hydrogen from escaping was an old one—the first balloon using this technology was one of the first balloons sent up into the air in 1783. While most early airships used rubberized fabric, this made sense only for nonrigid airships where the hydrogen balloon also served as the outer surface of the airship. The German rigid airships did not need as rigid a bag and, in fact, wanted to to be as light as possible, which led them back to goldbeater's skin. The switchover was further forced by the explosions of *Schwaben* and *L III*, which were both traced back to sparks made by the material. The *L 2*, whose crash had first brought Lehmann and his *Sachsen* to the navy, had been the first airship whose entire gas bags were made of goldbeater's skin.

Since the beginning of the war, all slaughterhouses were told to save this menbrane, which was a pouch of the cattle's intestine, located just before the colon, and larger slaughterhouses would have crews specializing in their collection. The membranes would be cleaned and packed in salt in barrels before being for processing. This consisted of scraping off all the excess fat, then soaked in water with some glycerine—to promote flexibility—in it, then washing it in a saltwater solution and drying it again.

The processed goldbeater's skin would be laid down with a small overlap, and after drying, this would make for an airtight connection. Once larger sections had been made, they would be glued down onto a fine fabric—usually cotton. A second layer of goldbeater's skin would then be overlaid to ensure that no gas could escape. This still meant that for the 1,800 square meters of cloth needed for a single layer for one gas bag, something like 12,000 cattle would lose their lives, so half a million for the whole airship.[7]

In 1915, Count Zeppelin had formed the Ballon-Hüllen GmbH—the balloon envelope corporation—in Tempelhof, a neighborhood in Berlin near the airport Pohl had worked over the previous years, to fill the demand for the new gas bags. A major issue for Zeppelin and his company was having enough people available who could manufacture the bags, even as the Zeppelin cruises around the Baltics. They were running advertisements in Berlin newspapers stating that they were looking for two hundred women to work for them.[8]

Thus a price of 100,000 marks was not too surprising, even if it was a huge amount of money back then. The salary that Pohl had accepted for his job in Berlin was about 3,300 marks per year; while student fees could raise that to 6,000 and possibly 10,000, that still meant ten years of work to afford a single bag.

The total volume of hydrogen the ship could hold in her nineteen ballonets was an astounding 55,200 cubic meters, which gave it a lift of 64,000 kilograms. With an empty weight of 36,000 kilograms, it could thus lift 28,000 kilograms of fuel, cargo, and crew.

The outer skin of *LZ 120* was also fabric, though fabric painted with a cellulose acetate dope, which caused it to contract to ensure there is no flapping which would translate into excessive wear on the Zeppelin. The fabric itself was then painted a dull gray. Originally, Zeppelins had not been painted at all, and the fabric had been allowed to darken naturally, leaving them a shade of burnt umber that became quite distinctive for Zeppelins. The reason not to paint was quite simple—the weight that this step would have added. During the war, however, questions of camouflage came up, and it was decided to paint them gray to hide in the clouds. As more Zeppelins were used at night, some were also painted black on the underside, while the top was left gray. *LZ 120* also had a somewhat mottled exterior due to the repairs done to its envelope over the previous year.

One thing that surprised Pohl from the start was how translucent not only the gas bags but the whole Zeppelin was. While under ordinary light they looked gray and impermeable from the outside, with the sun behind them, it was possible to see shadows all he way through them, and inside during the day, there was no need for any further lighting.

Parts of the outer skin was also completely transparent—with good reason. The crewman responsible for dropping bombs had to see what he was doing, so windows were set into the bottom of the hull. These windows were made, like the windows in the gondolas below, of Cellan, a variant of the cellulose acetate that was used on the outside of the ship. Manufactured by the German Celluloid Company, Cellan was similar to glass in its transparency and brittleness, but was also more prone to being scratched and otherwise losing its transparency. It had, however, one major advantage over glass for this particular use—it was considerably lighter and thus used wherever possible in the airship.

When the R class was designed, it had represented a huge step forward in Zeppelin technology, with a length 10 percent longer than the Q class that preceded it, while its almost 30 percent increase in diameter allowed for an almost 50 percent increase in volume, and thus a 60 percent increase in lift. By adding two more engines, for a total of six, the Zeppelin company's engineers ensured that the top speed was also over 10 percent higher than previous ships. In order to fit in these motors, side gondolas were added left and right of the ship. While Schütte-Lanz had introduced this concept in 1914, it was new to Zeppelins. It was thus no surprise that they, when they had appeared over England, had been given the sobriquet "super-Zeppelin"

In short, the R class was a distinct improvement over the previously built, so great that a Q-class Zeppelin that was already being built was scrapped to allow for the building of a new, R class, airship. This airship would have been given the hull number 70 and is the reason why the hull numbers do not quite line up with the actual numbers of Zeppelins built.

The first R class was hull number LZ 62. It first flew on May 28, 1916 and was commissioned *L 30* two days later and taken over by Horst Freiherr Treusch von Buttlar-Brandenfels, while the executive officer was Hans von Schiller, the first Zeppelin officer Pohl had met. Buttlar flew the Zeppelin to Nordholz, from where it would take part in the action of August 19, 1916, when the German navy attempted to shell Sunderland, a British seaport on the east coast, most of the way to Scotland—and almost exactly due east of Tondern. A fleet of Zeppelins was sent up to attempt to determine where British ships were stationed, so that the German ships could avoid a direct attack. The operation failed, not the least because the weather kept Zeppelins from fully doing their job—as well as simple mistakes in identifying ships that were made.

Immediately after this inconclusive sortie, *L 30* was moved to Ahlhorn, and two weeks later took part in one of the biggest raids of the war. On September 2, sixteen airships took off from bases all across Germany to bomb England. While Buttlar claimed that he had flown over and dropped bombs on London, starting fires and collapsing buildings, local reporting indicated that they had barely made it over British soil and had, in fact, dropped bombs on the small town of Bungay.[9] Another raid three weeks later had a similar result, while Buttlar claimed to have bombed London, nobody observed him, and there was indeed a real question as to where he spent the time over the English Channel. A similar result was achieved twice in the next couple of days, though this time, whatever prudence caused Buttlar to avoid flying over England was confirmed by what happened to his sister ship, *L 31*, during the latter raid when it was shot down by 2nd Lt. Wulstan J. Tempest flying a B.E. 2 airplane.[10]

A further attack on November 27 was aborted when *L 30* suffered engine failure almost immediately after takeoff.[11] A month later, Buttlar was replaced by Oberleutnant zur See Friemel. While the above anecdotes do not show it, Buttlar had completed fifty-four successful Zeppelin flights during the war, given the losses in the Zeppelin corps, not a bad record at all.

Other of the further sixteen R-class Zeppelins built were not so lucky. Five of them had been shot down during raids: the aforementioned *L 31*; *L 32*, which was shot down over England less than two months after its first flight; *L 33*, which crashed on that same raid; *L 34*, which managed to survive that particular raid but was shot down in late November 1916; and *L 39*, which was destroyed by French flak on its third mission.

Four further of the R class has been damaged so heavily in a landing that they had to be disassembled: *L 36* was damaged in landing on February 7, 1917; *L 38 was* damaged during forced landing; and *L 40* was damaged while landing on June 16, 1917.

This left nine still operating: *L 37*, *L 41*, *L 35*, *LZ 113*, *L 45*, *L 47*, *L 50*, which had flown for the first time just the previous month, as well as of course *L 30* and *LZ 120*.

As the new year began, the R class was already apparently obsolete. The relative ease with which British airplanes could reach the attacking Zeppelins meant that only airships that could fly higher than the airplane could would be used to attack England. Thus, on February 16, *L 30* found itself flying antisubmarine patrols. On April 5, it was sent to Tondern, then in May to Seerappen, where it was a stablemate of *LZ 120*. It was now under the command of Oberleutnant zur See Bödecker.

Zeppelin technology, like all technologies during this time, was moving fast, and even as hull number LZ 90 was being built in the shed in Löwenthal, a newer, better, class was being constructed a few kilometers south in Friedrichshafen. The new ship, while no larger than the previous one, was built with one goal in mind: to increase the height to which the Zeppelin could climb. In spite of the awe that the R class had inspired in the British, their airplane technology had rapidly risen to the challenge, and RAF pilots had managed to down four of the super-Zeppelins in the course of 1916, and each major raid on England during 1916 had cost the loss of at least one Zeppelin, making an improvement in technology of utmost importance. The first of this new S class—hull number LZ 91—flew exactly a week after *LZ 120*'s first flight. It would be turned over to the navy and was given the name *L 42*.

The German army, which had been reassessing its airship strategy for a while, decided that they could still use one of the older models, and so, after three test flights flown by the Zeppelin works, the new airship was turned over to Ernst Lehmann and his crew. It would be the first of two R-class Zeppelins to be taken on by the army. The second, and last, would be *LZ 113*, hull number LZ 83, which, in spite of the lower hull number, was actually delivered three weeks after its fellow R-class Zeppelin. It was not just the last R-class Zeppelin but the last Zeppelin that the army would get.

Lehmann's first flight in his new airship took place on January 31, 1917. It was a simple test flight that circled Friedrichshafen and returned to its hangar at Löwenthal. Two days later, the crew assayed the trip 550 kilometers northeast to Jüterbog, located southwest of Berlin. For the next month, the Jüterbog airport, with its two sheds, remained home for *LZ 120* and its crew. While the airship remained in the hangar, the crew practiced using Pohl's new Radio Direction Finding system. Lehmann was, in particular, pleased with the new system. He had understood the importance of not giving the enemy any chance to determine where a Zeppelin was. So careful was he about using the radio that he was listed as missing twice because he simply refused to break radio silence just to put the put other's minds at ease.

While Lehmann did start the engines during this month in Jüterbog, he did not actually fly the airship. The simple reason was that it was just too cold. In fact, there were times when it was too cold for the engines, and in order to get them started, they had to boil oil and pour it straight into the engines.[12]

Finally, on the last day of February, the weather allowed them to move. Their destination was Kovno, the Russian city that had been occupied by the Germans in 1915. It was an almost 800-kilometer flight, and they took off in the evening of the twenty-eighth, arriving the following morning.

Once the airship arrived in Kovno, it was loaded with 7 tons of bombs that were to be dropped onto Petrograd, and then the men waited for the weather to improve. In the end, Lehmann did not attack the Russian capital at all. While the winter continued to be brutal, it was not the cold that stopped them, but rather internal events in Russia, with the February Revolution leading to the March 15 abdication of the tsar. While the new provisional government was nominally prowar, the people—and particularly those rallying around the Bolshevik banner—were decidedly not, and fighting ground to a halt.[13]

Lehmann managed exactly one flight the first two months he was in Kovno, and that was more of a test flight than anything. In the meantime, the Germans had shipped Vladimir Lenin back into Russia, and his arrival on April 16 had shifted the internal fights into high gear. There was no need for any Zeppelins to add fuel to the fire—and, in fact, any attack might have been counterproductive to the German war aims by uniting the Russian people against a common enemy.

Instead, on May 4, Lehmann received orders to transfer to Seerappen, near Königsberg in East Prussia. He later described the the months that followed:

> There ensued a brief period when we, so to speak, were out of a job. Our LZ-120 was assigned to no more raids. We were able to continue our radio experiments; however, these flights served a double purpose, affording an opportunity to study all the various methods of landing a big ship. We practiced landings and flew almost as often as during my training days, and it was not long before we could handle the LZ-120 as familiarly as any expert with a motor car or a launch. I gave several of my officers opportunities to command the ship in these maneuvers and the best landing of a day was recognized by special honors in the mess room that evening. It was quite a sport.[14]

It was clear to Lehmann that the Zeppelin was no longer of use to the army. Even while they were waiting in Jüterbog to move to Kovno, the last army raid of the war was happening: *LZ 107* had flown over Boulogne, hidden in a cloud, and, using Lehmann's observation car, had dropped its bombs on that city.

On the western front, they were confronted by ever better armed and capable airplanes, especially with the new incendiary bullets that had been developed. Beyond that, new advances in airplane bomber technology had taken that role away. The Balkan front was not important enough to spend the money and manpower needed to keep airships aloft there. And the Russian front had disappeared entirely.

Only in patrols over the North and Baltic Sea was there any use for the giants of the air, and this was a role entirely suited to the navy and not at all the army.

LZ 120 was therefore to be turned over to the navy, though it was not considered modern enough to survive the rigors of the North Sea and was to stay in the Baltics. While they waited for the final handover, *LZ 120* was assigned to patrol duty in the Baltic.

> The job was to determine daily the presence or absence to enemy naval force in the Baltic, to keep a close check on the Russo-English submarine stations in the Gulf of Finland, patrol the sea for mines and observe the movement of merchant vessels along the Swedish coast. The routine was for us to be out twenty-four hours on a patrol and then rest for a similar period. We made a great number of flights that summer of 1917, mostly in wonderful weather which lent an atmosphere not unlike that of our peacetime operations. There was no incident of a military nature worth mentioning, and we had plenty of opportunities to try out new theories. One important series of tests lay in our practice of water landings for the

LZ 120

development of new equipment such as changes in the control cars, engine gondolas, water collecting apparatus, life-boats and other devices without which no active airship is complete.[15]

Prince Henry of Prussia visited one day that summer. Prince Henry was the younger brother of the Kaiser and a grandson of Queen Victoria. He was an admiral in the navy and had spent the war up until then as the commander-in-chief of the Baltic Fleet—a job that had disappeared with the outbreak of the Russian Revolution. He thus had time to tour the land, and spent the day with Lehmann looking over the airship as well as its new devices.

But mainly, Lehmann and his crew just enjoyed the "manifold beauties of the Baltic shores—blue skies, little white clouds, blue sea, and all this enveloped in the mellow haze peculiar to that part of North Europe."[16]

CHAPTER 13
JULY 29, 2:00 P.M.–JULY 29, 6:00 P.M.

The port of Libau from the air

As Pohl sleeps, *LZ 120* holds to its easterly course across the open Baltic Sea. At a steady speed of 50 kilometers per hour, they are due to reach their next destination in two hours. The weather has become slowly hazier, but still the visibility is almost 30 kilometers. Those of the crew currently awake are able to watch the approach of one of their sister ships from quite a distance away.

L 37 is, like *LZ 120*, an R-class Zeppelin. While it has a hull number that indicated that it was fifteen steps earlier than *LZ 120*, they had, in fact, been delivered only two months apart. The reason for this was that it had been the first airship built in the new factory at Staaken, and had been subject to severe delays in production—and is considerably heavier than other ships of its class. It can carry some 4,000 kilograms less than *LZ 120*, which is about a normal bomb capacity.

L 37 was thus obsolete even before it was delivered, and although it has been posted in various hangars along the North Sea from where raids to England have been flown, it has never participated in any of them, instead concentrating on reconnaissance flights, only one of which had seen real action. During one reconnaissance, they had seen a British steamer that had opened fire on them.[1] In late May 1917, it had been sent east, first to Seddin, but since the beginning of this month to Wainoden. Since its move east, it had been captained by Kapitänleutnant Paul Gärtner. While most of its flights had continued to be reconnaissance, just two days earlier, it had been involved in an actual attack.

The Åland Islands lie between Sweden and Finland, about 100 kilometers northeast of Stockholm, and thus well north of the where *LZ 120* has been flying of late. Though they are nominally part of the Grand Duchy of Finland, the islands had been turned into naval bases by their de facto owner—the Empire of Russia. The bases, in and around Mariehamn, had been used by both the Russians and the British, and were a prime target for bombing. The previous year, *SL 9*, a navy airship based in Seddin, had bombed the island, causing the deaths of seven men and a horse.[2]

Exactly a year later, it was *L 37*'s turn. It had departed Wainoden on the same day as *LZ 120* had taken off, on what was ostensibly a reconnaissance mission. Finding itself over the enemy naval bases, it dropped twenty bombs thereon, though without apparent damage. The news reported that fire had been returned both from shore and from the ships in the harbor, and the airship had fled without causing much damage.[3] It had been a long day in the air, however, landing in Wainoden again after midnight on the twenty-seventh of July. Now, this same airship, once again on a scouting mission, sails slowly toward *LZ 120* through the calm air in as peaceful a setting as one could imagine. The crews wave to each other as they pass.

Shortly after this meeting, Pohl awakes with a start. Above him the sun shines brightly in a deep blue sky. Checking his watch, he realizes that he has missed everything, and so immediately pulls out the notebook he had been using for the letter to his mother and sets about writing down his disappointment:

3:30 p.m. I slept through everything! The southern corner of Gotland as well as the meeting with L 37. Oh, well. The airships all look the same, I've seen enough of them, and I can't imagine that the lower third of Gotland is fundamentally different from the upper two, which I observed awake and with a telescope. It was just too nice sleeping in the sun in my little veranda in the stern, I had removed the canvas roof and had cooked in the sun under cloudless skies, stretched out lazily on my fur. But now I have to hurry forward, Libau is directly ahead of us.

Libau and its harbor are an enduring testament to the deep need the Russian Empire had for a warm-water port. Located at the northern end of the stretch of land that separates Lake Libau from the Baltic Sea, it is both the most southern Russian harbor on the Baltic as well as the most western of all of that empire's harbors. It is also the only Russian Baltic port that can be used year-round, over the last fifty years it averaged one day a year that it could not be navigated.

The only problem is its geography: a flat coast sloping very gradually into the sea. No indentation mars the straight line of the shore, no protected place for ships to anchor. Nonetheless, it was known to be used as a harbor as early as the thirteenth century, and in the seventeenth century, the first major works were done, building an inner basin protected from the sea by a wide jetty as well as a canal leading to Lake Libau. Moles were added about a hundred years later to protect this new harbor, but soon silted up. Shortly after the Crimean War, expansion began in earnest. The major work done was to extend the moles even farther into the sea. Further changes of this type were continued throughout the nineteenth century, especially after the completion of the railroad connecting Libau with the grain-producing areas of Ukraine in the mid 1870s, vastly increasing its importance as a harbor.

None of these incremental changes were entirely satisfactory, so in the late 1880s, the decision was made to finally build a proper harbor. This meant building a wide, U-shaped set of moles stretching 2 kilometers out into the sea. At the same time, a single mole in the center was built, so that the harbor could be used both my military and civilian ships, the former in the northern sector, the latter in the southern.

Work began shortly after the contract was signed in 1890, and required the building of a concrete plant that could produce 300 tons per day. This concrete was formed into blocks which were then placed on top of long spits made by piling up stones brought from elsewhere by barge and put into place by divers. Work continued for the next sixteen years, and it remained an important port throughout this time.[4]

Both the port and Libau itself have been in German hands since May 1915, when they had been taken by Army Detachment Lauenstein in the run-up to the Gorlice-Tarnow offensive farther south.

Even before this ground attack, it had been the object of an airship attack raid: On January 25, 1915, the airship *PL 19* had flown over the city. Built originally for the British army, the airship had been kept by the Germans after the outbreak of war. As a nonrigid airship, it was not well suited for the task that it was set, namely bombing the city. While it did manage to drop nine bombs weighing some 200 kilograms, it was brought down either by Russian artillery or because it had iced up.[5] Or maybe both.

Either way, four months later, the Germans took the city, returning it to German control for the first time since 1609. Even from the air, Pohl can see the results of the attack, and of Russian attempts to make it unusable for the Germans, on the area: giant piles of rubble, a destroyed drydock, and, in the harbor itself a sunken ship, of which only the smokestack and stern are visible. A number of smaller ships cluster around the sunken ship, though Pohl can not determine if they were trying to salvage the cargo or are attempting to refloat the ship itself. Germans are also busily rebuilding one of the drydocks; two floating docks are already back in action. There are also indications of current use by the Germans: two light cruisers, the SMS *Augsburg* and SMS *Regensburg* are tied up at the quay, as well as a whole flotilla of minesweepers.

Pohl continues to look down in fascination as they float over the whole town. The harbor is, as he would write to his mother a few minutes later, the most interesting thing that he has viewed from above in all of his time flying around in Zeppelins. He tries, and fails, to calculate how many hundreds of thousands of concrete blocks had been sunk in the endeavor. And he is stunned that "Russian disarray" could have produced such a marvel of engineering. Beyond that, the dichotomy of the two halves intrigues him, the northern half full of endless rows of barracks, plus officers's quarters, a factory, and the two largest structures: a mess hall and a church. The southern half, Libau itself, consists of mainly one-story wooden houses with a smattering of larger, more modern, homes interspersed.

Pohl returns to his notebook and writes down his impressions, ending with the comment about "Russian disarray." With this bit of racism out of his system, he goes to his satchel and makes an inventory of the food in it to make his lunch. The airship continues due south along the coast past Lake Libau, a narrow lagoon that stretches 20 kilometers down the coast. Beyond that are enormous forests separated from the beach by a narrow beach with only the occasional small town to interrupt the monotony. It is the perfect time to tend to one's stomach.

By this time, especially after having taken a solid nap, Pohl is feeling pretty good. The intestinal distress from the previous night is now only a vague memory, and the sunshine and wind he had been exposed to ensure that he is righteously hungry. He sorts through his food package and determines that he will not be able to continue to subsist on solely chocolate and cookies; he will have to attempt to eat some of the more challenging food—in particular, the bread that he felt had contributed, at least to some extent, to the night's terrors. In the end, he decides that there was no point in refusing to eat, that you just have to have faith that it would all work out. He cuts a slice of bread, covers it with a thick layer of lard, and adds some sausage. He washes it down with several cups of cold and, he notes with some trepidation, slightly sour coffee. It had, after all, been determined that the soup had fermented and this was what had led to the widespread suffering.

As Pohl finishes, he sees below him two large concrete moles jutting at an angle well into the sea. Where they reach land, the water widens into the top of a lagoon that stretches for kilometers south, and a few kilometers farther down on the north side of this water is a familiar city: Memel. This city of some 25,000 inhabitants was well known to all Germans as being at the very northeastern corner of the German Empire. In fact, its position in this regard had been fixed in 1841 by August Hoffman von Fallersleben when he wrote the poem "Das Lied der Deutschen," which, combined with a melody by Franz Joseph Haydn, had been a patriotic German song since then. The fifth line stated that Germany stretched from the Meuse (River) to the Memel (River).[6] While the use of the Meuse River was a bit aggressive—the river actually flows through Holland, Belgium, and France, with its closest approach being some 4 kilometers from Germany, the use of the Memel is appropriate: the river flows into the Kurisches Haff that Pohl could see from the air, and thus past the city and into the Baltic Sea. Twenty kilometers north of the city limits lies the town of Krettingen, through which the border with Russia Empire runs. The whole area has a strong Lithuanian influence, though Germans remain in the majority.

Memel was also, as he writes to his mother, a place that his father had known well—he had gone to school there, and had later taken ships from there to Stettin. The younger Pohl's real interest at the moment lies with the geological feature directly below him: the Kurische Nehrung. A 100-mile tongue of land only about 3 kilometers wide, it extends south from Memel in a long curve the bends slowly west. A narrow sandy beach extended along the entire western side, while on the other side, much wider beaches lead down to the Kurisches Haff, a body of water of over 1,600 square kilometers, while only being some 4 meters deep at its maximum. Between the two beaches lie closely planted rows of trees, interspersed with paths that invite strolling. Even from 400 meters in the air, Pohl can make out the trees and paths from his position in the armchair, the telescope he holds brings it all into focus. But for him, the main attraction is the spit itself, a joke in the creation, as he calls it.

Two-thirds of the way along the comes the largest town on the spit: Rossitten. Immediately recognizable by its large brick church, it lives, like the other villages on the spit, from fishing, but, unlike the others, has enough land around it to support agriculture. It is also known for its ornithological observatory. In the late nineteenth century, the ornithologist Johannes Thienemann had observed huge flights of migratory birds over the spit, birds that avoided open water would come together here. It was thus a prime location for the study of birds, and in 1901, Thienemann opened the first ornithological research station there.[7]

As Pohl writes of Rossitten and the fact that he has now seen the entire German Baltic coast from Libau to Lübeck, Captain Lehmann awakes above. Lehmann has slept over seven hours in his hammock and sets about taking one of his showers, then changes into a sporty shirt that was quite different from his usual military gear. He is feeling good as he descends into the gondola, and proceeds to the navigator's table, where he spends some minutes with his slide rule and a compass. At 6:30, he then settles down next to Pohl and says that they have been in the air for over sixty-six hours and have flown 2,163 nautical miles, which is just over 4,000 kilometers—or enough to make it from London to St. John's in Newfoundland: A transatlantic flight by any definition. Furthermore, they still have enough fuel for another forty hours, so that they will soon have flown the distance from London to New York.

This engenders a whole different discussion: how to improve life on board for the crew. That the airship is fully capable of a transatlantic flight now seems to be accepted by all. But the welter of garbage and chaos produced by each individual's briefcase and food bags is, without a doubt, in need of improvement. Bringing some sort of order into this would also be useful when using airships for four-day patrols.

Lehmann finishes up by telling Pohl that they are, once again, on a course for Glücksburg, and that he hopes to have him directly above his mother by 9:00 the next morning. Pohl replies that he will be on vacation starting at midnight, a morning spent over the house that he hopes to spend several weeks in will be almost as good, that he is happy to give up some vacation for this trip.

CHAPTER 14
THE DREAM OF THE ATLANTIC

The Wellman ship *America*, seen from the British ship RMS *Trent*. The anchor of the airship can be seen dragging through the water through the railing at the center bottom. *Library of Congress*

THE DREAM OF THE ATLANTIC

aptain Lehmann had far more in mind this afternoon than either setting a new flight record—which he had already done—or proving that the airship could be better used for reconnaissance by flying for one hundred hours—after all, the army was getting out of the airship business entirely. His real goal was much greater and much older: to prove that an airship could fly across the Atlantic. The distance from Frankfurt to New York City is about 6,200 kilometers. At *LZ 120*'s top speed of 100 kilometers per hour, it would take about sixty-five hours to cross the ocean; at the 60 kilometers per hour or so that the ship has been actually proceeding, it would take one hundred hours to do so.

Crossing the Atlantic by air had been a dream of aviators since the dawn of the balloon era. As early as 1836, there was a discussion about the feasibility of such a trip. While the current technology lagged far behind the plans, it was unsurprising that people were looking for a better way of making the voyage; crossing the Atlantic in these presteam days was a two-to-three-month ordeal, subject to the whims of the weather, in a cramped and poorly ventilated ship. Floating high above this was an obvious improvement over the current state of affairs.

The first person to publicly state their plans was England's Charles Green. A veteran balloonist with some 275 ascents under his belt, Green, together with Admiral Sir Sidney Smith, realized that there were steady westerly winds blowing at higher altitude, completely divorced from whatever direction the winds were headed at lower altitudes. The trick was, therefore, to have the balloon rise just high enough to get into this regime, without going too high.[1]

Green also proposed the use of what he called "carburetted hydrogen gas" (i.e., methane) as his lifting agent. This had the advantage of being much slower in escaping from the balloon, allowing for a longer flight, but with a density half of air, rather than the tenth of hydrogen, required a far-larger balloon for the same amount of lift.[2]

Green originally announced his plans in 1836, the same year that he had set a record by flying from London to Weilburg in Germany, a distance of 750 kilometers. Four years later, he went so far as to publish a picture of the balloon that would do the trick, a picture purported to being "exact." It showed a spherical balloon about 30-foot diameter with a small basket underneath, just large enough for a single passenger. In front of the basket was a two-winged propeller, in the back, a rudder. Dangling from the bottom, and stretching down into the water just a few meters below, is a rope. The last was one of Green's inventions: using a trailing rope to keep a constant height. Green called this a guide-line.[3]

The problems here were manifold. First off, the gas bag, when filled with methane, would have a lift of about 260 kilograms. Even the lightest canvas would mean a bag that size would weigh some 150 kilograms, leaving only 90 kilograms for the passenger, the basket, and the guide-line.

The balloon is shown to be about 5 meters above the water, far below the 10,000-meter altitude in which the jet stream which Green hoped would blow him across the ocean is situated.

It was thus probably just as well that Green never attempted this foolhardy endeavor. He suffered major injuries the following year in a balloon accident, and although he claimed that this would not stop him from his transatlantic voyage, and, in fact, repeated his claims in 1846, he never did make a serious attempt.[4]

On the other side of the Atlantic, John Wise, Green's American counterpart, was thinking along similar lines. In an 1843 article which he requested that all newspaper publishers put in their papers, he outlined a plan for crossing the ocean in a balloon of 30 meters in diameter, and made of cloth that had been impregnated in some way to keep the hydrogen in it for weeks. Underneath was to be slung a sailing vessel, for use in the unlikely case of a water landing. Wise hoped that he would be supported by Congress in this endeavor; failing that, he asked that the "wealthy merchants of Philadelphia and New York should take it in hand."[5]

The trip was to take place in the summer of 1844, so Wise's supporters in New York were stunned to read in the *Sun* of April 13, 1844, that a balloon with eight passengers, including Thomas Monck Mason, who had accompanied Green in his flight to Weilburg, had arrived in South Carolina after traversing the Atlantic in three days. Further details were to be had in an extra the next morning.[6]

The extra, which was finally delivered around noon to the large crowd that had gathered, described the balloon in great detail—essentially, a larger version of the Green balloon. It also gave a blow-by-blow account, from the aviators' takeoff from Wales, with the destination Paris, and their realization that the winds were actually pushing them in the opposite direction, and thus their decision to push on and make it across.

The reaction was mixed. Some believed, others scoffed—particularly as the *Sun* had, not ten years earlier, published a series of articles purporting to describe life found on the moon. As it turned out, the doubters had it right: the whole thing was a hoax written by none other than Edgar Allan Poe, less than a year before the publication of "The Raven" would make him a household word.[7]

Among the supposed passengers in Poe's story was one William Henson, who had been working on a steam-powered airplane for a number of years at this point. Henson had managed to build a model which actually worked, in that it managed to get off the ground once—before crashing into a wall. This success led them to immediately incorporate the Aerial Transit Company, with plans of taking passengers across the ocean. A 1902 book succinctly states the results: "Be it here recorded that the machine did not cross the Atlantic."[8]

It would be another fifteen years before there would be another burst of enthusiasm for transatlantic voyages; even Giffard's 1852 flight did not noticeably encourage further work in that direction. The year 1859 would, however, produce a bumper crop. The most important was a trip by John Wise and others, in a balloon portentously named *Atlantic*. Wise had the forethought, however, to take off from St. Louis, in order to show that using the jet stream would be tend to keep the balloon moving in an easterly direction.

Thus, in the early evening of July 1, Washington Square, St. Louis, found itself full of people, there to watch the takeoff of the balloon. The crush surrounding it turned out to be a real problem, as the aeronauts could not adjust the "fan-wheels" mounted on the outside of the balloon, which allowed for the raising and lowering of the balloon without losing ballast or gas. Otherwise, the balloon was well stocked, including "champagne, sherry, sparkling catawba, claret, madeira, brandy and porter." Shortly after takeoff, the others noticed that Professor Wise was unconscious in the bottom of the car. He had stayed too long directly underneath the balloon's exhaust, and had been overcome by the exiting hydrogen. Having revived their leader, the aeronauts flew up and over the Mississippi, and then up into the jet stream. Although they found themselves making good time, and in approximately the right direction, it was also quite cold, so they came down to a lower—and warmer—atmosphere, where they "began a siege on the eatables and drinkables."

The flight continued on through the night, with the passengers sleeping in stages, while keeping the balloon off the ground through the judicious release of ballast. Around sunrise, the passed over Fort Wayne, Indiana. The sun warmed the balloon, sending it to higher elevations again as they passed over Lake Erie. Eleven a.m. saw them within sight of Niagara Falls, and about a mile up.

At this point, the plan was to land, drop off two passengers, take up ballast, and continue to the Atlantic. Instead, as it reached lower altitudes the balloon was stuck in a windstorm, and they found themselves pushed out into Lake Ontario. Throwing all manner of articles out kept the balloon out of the water until they could pass over it, landing in the forest that ringed the lake, crashing through 1 mile of it before they could bring the balloon under control.

They had landed near Sackett's Harbor, New York, for a total flight of a little over 1,300 kilometers, although passenger William Hyde, who wrote a long article published in the *St. Louis Republican* a few days later, claimed that it was 1,500 and possibly as far as 2,000 kilometers. The time of the trip was a very respectable nineteen hours and forty minutes.[9]

Their trip was thus about twice Green's flight in 1846 and about 4,800 kilometers short for a transatlantic flight.

Two others who made noises about a transatlantic trip that year were John Steiner and Thaddeus Lowe. Both were well-known balloonists, and both wanted to be the first to cross the Atlantic in an airship. Steiner's plan was for a 100-meter long, copper-bottomed dirigible. Newspaper articles of the day spoke uncritically of his plans, in spite of the obvious flaws in the story. For one, Steiner did not actually have any money for his project but was holding out for the—unlikely—appropriation from Congress, for another, his numbers displayed some elementary mistakes. It was thus hardly surprising that Steiner's plans rapidly sank out of sight, never to be seen again.[10]

Lowe, on the other hand, got much further in his plans than anyone before him. The newspapers followed him as he built his massive airship *City of New York* near its namesake city. Excitement reached a fever when, in late October 1859, inflation of the airship began in what is today Bryant Park, in New York City. Crowds streamed in all day to see the airship, the boat attached below, the engine that was to power the dirigible across the Atlantic, as well as the "fur coat, cap, shows, and gloves, which Prof. Lowe is to wear in the cold regions of the upper air."[11]

Fortunately for those seeking to see the balloon, and those making money from them, the weather showed no signs of improving. Throughout November, Lowe waited—and the crowds kept coming, each depositing their twenty-five cents in order to see the airship. On Thanksgiving, the weather turned ugly, with heavy wind, and Lowe used this as an excuse to shut down the whole enterprise until the next year.[12]

In August of the next year, Lowe was exhibiting his balloon again. This time, he attempted to collect the quarters of Philadelphians.[13] Throughout September, the public had its chance to view it, while Lowe waited for the proper moment for takeoff. Saturday, September 8, was the original date planned, but the wind caused the balloon to burst, setting back his plans.[14] A second attempt was made on the twenty-ninth. The inflation proceeded apace, and at 5:00 a.m. everything was ready for liftoff—when the balloon burst again. This time, it was determined that the fabric of the balloon had rotted from exposure and handling. The *New York Times* finished its article with the words "This unfortunate denouement will probably terminate the great experiment, for a time, at least, until parties can be sufficiently interested to raise the funds for another balloon and trial."[15]

Lowe came back the next year with another balloon. This time, however, he decided to follow in Wise's footsteps, and to attempt a flight from the middle of the country to the Atlantic. It turned out to be quite successful: Lowe even decided to start when the wind was unfavorable to him, to prove that the winds in the upper atmosphere would push him in the right direction, and that is exactly how it came to pass. Unfortunately, his timing was poor. Taking off from Cincinnati, he found himself nine hours later in Pea Ridge, South Carolina—behind enemy lines, as the state had seceded from the Union six months earlier.[16] Lowe was cast into jail and only released home several days thereafter.

It was not an auspicious result; only Lowe's subsequent work for the US Army helped rehabilitate both his and Steiner's good names.

The postwar period was a quiet time for American aeronauts. Into this slack period came Alexander Chevalier, a French balloonist convinced that he could fly from the United States to Europe in his balloon.[17] Chevalier went as far as to make some test flights from New York in late May 1869. During one, he found himself being carried toward the ocean and chose to land in Flushing rather than to continue before fully prepared. He determined that the fourth of July would be an auspicious date to begin his flight.[18] And then? Nothing. No further details emerged, and so it appears that this flight never took place. Chevalier appeared again the next year, taking up paying passengers in his balloon, his dreams of crossing the Atlantic on hold.

Dupuy de Lome's successful flight in 1872 immediately prompted the usual overeager enthusiasm, with the *Daily Phoenix* of Columbia, South Carolina, echoing what many said:

> The balloon is said to have obeyed the helm with the utmost alacrity, and to have progressed readily in the teeth of the wind. If this goes on, railway and steam packet stockholders must prepare for a fall. London and Paris will become a three days' journey from New York when the wind favors.[19]

In the wake of de Lome's flight, numerous aeronauts took up the challenge, including, once again, John Wise, who teamed up with Washington Donaldson, who had "electrified the people with his ballooning feats" and had made plans to cross the Atlantic in the airship *North American*. Wise convinced Donaldson to join forces and, after being snubbed by the Boston Common Council, approached the New York *Daily Graphic* newspaper and convinced them to subsidize the enormous balloon, which they could name after themselves in exchange.[20]

On June 27, 1873, the three parties signed an agreement under which the Graphic Company (owner and publisher of the *Daily Graphic*) would, over the next year, build and equip a 130-foot balloon. Wise and Donaldson would be "personally superintend and direct the construction of the balloon according to their utmost skill and judgment." Once the balloon was completed, they were to "make a public ascension … accompanied by such other persons as may be designated by The Graphic Company; and, making such ascension, they shall directly and without any delay or evasion, seek the elevation of the eastern air current; there to remain until land shall have been made on the eastern side of the Atlantic Ocean."[21]

The balloon was finished in September 1873. The first two inflations ended in failure. While the first was aborted by Donaldson, the second caused the balloon to burst. Nonetheless, the Graphic Company turned it over to Donaldson, who immediately rebuilt it, making it half the size it had been previously. On October 7, the balloon was inflated successfully, and Donaldson and the two representatives of the Graphic Company, Alfred Ford and George Ashton Lunt, "rose gracefully" from its starting point in a baseball field in Brooklyn.

For the next few hours, all seemed well, and they passed over Glen Cove, on Long Island, at what was estimated to be a mile an hour—a rate that would have taken them across the Atlantic in under three days. Unfortunately, in order to keep aloft, Donaldson found himself throwing over more and more of his precious ballast. In the end, they found themselves returning to earth at Canaan, Connecticut, at 1:25 p.m., having traveled less than 70 kilometers in just over four hours.

In returning to solid ground, Donaldson and Ford jumped from the balloon, while Lunt stayed aboard. He jumped when the great airship encountered another tree. Sadly, in contrast to Donaldson and Ford, Lunt was fairly high up, crashing down through a tree before hitting the ground. Lunt died of his injuries the following April, while Donaldson continued on as a balloonist, dying two years later over Lake Michigan, having never attempted to repeat his flight.[22]

Another attempt in the mode of Professor Wise was attempted in 1881. Samuel Archer King was, at the time, one of the best-known balloonists in the country, and he too wanted to show that a transatlantic flight was possible by flying from Minneapolis to Boston. On September 12, his enormous hydrogen-inflated balloon took off. It was late in the afternoon already, and the flight was almost immediately doomed by the need to dump ballast simply to stay aloft. Thus King decided to land, having made it no farther than St Paul.[23]

Most of the attempts at flight over the next few years got no further than the planning stage. Some actually got as far as trying to raise money for the venture; none actually took off. The closest any one came was the airship *America*, which was designed by Peter Campbell.

Campbell, a jeweler by trade, had been intrigued by the pedalpowered airships that were being shown off around the country at the time. He first made the news in early 1888 with a small, clockwork-powered model, which he flew in the confines of his store. By the end of this year, he had a full-size version built, in which the aeronaut James K. Allen flew for about 10 kilometers, during which "with but few minor exceptions, the machine obeyed the actions of the various propellers."[24]

With this minor success, Campbell found himself thinking big. A letter sent to him from England pointed out that this meant that a flight across the Atlantic was possible, though a larger airship would be necessary.[25] Instead, Campbell decided that all he needed was a new pilot, hiring Edward D. Hogan, "one of the most daring aeronauts of the age,"[26] who had completed more than four hundred successful balloon ascents.[27]

Hogan was to demonstrate "the practical worth of Mr. Campbell's invention," after which he intended "to make a voyage, if possible, to Europe."[28]

On July 16, 1889, Hogan took off for a brief flight; the main purpose was simply to show that the airship would work with coal gas, as well as the hydrogen that had been previously used.[29] Almost immediately, things went awry. The balloon shot up, and began heading north and out of sight. That evening, a balloon was seen over Providence, Rhode Island,[30] though it was not clear whether this was Hogan or not.

The next sighting was well out over the Atlantic, at a point about 250 kilometers due east of Atlantic City, New Jersey. A passing ship noticed the balloon and steamed over to see what was going on.[31] By the time they arrived, the balloon was dead in the water and there was nobody nearby. It was assumed that Hogan had been overcome by the gas from the balloon and fallen into the water. His body was never recovered.[32]

Eight years later, another—slightly different—attempt was made to fly between Europe and the United States. The balloonist was Solomon Andree, and he was accompanied by two passengers. In their case, they tried to go via the North Pole. On July 11, 1897, Andree took off from Spitsbergen, and was last seen traveling in the northerly direction with good speed.[33] It was to be the last anyone would see of the balloon or its three passengers. The authorities spread flyers throughout Canada, particularly its northern reaches, with pictures of what to look for. Rumors that the balloon had been seen swirled for months. In September, a message came from Russia that a balloon had recently been sighted in Siberia, almost 4,000 kilometers and two months after takeoff.[34]

Over the next ten years, no further attempts were made to cross the Atlantic. Numerous plans were made, but no actual airships were built. Some of the plans were simply fantasies; some were attempts to separate investors from their hard-earned cash. And with some, it was not clear what was going on. One of the more remarkable endeavors was started by Thurlow Weed Barnes and Lewis Nixon, who incorporated a company grandly named the Aerial Navigation Company of America, with plans to build 800-foot ships carrying a hundred passengers across the ocean.[35] In spite of the fact that the most successful airship builder, Graf Zeppelin, had yet to put any airships into passenger service, Barnes and Nixon were convinced that they would soon be flying passengers across the ocean—even though they had never even flown in an airship. The two men's pronouncements were given more weight than they deserved due to Barnes's success in building trains in China, and the fact that he was the grandson of Thurlow Weed, who was instrumental in getting Abraham Lincoln the nomination for president in 1860, while Nixon was a famed naval designer and owned several shipyards.

For several months, their plans were publicized in newspapers across the country, and eventually, they were insisting that the airship would be 850 meters long, carry 2,500 passengers, and cross the Atlantic in two days.[36] At this point they combined forces with one Edward J. Pennington, who had been active in the early 1890s with a harebrained scheme to fly across the Atlantic. Pennington had been one of those whose main interest was fleecing investors, and had disappeared long before his investors saw any return whatsoever, shortly after showing a very simple airship that was capable of flight—but only indoors.

And now, here he was again, teaming up with two who should have known better. The first reports, in late 1908, quoted Nixon extensively: "We expect to start the construction of this airship almost immediately. It will be 700 feet long, with a diameter of eighty feet and passenger room for 100.... Besides its passengers and armament, the ship will be expected to carry food and fuel enough for a trip across the ocean."[37] Others added that Thurlow Weed Barnes "expected the first of the great airships to be launched within the next twelve months"[38]

In fact, within twelve months, the whole company had disappeared in a cloud of acrimony. A single article in the *New York Times*, published in June 1909, precipitated its downfall. The *Times*, less credulous than its competitors, noticed that this was the same Pennington who had shown himself excellent at moving money from the pockets of his investors into his own, and very little else, twenty years previously.[39]

His supposed partners wasted no time in throwing Pennington to the wolves. Nixon "denied . . . that he was in any way interested in the company. He said he wished it made clear that he had no connection of the financial organization of the concern and knew of it only through having been asked to look at the plans for a dirigible ship similar to the Zeppelin airship." Barnes, for his part, "was not accessible." In short, a far cry from their enthusiasm from just six months earlier.[40]

Pennington knew the jig was up, but refused to depart the stage gracefully. Instead, he pressed a libel suit against the *Times*, something that did not turn out well. Just the headline of the article in which the *Times* described the trial says everything: "Pennington Hazy about His Career." It did not get much better from there, with Pennington denying any more connection to the company than Nixon or Barnes had claimed to have in June. Suddenly, Pennington was simply the engineer, and the others were responsible for the financial misdeeds.[41] In short order, the judge in the trial threw it out, calling it a "farce."[42]

Pennington, Nixon, and Barnes thus joined with dozens of other would-be Atlantic flyers in that they talked a good game, but could not even get off the ground, let alone fly across the ocean. Their names are buried in newspaper archives around the world: Schroeder, Krueger, de Bausset, Jovis, Fest, Wolff, Barton, Custead, Godard, Capazza, Thomas, Wortscher, Bliven, Johansen, Learmouth, Fielding, McCready, Schultz, and Roenne.

In 1910, however, finally, a real attempt was made. Walter Wellman's airship *America* not only took off but had some real hope of actually crossing the ocean.

Walter Wellman was a journalist who found his stories leading him on to ever more remarkable adventures. After two polar expeditions using old standbys of ships, sleds, and dogs, Wellman built an airship to take him to the North Pole. The money was furnished by his employer, the *Chicago Record-Herald*, and the expedition was thus named the Wellman-Chicago Record-Herald Polar Expedition. In 1906, Wellman and his crew headed for northern Norway, to Spitsbergen, almost at 80 degrees north and thus about 1,000 kilomters to the North Pole.[43]

The time was spent building an enormous hangar for the airship he had named *America*, and thus only toward the end of the summer was there any hope of starting, but mechanical defects denied any chance of taking off.[44] During the winter 1906–7, Wellman had the airship rebuilt and returned to Dane's Island, now certain of success. This time, it was the weather that wreaked havoc with their schedule, and it was not until early September when they could take off. After a flight of only about 60 kilometers, however, Wellman discovered that the compass had broken, and they found themselves lost in a snow squall. Reluctantly, Wellman had the airship land, and was rescued by the two steamers who had been following along their flight.[45]

Two years later, Wellman tried again. This time, the airship made it only 50 kilometers before the equilibrator—a long line that was to keep the airship from getting too high or too low—broke, sending the airship shooting into the air. Only a quick hand on the safety valve, releasing gas from the envelope, could keep them from climbing too high. A temporary equilibrator was rigged, and the airship began to limp south again until reaching the edge of the ice fields and a steamer that had seen them struggling. Once again the airship was towed back to its hangar, where as second tragedy struck: a gust of air caught the balloon, popping it and thus wrecking any chance of trying again that year.[46]

Instead, Wellman turned to another challenge: flying across the Atlantic. After rebuilding *America*, including adding a second engine, he moved to Atlantic City in the summer of 1910 to await favorable weather. In contrast to previous announcements of transatlantic flights, which had been received with utmost credulity by the news media of the day, Wellman's plan earned a surprising amount of scorn from newspapers across the country. Some felt that it was all a publicity stunt;[47] others cracked that the obvious next thing for Wellman to attempt was a flight into the crater at Vesuvius,[48] while even others suggested that Wellman take a boat[49] or to learn how to swim.[50] This attitude may well have come from the fact that the expedition was being supported by three newspapers: The *Chicago Record-Herald*, the (London) *Daily Telegraph*, and the *New York Times*. Unsurprisingly, these three newspapers were much more supportive in their pages than others, spending large amounts of space on the minutiae of the preparations.

Finally, at 8:05 a.m. on October 5, Wellman and his five crewmembers—and a cat named Kiddo who had stowed away—took off from Atlantic City. As in previous trips, Wellman had a ship tow his airship out into the ocean, a particularly wise decision in this case owing to the heavy fog blanketing the sea. Just as they were getting ready to detach themselves from the ship, Wellman had second thoughts about having a cat on board, especially as Kiddo seemed to be restless and out of sorts in the swaying cabin. Wellman ordered the cat to be put in a bag and sent down by a rope to ship below. He then sent what is generally considered to be the first-ever radio transmission from an airship to the ground: "Roy, come and get this goddamn cat." By the time Leroy Chamberlain, Wellman's secretary, had made it out to the airship, the sea was too rough for any feline transfer and the airship was on its own, still with the cat on board.[51]

For the first hours, all went well. After about two hours, they stopped the engines to send a message back to Atlantic City. The message was banal, "All well on board. Machinery working well," and not exactly accurate. Vaniman, the engineer, and his assistants Loud and Aubert had been working nonstop to keep them running at all.

But, for now, they were working. With the engines back on, the airship began moving steadily to the northeast. Unfortunately, by the afternoon, trouble reared its head: the main engine broke down. Vaniman posited that sand had gotten into it during the time waiting for favorable weather in Atlantic City. Knowing the nature of the problem did nothing to repair it. According to Vaniman, "It was no good and could be thrown overboard for ballast."

The members of the expedition remained hopeful, however. After all, there was still a second, smaller engine, which had performed admirably thus far. In fact, it continued to run throughout the night, though Wellman was shocked to see the numbers of sparks flying out of it—much too close to the enormous envelope of gas keeping the ship in the air. Vaniman was more sanguine, pointing out that the engine had been producing sparks like this from the beginning; it was just that during the day you could not see them.

During the night, the airship also almost ran into a schooner, but quick thinking on the part of the helmsman kept disaster at bay. Early the next morning, the motor was shut off briefly, then restarted, then stopped again when it was determined that the wind was blowing the *America* in approximately the right direction. For the next two days, the airship was essentially at the mercy of the winds. In spite of this, they continued to make steady progress to the northeast, getting slowly closer to the European continent, with the engine used sparingly.

By the next afternoon, in spite of the care taken over the engine, it too, was broken, and it was clear that there was no hope of reaching Europe. With the wind shifting, it now seemed more likely to reach Bermuda. Instead, at 5:00 a.m. on the eighteenth, members of the crew sighted the steamer RMS *Trent* and managed to signal it using first Morse code on a signal lamp, then communicating via radio. The *America* dropped down to the water, where the crew unsnapped the balloon, which bounded away over the waves, while they drove the boat that had been suspended under the balloon over to the *Trent*. The airship had made it to a point 600 kilometers due east of Hatteras, and thus almost exactly due south of the easternmost point in the continental United States.

Everyone, even the cat, survived with no injuries. Only the *America*, and presumably Wellman's pride, were lost that day. If nothing else, they had managed a flight of more than seventy hours and traveled a distance of more than 1,500 kilometers.[52]

Nonetheless, this would be Wellman's last flight in an airship. Vaniman, was, however, undeterred, and ended up paying for this with his life. He had a new airship built, which he named *Akron* for the home city of its two builders. Vaniman's great improvement was a second interior bladder that could be pumped full of air to reduce the size of the balloon holding the lifting gas, thus reducing its lift and simplifying the regulation of altitude.[53] Its other innovation was designing it to run on only half the engines at a time, ensuring that they would not burn out as *America*'s had done.[54] This was, essentially, what Lehmann was doing during *LZ 120*'s flight.

The balloon was built in Atlantic City, and on July 2, Vaniman and four others, including his brother, went up for a trial flight. For the first few minutes, all was well. The crowd below could see the airship slowly rise, kept under control by its captain. At about 600 meters, the airship apparently encountered warmer air and, to the horror of those below, burst, sending the five aeronauts plunging down to their death in the ocean.[55]

The following year, a German American businessman named Joseph Brucker raised money from the Swiss Suchard company for purposes of a transatlantic flight. An airship was actually built but began to leak even before it had its first test flights. In the end, its flight was indefinitely postponed, like so many before it.[56]

The following year, for the first time, the Zeppelin company began talking of an Atlantic crossing. While up to then the announcements in this direction had come from any number of wild-eyed dreamers, who foresaw immediate transatlantic flights in Zeppelin's future even before he had lifted off for the first time, this time, it was direct quotes from the count himself that drove the coverage. As always, the count was cautious in his prognoses, saying only that he thought that this flight might occur in the summer of 1915.[57] And, had the war not broken out, it was not out of the realm of the possible that this might have happened. Instead, of course, the bulk of the energy within the Zeppelin organization went into very different research, and only with Lehmann's flight was there some sense that this goal might, sooner rather than later, be achieved.

CHAPTER 15
JULY 29, 6:00 P.M.–JULY 30, 2:00 P.M.

The East Prussian seaside resort of Kranz as seen from the air

A s *LZ 120* reaches the end of their two-hour flight along the Kurische Nehrung, the city of Kranz becomes visible on the port side. This seaside town, which they had last visited from the air the day before their departure, lies 400 meters below them and basks in the late afternoon sunshine.

Lehmann prudently opts to turn west at this point. He is worried that some of his superiors either in Königsberg or Seerappen, about 25 kilometers south of them, will see them and order them back home. After all, he has completed the mission that he originally had sold them on, and the fact that they are now simply trying to extend the time and see what the maximum time and distance a Zeppelin can fly was not exactly in the original orders. That their being spotted is a justified fear is validated by the fact that they can see *LZ 120*'s hangar mate, the Navy Zeppelin *L 30*, flying south of them on a training flight over Königsberg.

Pohl expresses disappointment in their change in direction; he had been hoping to see his friend and colleague Max Wien and family at their estate on the southwestern corner of the Samland Peninsula, but understands that one should not tempt fate. He has as little interest in having the flight cut short as any crew member. Instead, he has the opportunity to see Rauschen and Georgenswalde, two resorts on the north coast of Samland. While Rauschen had originally been a grist mill, and become a spa and resort in 1820,[1] it has since become famous enough to be visited by the German Kaiser—who had demanded that the embankment be beautified. It is a unique place in that the city was situated on a high bluff above the beach, so that the city fathers had decided that it was necessary to build an aerial lift to take visitors to the water. Those that risk the trip on it, or take the winding path to the beach, are rewarded by a wide beach backed by an extensive boardwalk and a long building containing changing facilities.[2] The beach is well attended, in spite of the war raging all around it. South of the seaside resort lies the old city of Rauschen, well protected from the fury of the Baltic Sea winters and directly on the millpond that had long been the city's economic engine. Beyond the pond lie royal forests that add to the restful nature of the area.

Georgenswalde, just a few kilometers west of Rauschen and connected by train tracks running at the top of the dunes, has a very different history, having been an estate for most of its life, and first mentioned as a seaside resort 1898.[3] Just before the war, a large health resort, which dominated the landscape as seen from above, was added to its amenities. Behind the spa hotel lies an open area for use by the guests to walk, while the front is dotted with umbrellas shading those taking a rest with a drink while looking down over the ocean.

Pohl examines the two resorts from above and, given that it was possible that some of his family are on vacation there, waves a flag at them as he flies by. It is not completely out of the question that his waving might be in vain. After all, his father had been born less than 150 kilometers east of here, and while he had made his way west, many siblings and cousins remain. They had survived the war, which had raged through the area, especially the town of Eugen Robert Pohl's birthplace of Gumbinnen, early in the war, but since then, life had settled down to its usual rhythm, which included summer vacations here on the Baltic Sea.

Pohl returns to his writing as the Zeppelin passed Brüsterort, located on the northwest corner of the Sambian Peninsula. Easily visible to Pohl from his position is that famous lighthouse, which had been described in a recent novel as the "slim lighthouse of Brüsterort, which stands on a dark peninsula as if on a giant jetty." At night, the novel continued, the light looked like a "large, red-flashing eye of a predator."[4]

Located as it is at the top of a 36-meter cliff, the lighthouse protects ships far into the sea. That this was a dangerous corner had been clear since the early eighteenth century, when a warning lamp was installed—a vast improvement over the top of the church tower nearby that sailors had used to orient themselves at that time. A hundred years later, the warning lamp was replaced with a light beacon;[5] then in 1846 the current 14-meter-high lighthouse was built, a light that can be seen some 22 nautical miles over the sea.[6] From his perch, Pohl can look straight down on the lighthouse, with a good look at the white, crumbling cliffs to boot—and the stone reef that makes the area so dangerous.

Looking to the south, Pohl sees the town of Palmnicken, known for its amber works. In spite of it being Sunday, the chimneys of the factory are smoking, making electrical insulation from amber for the war effort, Pohl surmises. This stretch of coast is known for its amber deposits, and the mining rights are reserved by the country. Travel guides caution visitors against picking up larger pieces.[7]

The airship then heads due west, with destination Lolland in Denmark. It will be over water for some time, so with no further interesting beaches to see, Pohl decides it is time for further adventures on board. Wrapping himself in his sister's scarf, he makes his way back into the keel of the airship and to the ladder leading to the top of the airship.

After a few minutes of enjoying the view from up top, he pulls out his notebook and continues his letter:

I'm sitting up on the platform, right at the front behind the windscreen. There is barely a breeze to be felt, and I can see all around me only blue sky and water, to my right the golden reflection of the sun and of the ship only the front quarter of the bulging back. I can't see the highest point of the ship, the curvature of the new ships is too great.

As he writes, he overhears the three crewmen seated behind him and writes down their conversation. They are talking about last night's intestinal disasters, and each of the three has a different story to tell, stories that appear far funnier in the bright sunshine in the mild breeze on the top of the ship than they had in the dark night. One had been on the top of the ship when he had been struck, and had had to climb down the 25-meter tube to find some relief. The second had been too frightened to leave his hammock, uncertain whether he would be able to make the transition to the relative safety of the gangway in his state. The third, however, wins the round: he had actually been ordered away from the restroom by a superior officer, in this case first officer Schehl. Much laughter ensues, aided by the fact that everyone has been on the mend since midday, that the fermented soup is no longer a danger to anyone.

As he writes, Pohl notices that the setting sun is no longer directly ahead, but has turned some 30 degrees to the north—they are no longer heading west, but southwest. He deduces that they are headed for Köslin and Susanne Lehmann once again.

He is proven right as the next geographic feature they approach is the un-mistakable—or, as Pohl had written of it the previous year, "peculiar"—shape of the Hel Peninsula. Jutting some 30 kilometers from the northwest corner of the Bay of Danzig into the center of that body of water, it is less than 300 meters wide for much of its length but widens to almost 3 kilometers at the end, which is also where the town of Hel is located. Until the seventeenth century, the pen-insula had actually been a series of islands that had eventually been connected by sand being washed between them, and even today, major storms occasionally break through the narrowest sections and turn it back into an island. Its name has nothing to do with the Christian afterlife but refers, rather, to the goddess of the dead in Scandinavian mythology.[8]

Lehmann turns west as they reached the town of Putzig, located at the base of the Hel Peninsula. This small town of some two thousand inhabitants had four years earlier gained some fame for being the base of half of the newly created German navy flying corps. While the lighter than air crew were stationed at Johannisthal, just outside Berlin, their heavier-than-air compatriots and their handful of planes were relegated to this backwater.[9]

As they continue along the shore of the Baltic, the sun begins to sink in earnest. Pohl is enraptured looking down, struck by the coast in general and the sand dunes in particular. He can make out the traveling dunes below, moving relentlessly some 5 meters a year to the east, overwhelming the forests that try to stand in their way, and entirely ignoring human attempts to slow their advance through judicious plantings.

The dunes below were named by passing sailors "large wool sacks" in times past, a name that while now registered on maps is no longer used by the locals. Just past the dune is the town of Leba, located on the shores of the Baltic Sea between two lakes, Sarbsker to the east, Leba to the west. The peaceful town below belies a turbulent past, with the weather wreaking havoc on the Leba River, which flows from the eponymous lake to the sea, past the city. Not only is the mouth of the river constantly on the move, but the whole town had to be moved from the western side of the river to the eastern in 1572 after it was destroyed by sand and water. Even today, some remnants of the old church can be seen poking through the sand, much as dead and dying trees can be seen poking through the leading edges of the traveling dunes.[10]

The next 30 kilometers are entirely bereft of life, with not even a single house, until finally the town of Rowe appears in the last light. Pohl has just had the thought that this remote village would make for a perfect summer resort when he detects numerous people in white bathing suits below. They, in turn, have become aware of the airship some 400 meters above and wave heartily. Fifteen kilometers past Rowe, they passed over Stolpmünde. Originally a fishing village[11] and the harbor for the city of Stolp, 18 kilometers south by air or about twice that if you traveled along the Stolp River, it had been one of the major seaside resorts in the late nineteenth century,[12] but today has lost out to newer resorts, only its spa and hotel with a surrounding park rate a mention in current travel guides.[13]

It is here that Lehmann turns a few degrees to the south and thus travels the last 50 kilometers to Köslin over land. By now, it is entirely dark and Pohl is unable to make out anything of the countryside below. Once in Köslin, however, this changes: Lehmann brings the airship down to 200 meters, turns on the Zeppelin's spotlight, and trains it on the window behind which he knows his wife to be. He then flashes the light on and off until eventually—Pohl tactfully refrains from writing exactly how long this takes—Frau Lehmann turns the lights in her room on and off a few times to indicate that she was aware of this attention. Satisfied, Lehmann orders the airship to turn a few degrees to starboard and continue on its mission.

A half hour later, Pohl is back in his favorite spot and soon fast asleep. As he sleeps, *LZ 120* heads west at a steady 35 km/h, passing back out to sea, over Rügen, Hiddensee, past Zingst, and back out into the open water.

As they fly, the weather turns progressively worse, from clear skies to patchy fog, to drizzling and finally to rain. In order to avoid this, Lehmann orders the airship to ascend from its usual 300-meter altitude to 2,000—something that Pohl sleeps through unaware, even as the sun rises.

Far below lies the Danish town of Gjedser, on the very southern tip of the island of Falster. While they had attempted to reach this point numerous times in the previous three days, the weather had always made it impossible. And even now, though it is after sunrise, the weather makes it impossible to make out, especially from this height. The small island, home to only 36,000 people, had become of vital importance ever since the United States had ceased trading with Denmark for fear that US goods would get from there to Germany. Thus both Germany and Denmark are now looking to the farms here that produce animals and sugar beets to feed them.[14]

Pohl awakes at 7:30 and notes with satisfaction that they are still headed in the right direction, even if the weather is now downright unpleasant. They are just off the north coast of the island of Fehmarn, a small, flat island dominated by cattle pastures,[15] and the town of Marienleuchte, which is mainly known for its remarkably squat lighthouse that dates back to 1832.[16] He enters the keel of the airship, happy to get away from the rain, and makes his way forward.

In the gondola, he is greeted with a disappointment. Lehmann, who is busy calculating at the navigator's table, announces that the weather does not allow them to continue west, and that therefore a flight over Glücksburg is out of the question. Instead, he sets the course to the southeast and the town of Warnemünde. As they fly, the weather improves from rain to drizzle, and but as the airship is now 1,000 meters in the air, little can be seen of the German coast as they arrived.

They leave Warnemünde on the starboard side as they head east along the coast. Pohl looks for signs of the naval aircraft that had been brought here, but the weather is keeping them on their pontoons far below. No chance to see the city's lighthouse, either. The city, an exclave of the city of Rostock, a few kilometers up the river, lies buried in fog.

Maintaining altitude, Lehmann steers the ship back to Zingst, where Lehmann has the ship fly an extra turn before aiming the ship directly north and Copenhagen. They soon reach the island of Moen, and Pohl peers down to see the famous Klints: chalk cliffs on the easternmost point of the island. The tallest, the Hylledalsklint, is 128 meters high, but all are worth a view.[17] Pohl has been alternating looking out of the window and adding to his letter as they fly, but just as he is about to write about the cliffs, the motor in the rear of the main gondola is started. In the ensuing noise and turbulence caused by this, Pohl's handwriting—never good under the best of circumstances—becomes an unreadable scrawl.

He apologizes for this in the next sentence but never does get around to describing what he has just seen. Instead, he is distracted by another circle that Lehmann flies, this time around the German battleship SMS *Lothringen*. This ship of the

Braunschweig class had been made obsolete just a few years its commissioning by the launch of the HMS *Dreadnought* in 1906. The British ship was almost 50 percent larger and 20 percent faster than its German predecessors.[18] Nonetheless, *Lothringen* was still part of the German navy at the beginning of the war. It was deemed unfit in late May 1916, just before the Battle of Skagerrak (Jutland), and now bided its time as a guard ship, surrounded by antitorpedo nets.[19] It is these that Pohl and company can make out easily, even from their altitude.

They never quite make it to Amager, an island just south of Copenhagen that is slowly being encroached by that city.[20] Instead, Lehmann turns east, toward Sweden, and flies down the coast. Around Falsterbo, a town located on a peninsula of the same name that reaches far into the Baltic Sea on the southwestern corner of Sweden, Pohl looks up from his writing and notices that he can see every one of its house even without his trusty telescope. The weather has been steadily improving as they flew, and the haze that surrounds them does little to disturb their view. Pohl particularly notes that the increased height that they are currently at makes it much easier to determine the depths of the water over which they are flying; he felt that he could draw a depth chart solely from the shades of blue that he can see below. As they continue to fly along the coast of Sweden, Lehmann has them rise to 2,000 meters again, something Pohl notices immediately as his ears begin to pop and that he is starting to get cold, in spite of his fur coat. He is intrigued in what other ways the altitude is affecting him, so he downs his pencil and presses two fingers against his other wrist. He compares his pulse against his watch and is pleased to note that his heart is beating only fifty-five times per second.

Further consultation with Lehmann confirms that they have now flown over 5,000 kilometers and that there is no reason to believe that they will not finish out a full hundred hours in flight. Pohl puts away his notebook and goes back to enjoying the view, taking in this stretch of the Swedish coast, which is the last part of the Baltic coast that he has yet to see.

CHAPTER 17
THE FUTURE OF ZEPPELINS

Aufstieg bei Manzell
4. August 08 morgens.

Im Fluge.

Auffahrt, Flug u. Ende des Zeppelin'schen Luftschiffes Modell 4.

Katastrophe bei Echterdingen 5. Aug. 08.

Postcard showing *LZ 4* in flight and after its accident in Echterdingen, August 5, 1908. During what was supposed to be a twenty-four-hour flight, one motor needed to be repaired. The airship landed and was tied down but was caught by a gust of wind, torn from its anchorage, and had to be landed again. During the landing, the airship struck trees, and some of the gas bags were punctured and it caught fire. *Bain News Service Photograph Collection / Library of Congress*

I n spite of the undoubted achievement of Lehmann, his crew, and his airship, their voyage had also clearly shown some of the drawbacks of airships. Some of these could be solved through better technology; others were simply intrinsic to the idea of filling an enormous balloon with light gas and pushing it through the air. All of these were issues that Lehmann would have to wrestle with in the next phase of his career, and he was probably better aware of the shortcomings than anyone else.

The first issue that he would have to solve was the question of the engines. While they were now undoubtedly the "light handy Instruments to give . . . Motion" that Benjamin Franklin had written about 135 years earlier,[1] and the improvement over those from even the early days of the Zeppelin corporation was astonishing, but the fact was that even the engines installed in *LZ 120* had their issues, that engine breakdowns were common on Zeppelins—the fact that they had to stop all engines and float through the air for a while on two separate occasions to fix the engines made that abundantly clear.

While the repairs to *LZ 120* had been, at worst, a delay, loss of engines had been a significant issue throughout the airship era, and deadly in some cases. On February 17, 1915, the navy Zeppelins *L 3* and *L 4* had taken off from Fuhlsbüttel near Hamburg to look for enemy ships on the Danish west coast. About four hours after takeoff, one of *L 3*'s engines broke down. They had traveled about 350 kilometers north at this point. Given the winds that the North Sea has during the winter, the captain made the decision to turn around. Battling headwinds on his way south, he had made only about 70 kilometers in the course of the afternoon when the second engine broke down. Lieutenant Commander Hans Fritz knew that there was no hope of getting back to safety, so instead steered toward the Danish island of Fanø, where he brought the airship down hard, breaking its back. The captain then had the crew destroy first the documents on board the airship, then the craft itself. Fritz and the rest of the crew were found by the Danes and had been interred ever since.[2]

While motors had become more reliable in the two and a half years since then, and in spite of the best efforts of Mr. Maybach and his company, airship motors were far from the efficiency and reliability that they required for a flight across the Atlantic. While some reliability could be engineered in by adding redundant engines, this would also increase the weight of the airship and therefore its ability to carry paying passengers. This was, on the other hand, also an eminently solvable problem. Motor reliability had increased dramatically over the forty years since Nikolaus Otto, Gottlieb Daimler and Wilhelm Maybach had created the first internal combustion engine, and there was no reason to believe that improvements in this direction would cease. Time and further research would bring the answers.

Another problem Lehmann foresaw but hoped for improved technology was that of the internal ballonets. Keeping the lifting gas safely inside the airship instead of leaking out and losing lift required at this time the death of hundreds of thousands of cattle, plus of course a very well-trained team to turn these intestinal parts into usable airtight bags.

Worse was the fact that the very act of flight degraded the ballonets. As the airship moved through the air, the continual vibration produced by the engines rubbed the envelopes against the ribs and wiring of the airship, scouring tiny holes throughout. Once landed, the riggers would have their hands full examining every part of the fabric for these holes and patching them. Lehmann already was planning on having a complete survey done of the fabric, their report would be added to the final analysis of the flight that he was planning on writing after landing.

Another issue, though not one they had to deal with over the last four days given the serene weather they had been flying through, stemmed from the fact that the goldbeater's skin was made from an animal: The membrane tended to either attract insects, grow mold—bad enough if it increased the weight of the ballonet—or putrefy, which would degrade the envelope to the point that it could no longer hold hydrogen.[3] These issues had particularly struck Zeppelins laid up during the long winter months suffused with the high humidity that characterized those months in northern Germany, and often the crew would have to take out an airship for a flight simply to dry it out.

Other solutions to the question of gas-proof bags, usually involving rubber, had all proven to be far too heavy, and the danger posed by rubber and its ability to create sparks was also not to be ignored. While the end of the war would most likely make the raw material easier to acquire, the real cost was the construction of the balloons, something that would be unlikely to get cheaper. The only real hope lay in a new technology, and thus far there did not seem to be a possibility on the horizon.

Even the outer skin of an airship was far from troublefree. While the substance, cotton, was well understood and unproblematical, it did tend to soak up water and thus increase the weight of the ship capriciously. Even worse, if the crew then dropped ballast to make up for this increased weight, then the drying out process that was sure to begin shortly thereafter was certain to lighten the airship enough to necessitate the release of some of the precious lifting gas.

The moisture, along with adding weight, also damaged the outer skin in other ways, causing the patches that had been added to the outside to either fix holes or cover up the fastenings that connected the larger sections of the envelope to peel off. Flying around with swaths of fabric flapping in the breeze was both unsightly and increased the drag on the airship. While rain was the main culprit here, just high humidity could make life on the airship very unpleasant.

Vexing, too, was the question of lifting gas. While there were many options—the German chemist Hugo Erdmann had counted fifteen in 1909, ranging from cold air (no lifting power) to hydrogen, which could lift 1.2 kilograms per cubic meter—most of these were either dangerous, lacking in lifting power or both and the rest, with one exception, required continual application of heat to remain lighter than the surrounding air.[4]

The hydrogen that had kept the German airship fleet in the air from the beginning had the major issue in its flammability. A small leak coupled with any stray spark and the airship would go up in flames. The second naval Zeppelin had been destroyed all the way back in 1913 when hydrogen leaked from the bag, was sucked into the airship's engine, and ignited. The result killed the entire crew.

A similar event had destroyed *L 18*, the first airship that Pohl had been on, just two weeks after her first flight. After being flown to its new base in Tondern, Capt. Max Dietrich requested that the bags be fully inflated. During this procedure, an explosion in a gas line started a chain reaction that ended up burning up the airship. The fire raged for about one and a half hours and killed not only a crewman but six workers from the 1st Marine airship troop.[5]

The flammable bullets that the English had deployed with such devastating effect owed their power entirely to the nature of hydrogen gas. On the other hand, hydrogen had, by far, the greatest lifting power of any gas, and thus required a smaller envelope to carry the same cargo.

Far better from a danger perspective was helium. Utterly inert, it could be exposed to any flame without posing any danger. As early as 1896, scientists interesting in further flight were intrigued by its properties, that it was 90 percent as effective a lifting gas as hydrogen without that substance's downsides. There was just one problem: actually procuring the gas. Prewar, the best source was thorianite, a rare mineral found in Ceylon which, when ground up, would release helium. It had also been noticed that some hot springs released helium along with other gases, but this source had not yet been harnessed.[6] None of these sources were viable, though; the largest single collection of this gas was a four hundred liter container at the University of Leiden, a far cry from the 50,000 cubic meters needed for an airship.[7]

The next lighter gas Erdmann suggested was borane, a highly unstable and reactive compound almost completely unsuited to any application if this sort—and at three times the weight of helium, not a great lifting agent to begin with. The next two gases—methane and ammonia—were similarly problematic.[8]

In short, in order to build safe airships, either the flammability of hydrogen would have to be reduced or helium produced in large quantities.

What Lehmann could not know was that, far across the ocean and in the arid American southwest, drillers for methane gas had noticed that the gas that their rigs were producing contained up to 1 percent helium. While this byproduct was not of much interest to them, others calculated that this source of the inert gas would reduce its price by a factor of thirty thousand and make taking off strapped to a balloon of helium a real possibility.[9]

However, whatever the gas used, the fact remained that airships would be very fragile, or they would be far too heavy to fly. While the amount of hydrogen needed to lift a normal person is only a 2.5-meter sphere, the weight of any envelope is not insignificant and must also be accounted for. In the case of *LZ 120*, while the lift of the gas on board was over 66,000 kilograms, about half of that was lost to the weight of the airship itself. Over half of the remaining lift went to fuel, and in fact, the weight of the twenty-nine passengers on board made up less than 10 percent of the available lift. In spite of this, Zeppelins had time and again been shown to be extremely fragile. Being hung up incorrectly in their hangars or simply being pushed against the door of the shed while being walked in was enough to require extensive repairs or simply dismantling the ship and building a new one.

In the case of the *Deutschland II*, hull number LZ 8, and the second airship that the Zeppelin company built for DELAG, it was a gust of wind that pulled the airship out of the hands of its ground crew as it was being taken out of its hangar. It was bent in half, with the forward section coming to rest on top of the hangar. Fortunately, while there were passengers and crew on board, they were able to climb down safely on a ladder.[10] The accident highlighted the fragility of these airships, but any attempt to strengthen the ships against these sorts of minor accidents would wipe out that little bit of lift necessary to actually take people on board.

Other issues that Lehmann and others had been struggling would become moot again in peacetime, in particular the current need to bring an airship over its target without alerting those below. Throughout the war, the Zeppelin attackers had to pay close attention to the moon, as a bright moon would light up their airships and signal their presence to the defenders. Assuming that the moon was shining at night, about four to six days around the new moon would be the safest to attack. Otherwise, about half the time the moon was below the horizon and it was thus possible to attack. This shut down about one-third of the time as unsuitable for attack. Lehmann himself on his very first attack in the war, a flight against Antwerp, had to squeeze the actual time over the city into the brief window between moon set and dawn. In this case, he managed to drop bombs in the twenty minutes available to him, but throughout the war this particular issues would bedevil the Zeppelin pilots.

It was much easier was to fly undetected when there were clouds. While the soldiers below might hear the airship flying overhead, any shot taken at it would be entirely at random, and the likelihood of a direct hit was exceedingly low. Of course, this went both ways—the airship crew had no idea where they were, either. Two innovations in the course of the war helped to mitigate this problem. The first was Lehmann's observation car, which allowed a spotted to descend below the cloud layer and direct the fire. Lehmann had had success with this in their attack on Calais in March 1915. While their attempt to bomb England that day had failed, they had been able to bomb the French city on their way back to their home base.

Where of course even Lehmann's invention failed—and, indeed, had failed on that flight—was in low-lying clouds and fog. The observation car was only useful under very particular circumstances, and thus again limited the use of Zeppelins in war.

The second innovation was of course Professor Pohl's radio direction finding equipment. It was, however, not precise enough to allow for a targeted attack, but did ensure that an airship kept from determining its location by clouds could find its way back home safely. This innovation was of great interest to all airship pilots in peacetime as well.

When Count Zeppelin first lifted off from Lake Constance in 1900, the dream of heavier-than-air flight was still exactly that—a dream. While hundreds had attempted this kind of aviation, the results so far were not impressive. It would be over three years after LZ 1 lifted off that the Wright brothers managed a brief hop of 260 meters in their flyer—not that much farther than the length of *LZ 120*. By then, the Lebaudy brothers had designed, built, and flown an airship that could cover almost 100 kilometers at a stretch. For the time, the airship seemed to rule the air. This would not remain the case for long, and especially since the beginning of the war, the airplane technology had increased in leaps and bounds.

The first intimation of this came on June 7, 1915. While Zeppelins had been injured and destroyed by ground fire, they had thus far managed to avoid being brought down by air. On this day, the army airship *LZ 37* was returning to it hangar in Gontrode, Belgium, after a failed attack on England that had ended with a bombing run on Calais. As *LZ 37* began to sink toward safety, Flightsublieutenant Reginald Warneford in his airplane climbed above the airship and dropped six bombs on it. Five missed their mark; the sixth crashed through the skin and aluminum skeleton and exploded deep inside the hull.[11] Only one crewmember, who rode the gondola down and then was ejected into a nun's bed in a nunnery it hit, would survive.[12] It was the first time that an airplane had bested an airship, but it would not be the last. While Zeppelin captains knew that by keeping their airships high above the earth, they would be safe from attack, the ability of airplanes to follow them to these altitudes continued to expand. Thus the introduction of the height climbers, which ended up at the very outer reaches of where humans could survive high above the earth. But even here airplanes could follow. It was a race for height that the airships could, in the end, not win.

Airplanes had already gone on the offensive against the Zeppelins. A little over two months into the war, on October 8, 1914, two Sopwith Tabloids took off from Antwerp, which was just about to be captured by the Germans. The planes, named for their small size, were flown by Squadron Commander Spenser Grey and Flight Lieutenant Reginald Marix. Their targets were the Zeppelin sheds near Cologne and Düsseldorf, respectively. While Grey never found his target, instead dropping his bombs on the local train station, Marix found the airship hangar with no problem and dropped two bombs on it from 200 meters. Both found their target. The shed collapsed and a giant burst of flame indicated that not only had the shed been destroyed, but the airship inside. It was the end of the army *Z IX*, which had been the last Zeppelin delivered before the outbreak of the war, and who had bombed Antwerp not two months earlier. Marix's airplane ran out of fuel before making it back to Antwerp, but he managed to find a bicycle and reach the airfield before Grey, who would return and land safely. They were told that the German attack was imminent, and left the airfield via car. The two pilots would escape to fight another day.[13]

Even as the ability of airplanes to attack as well as defend against Zeppelins was improving, so were they ever better able to take on the assignments of the airships. In March 1917, the German army had received new Gotha G.IV bombers, which had a range of over 800 kilometers, putting London well within reach of the German airfields in Belgium. On May 25, 1917, twenty-three of these new airplanes took off from two airfields near Ghent, with London as their target. Cloudy weather over London forced the armada to divert to secondary targets along the coast, but almost 100 people were killed on that day. A little over two weeks later, a similar attack reached London itself, with a predictably large number of casualties. In both cases, the attacks had come during daylight hours, contrary to the experience up until then, when the bombs had fallen at night.[14]

London air defenses soon learned to defend against this new form of attack, and so by early fall, the airplanes were, like the Zeppelins before them, coming at night. This resulted in the same issues in finding not only their targets and their way home as with the airships, but the pilots had made it clear that this was a force to be reckoned with, especially since each airplane required a crew of only three and could hold 500 kilograms of bombs, a little less than half of what Lehmann had on board *LZ 120*.

These bombers were also about 30 percent faster than any airship, and other aircraft were significantly faster yet again. Pohl had himself experienced 180 km/h in a Rumpler craft. There was no doubt that, whatever deficiencies airplanes had in contrast to Zeppelins at the beginning of the war, they had overcome these and more; the future would belong to heavier-than-air aircraft.

Even for the civilian purpose which Lehmann foresaw, the new airplanes were rapidly closing the gap between current capabilities and what was necessary for a transatlantic flight. The latest German bombers had ranges of close to 1,000 km, half of the distance over water that they would have to fly between the Azores and the southeast corner of Newfoundland, which would be the first land on the American continent they would reach. Given the speed of development in the fourteen years since the Wright brothers' first flight, there was no reason to doubt that this gap would be soon closed.

While there was no question that any flights of this nature might take less time, but would be considerably more uncomfortable, the fact was that the ships crossing the Atlantic had improved markedly in the seventy-seven years since Green had first dreamed of doing so by air. While at the time, it took more than thirteen days to make the crossing,[15] five years before the war, the *Mauritania* had made it across in just over four days—and in a style that would have been unimaginable to those who had crossed the ocean in 1840.[16] Lehmann would have to make sure that the passengers experienced a similar level of luxury; the wicker chairs and detritus-decorated tables would not be an option, nor would a couple of hammocks stretched over thin fabric be acceptable to passengers paying huge sums for the privilege of flying over the ocean.

The biggest issue facing the Zeppelins was, without a doubt, the weather. A successful as the flight had been to this point, they had failed to reach a specific target several times, never making it, for instance, to Glücksburg. Furthermore, a number of low-pressure systems had kept *LZ 120* out of the eastern Baltic Sea for much of their flight, and in the end, it was an impending storm coming in from the west that Lehmann had to keep a sharp eye out for.

The weather had been an issue with airships from the start. Originally, the major problem had been wind of almost any strength. The first airships could overcome only the lightest breezes, and anything stronger would keep the airship on the ground.

Even as motor technology improved, weather could still be treacherous and often led to disaster. LZ 4, built for the military in 1908, survived a broken engine during its twenty-four-hour endurance flight attempt by landing in a clearing for repairs, but could not overcome a strong gust wind which detached it from its moorings and flung it into the trees surrounding the landing site. It burst into flame and was destroyed.[17] It was hardly the only Zeppelin to suffer the same fate. LZ 5, built with money donated after the previous tragedy, was destroyed when a storm came through while it was moored.[18] Four years later, the first Zeppelin crash resulting in casualties was also caused by the weather. The brand-new navy Zeppelin *L 1* was taking part in maneuvers in the North Sea when it encountered a hurricane. The sudden decrease in temperature caused the hydrogen to lose lifting power, and in spite of all attempts to lighten the airship, it crash-landed some 30 kilometers from the German island of Heligoland. While some of the crew were able to rescue themselves by leaping from the gondola, those that stayed inside all the way into the water were killed. Among the dead were the commander of the Marine airship division, Capt. Friedrich Metzing, and the captain of the airship, Captain Hanne.[19]

Airships had also been lost due to lightning strikes. The navy airship *L 10*, for instance, was flying toward Nordholz on September 3, 1915, after a reconnaissance flight over the North Sea, when she encountered a thunderstorm. The ground crew was looking in the direction where they expected her and saw a "large flash of flame like that of an explosion, which left a large cloud of smoke," Peter Strasser later wrote. Others, closer to the impact, indicated that it had indeed been a lightning strike that had caused the explosion. All nineteen on board perished, the first navy airship crew to die in the war.[20]

Beyond the unpredictable nature of storms, which could, to some extent, be monitored and avoided, there was one other weather-related issue that had bedeviled the Zeppelin corps since the beginning. This was that steady winds at the airfields could prevent an airship from being brought into its hangar. The vast area of the side of the airship meant that even low wind speeds could generate enormous forces, which could keep the ground crew from walking the ship into its shed. Calculations had shown that the pressure from a moderate wind could produce a force to the side equal to that of the lift of the airship—and actually produce about that much lift. Thus, for those hanging on to the ship from below, they would be dragged not only in the direction of the wind but upward as well—a very dangerous situation for all involved.

It was for this reason that one of Count Zeppelin's first hangars was built not on solid ground but on the water. This meant that the shed could be turned directly into the prevailing winds, so that the airship while being hangared would be presenting its shorter end toward the wind and would thus not be as affected. Later, this method was applied on solid ground as well. The first of this kind was built in Berlin-Biesdorf and had been used to build a Siemens airship from 1907 to 1909. Until the war, it was used by a Groß-Basenach airship, but was too small for large airships that had dominated since the beginning of the war. The other rotating shed was a the largest airbase of the war in Nordholz and built in the first month of the war. It would be an important element in the attacks against England.

Worrisome for Lehmann at this moment was that the shed at Seerappen was not of the rotating variety, and thus it was important that they arrive home before the wind picked up to the point that they would not be able to enter the hangar. While he still had a fair bit of fuel left, it was not clear that they would be able to fly around until the weather died down and they could land safely.

Fortunately, the weather was still holding; if the wind were to pick up, his only option would be to turn on all six engines and hope to race the weather back to the shed.

CHAPTER 17

JULY 30, 2:00 P.M.–JULY 31, 4:40 A.M.

The fort in Pillau, on the Baltic Sea, near their final destination of Seerappen

While Pohl is enjoying the view of the coast, Lehmann decides to practice bombing. The airship has been running on one motor for the past couple of hours, and they are slowly drifting down to 100 meters again. Now, Lehmann, looking down through the clear air below, declares a couple of logs floating in the water below to be enemy submarines. After calling everyone to battle stations, they drop 50 kilograms of bombs on the innocent logs, scoring at least one direct hit. Whether they have reacted quickly enough to disable a submarine before it would have had time to fire its cannon at the airship is unclear, but Lehmann is satisfied that they have, at least, practiced this maneuver and would be able to repeat it more quickly in future. With this practice under their belt, they continue on up to the middle of the island of Öland.

Along the way, they observe two German convoys: one with ten ships, the other with five. They seem to Pohl to be almost impregnable in their formation, especially with the escort ships surrounding them.

Around 3:30, it is time to turn south. They reach the German coast near Rügenwalde, a town of some six thousand souls 3 kilometers up the river from the Baltic Sea[1] and, in spite of the similar name, more than 150 kilometers from the island of Rügen. From here it is another 30 kilometers to the west to Köslin and the opportunity to visit Frau Lehmann one last time; then they turn east and begin to make their way back to home, cruising along at some 90 km/h. Pohl asks for permission to use some of the leftover fuel to clean a good-sized oil stain off his trousers. In spite of the 20,000 liters already burned, there is plenty left, and permission is readily given.

With landing in sight and all systems running smoothly, Lehmann gives the order to dump 500 kilograms of ballast—the first time in the whole trip that he has done so. So far the loss of lift from escaping gas had been countered by the fuel burned to push the airship through the air, and thus the airship has been at equilibrium. Coming up is, however, one last maneuver that requires the ship to be lighter. Since they are over water, losing 500 liters of water ballast is an easy decision to make.

Far to the west, the sun is beginning to head to the horizon. Sunset is always a magical moment on board the ship, as the hull is bathed in golden light, while far below, the countryside is already in darkness. It is a moment that never failed to stop Pohl in his tracks, but he has thus far been unable to capture its full magic in words.

It is time for Pohl to finish his letter. The shipboard clock says 8:30 p.m. and landing is scheduled for 4:00 a.m.; now is the opportunity to add a few concluding thoughts and then to try to get some sleep in a night that is certain to be cut short. Pohl digs out his trusty pencil and opens the small notebook that has served him so well thus far. Composing his thoughts, he looks down to see that they are near the town of Stolpmünde once again.

Pohl brings pencil to paper. He apologizes once again for the type of paper he has used, he hopes that this lengthy letter will make up for the many times that he has failed to write his weekly report, he looks forward to seeing both his mother and sister soon, and ends it: "End: 8:45, 30.7.1917 near Stolpmünde."

With this task completed, he returns to the gun platform and, if possible, sleep.

The airship continues east, out over the Bay of Danzig and the Hel Peninsula, and heads toward the Samland coast, running through the moonlit night at a steady 45 km/h. Pohl sees none of this below. He is lying on his back in the gunners nest, letting his eyes wander around the darkness and reflecting on all that he has seen and done over the last four days. He feels overwhelmed and decides that he needs to share his thoughts with his mother. He pulls his trusty notebook out of his pocket to add an addendum to his letter.

11 p.m. My Murl, it is unfortunate that I can't get you on board for at least a few minutes, so that you can get a sense of the beauty of such a flight. I could stand here in the stern for hours, wrapped in my fur, and let the cool night air swirl around my head. How soothing it is! The moon is in the southern sky, from the north come dark clouds, I can make out the west Prussian coast as a dark strip below, otherwise just stars and water. I will be sleeping without my cover again tonight. Good-night, my little flashlight is dying, I can't continue chattering at you!

He wraps himself into his familiar blankets and lies back again, watching the stars move slowly across the sky above. It is, he feels, utterly inappropriate to sleep at a time like this; he needs to take in the moment as best as he can, given that it is quite possibly the last time he will be able to fly in a Zeppelin. He then begins a rough calculation to see if it would be possible to continue flights like this after the war, for a civilian audience. It would be, he feels, a terrible pity if flights like this had to end.

At 11:30, he tries his flashlight again and finds that it is producing enough light for him to add a further addendum, in which he writes down his thoughts. He then settles back and goes to sleep.

He is woken at 3:00 a.m. by the ringing of the telephone, one of three communication devices on board. The simplest is a system of pipes that allows communication in and near the gondola by the simple expedient of talking through them. It is through this that the bombardiers kept in touch with the gondola. The second is the machine telegraph, which allows only for simple signaling—what the motors should be set to at that moment, coupled with a bell that would alert the mechanics to check the face of the telegraph for new instructions. Last but not least is an actual telephone that allows those in the machine gun nests above and aft to communicate with the captain far away in the gondola.

Down the wire from the gondola comes the instruction to stay where he is—for the final landing, every weight in the ship had to be carefully accounted for, so that the ship will remain balanced. Pohl quickly acquiesces, hangs up, and takes the opportunity to get his bearings. Up above is Jupiter, down below Pillau, at the north end of the Frische Nehrung, a 65-kilometer, curved stretch of land that separates the Baltic Sea from the Frisches Haff, a large and shallow lagoon similar to the Kurisches Haff north of the Samland Peninsula.

While this area had been important from the fourteenth century on, its real history began in 1479, when an enormous storm broke through the Frische Nehrung und created a passage between the Baltic Sea and the Frisches Haff. While at first quite narrow, by 1510 it was navigable and became an important passage to the city of Königsberg. Soon thereafter, a defensive stronghold was built to protect this important waterway, and during the Thirty Years' War, Gustav Adolph of Sweden built further fortifications here, including the five-pointed fort that still dominates the view from above.[2]

Pohl digs out his notebook again and continues to add to his letter, adding that he is also in the process of packing up his blankets. As he writes, he feels his ears pop again: the airship is rising. They are getting to an altitude where the gas expands to the point where the overflow valves release some hydrogen. While this is also possible to do by using the vents that can be controlled from the gondola, here they are hoping to use the automatic vents at the bottom of the bags, as that will force out the "dirty" hydrogen (i.e., hydrogen mixed with other gases), leaving the "clean" hydrogen at the top of the bags for use in the next flight. Over the course of four days, outside gas—nitrogen and oxygen in the main—has managed to work its way into the ballonets, either through the small holes that existed in spite of the riggers's best efforts or at the connectors. These heavier gases have been pooling at the bottom of the balloons, near the emergency relief valves.

Blowing off some of the hydrogen is also necessary because the ship is a fair bit lighter than it had been at the beginning of the flight, having burned thousands of kilograms of fuel in the process—and thrown away some of the water taken along as ballast, or even the weight of the bowl that Schehl had lost overboard two days earlier. With the current equilibrium, it would be impossible to bring *LZ 120* all the way to the ground. Thus valving some gas is necessary, and allowing it to rise high above the earth the best way of doing so.

They rise through 2,000 meters—the highest altitude they had reached in the course of the trip, and thus where the air is thin enough to expand the bags to their fullest. It starts to get cold: 8 degrees Celsius, considerably colder than the 15–22 degrees that they had enjoyed through most of the previous four days. It is, Pohl writes, getting too cold to write. They eventually reached 2,800 meters, a half kilometer higher than their previous maximum. Pohl can tell when the gas began to release, as the hydrogen makes a grumbling sound as it escapes, a dull music that any airship crew member knows well. As the gas escapes, the ship begins to sink again, a self-regulating process that makes this method of blowing off hydrogen a far more precise one than simply opening the upper emergency valves.

LZ 120 continues east, across the bay leading to the town of Fischhausen at the north. Pohl's colleague Max Wien's estate—which they had hoped to, but failed to, overfly—is part of this town. On the other side, it arrives at the entrance of the Königsberg-Pillau maritime canal. While originally goods headed to Königsberg had to be transshipped in Pillau, on November 15, 1901, after more than twenty years of planning and work, this canal opened. It allowed ships to transit the shallow lagoon, passing through a channel that had been built along the northern shore of the Frische Haff and could be, in contrast to the lagoon, be kept dredged deeply enough to allow it to be used by oceangoing vessels.[3]

They follow the route of the new canal in a generally northerly direction. Where it turns to the east to head straight toward Königsberg, the airship continues straight, the last 5 km to Seerappen and its hangar.

The navigator makes a last notation as to their height, 2,800 meters; speed, 0; and the distance they have traveled over the last hundred hours, 3,300 nautical miles, or almost exactly the distance from Frankfurt am Main to New York City. Lehmann, his crew, and his airship have together smashed the record for distance traveled—not that anyone was prepared to celebrate at this moment. Their airfield is still dizzyingly far below them, and there is still the question of the landing to answer.

Pohl huddles in his coat and waits for the ship to warm up as it returns to the ground. As they float down, the eastern horizon begins to show the first signs of dawn, and by 3:55, he is ready to write again—and can do so without the aid of artificial light. Not far below is their hangar, surrounded by farms clearly visible in the predawn light. It is a limpid day, the perfect flying weather—and the flight is almost over. Pohl takes a moment to fix the scene in his memory, letting his eyes sweep across the landscape.

Up front, Lehmann orders the antennas that streamed down from the front of the airship to be retracted, and the landing lines to be deployed. He ensures that the airship was light, not heavy, since he wants to avoid having to make the troops below have to catch the airship as it descended, a maneuver that he know ends up with bloody fingers and bumped heads. Instead, the men below will take the lines and add just enough weight to make it have no lift at all, at which point it can be easily handled on the ground.

Down below, 250 men from the VI. Marine Airship troop stream out from the hangar into the crepuscular light. They arrange themselves on the open field and prepare to grab for the lines that will be dropped. Lehmann orders all six engines to be turned on, for only the second time since takeoff. At the very front of the ship, two portholes opened from the bottom of the airship and out fall two bundles of ropes that snake toward the ground.

Lehmann brings the airship down toward the ground, slowly approaching the men below, but they were unable to grab ahold of the lines. Lehmann orders the airship to go around a second time, and this time, the men are able to take up the lines and bring the giant airship back safely to earth. The time is 4:40 a.m., 101 hours after takeoff, and ends the longest time any humans have ever spent untethered from the earth. No airplane, balloon, airship, or glider has ever been in the air for this length of time—or, in fact, anything even approaching it: They have more than doubled the longest time aloft and almost tripled the distance traveled by *North Sea 1* earlier that year. The navigator adds one final entry into the log marking this achievement and finishes securing his tools, while Lehmann orders all engines to stop.

With the Zeppelin now safely back on earth, the sliding door on the side of the gondola, firmly shut for the last four days, is rolled open and Pohl steps down onto the ground with shaky legs. After four days of constant movement under his feet, it now seemed that the solid ground is moving, as well. He shakes himself briefly and walks over to the mess hall.

The ground crew, now arrayed around the entire ship, waits for instructions. Their commander makes sure that there is no wind and gives the order "Airship to the shed, march!" Step by step, the troops carefully walk the airship bow first toward the hangar, whose front doors are wide open, while its rear doors are cracked to allow air being pushed forward by the airship to escape. The crew stops just outside the open doors, awaiting final orders.

The airship crew remains in the airship, with engines idling. Until the airship is firmly inside its hangar, there is the remote possibility of it being torn away by a sudden gust of wind. Thus, for the time being, everyone remains at their duty station. Outside, the ground crew strains against the ropes until the order "Airship into the shed, march!" sounds. The giant airship disappears into the hangar, and the great doors are closed behind it. Only now does Lehmann order the engines to be shut down and has the crew stand down.

While the crew disembarks, the ground staff replace their weight with sacks of sand, so that the airship floats just below the ceiling of the hangar, ensuring that that it did not deform while waiting for its next flight.

Inside the mess it is warm, dry, and filled with the smell of coffee brewing. The crew is assembling, tired but elated by their record-breaking trip. Pohl gets a cup of coffee, then sits down at a table and pulls out his notebook one last time, writing:

4:55 a.m. The sun rises, in the mess the coffee is steaming. As I write this, I hear from the next table "Oh! The professor is writing a book *101 Hours in an Airship*!" And with that, a final farewell!

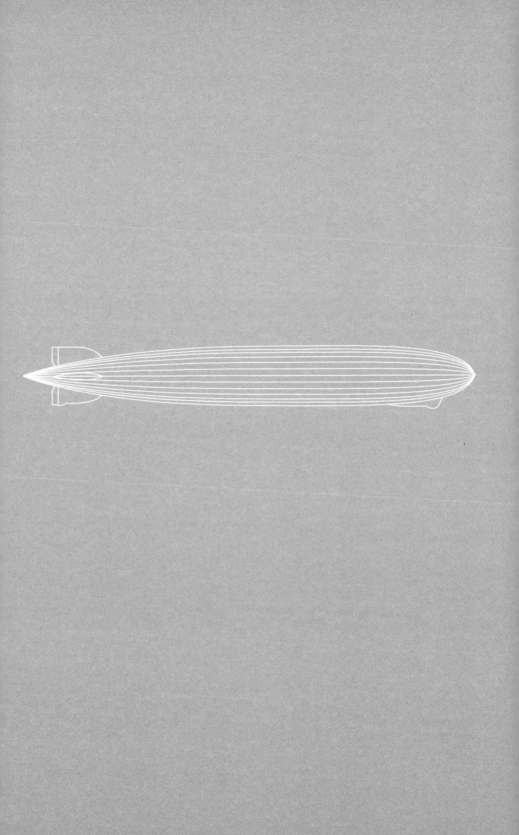

AFTERMATH

The gondola of the British airship *R 34* on the ground in Mineola, New York, on July 6, 1919. *Library of Congress*

Just about the same time as they were landing, and 1,200 kilometers west of Seerappen, allied guns opened up on German positions near the town of Ypres. After the initial attack, allied soldiers began to advance on the German lines. It was the beginning of a long-planned attack on the western front, partially as an answer by the Allies to the loss on the eastern front. It was reasonably successful, for a time, though later the Germans counterattacked, regaining the ground. While the treaty of Brest-Litovsk, signed between Germany and Russia on March 3, 1918, would free up large numbers of German troops from the eastern front, the Germans also knew that they had to attack quickly, before the United States soldiers began arriving in significant numbers. While a huge advance northeast of Paris in the summer of 1918 would bring the Germans closer to their goal of capturing the French capital than any time in the previous four years, this attack, too, was stopped. And as summer turned to fall, the arrival of large numbers of US soldiers allowed the capture of St. Miheil, along with numerous other salients. By the end of September, the allies had straightened out the line through Belgium and France, and had enough soldiers on the lines to begin a broad attack. The Germans, by now vastly outnumbered, began to retreat, slowing down the attack as best they could but unable to stop or counterattack against the onslaught. The German high command began seriously thinking about the possibility of negotiating for peace.

October brought a number of breakthroughs, by the United States in the Meuse-Argonne region and by the British near Le Cateau. While the German army continued its skillful retreat, farther east, the situation became ever more dire. Both the army and the whole government were on their last legs.

There were no magic weapons. The closest was the simple truck, which the Americans arrived with in large numbers, which allowed the allies to take advantage of the breakthroughs the troops would manage to make in German lines. At 5:45 on November 11, the Germans and allies signed an armistice, to take effect at 11:11 of that day.

Around the world, countries began to take stock of the cost of the war: some 10,000,000 soldiers dead, plus almost as many civilians. Huge swaths of land stretching through Belgium and France turned into a nightmare of mud and death. Towns wiped completely off the map. The horror of war ran deep through all those involved in the writing of the Treaty of Versailles, which finally and formally ended the war, charging Germany with the blame and demanding punitive reparations to atone for their sin.

Around the world, families that had been affected by the turmoil of war began the slow process of figuring out how to move forward again. Some were lucky, and able to pick up where they had left off four years earlier. Others had to begin to learn how to make do without their husband, father, or son.

Those that had spend four quiet days aboard *LZ 120* were among those affected.

Almost immediately upon landing, Lehmann turned *LZ 120* over to the navy, who put Johann von Loßnitzer in charge. While Loßnitzer had begun the war in the trenches on the western front, he had then switched to the airship troops. The first post-Lehmann flight was an interesting one in that there were two landings involved. The airship took off on what was listed as a reconnaissance flight on August 8, landing 200 kilometers north in Wainoden, then took off the same day for a flight to Seddin, 350 kilometers to the southwest. The last flight of the day took them the 200 kilometers west and back to Seerappen. Six days later, this was followed by another reconnaissance flight, then one last training flight before the airship was transferred to Wainoden. The reason for this was that the German military was preparing for one last attack on the eastern front, an operation to complete what had been begun with the capture of Libau two years earlier.

The action was named Operation Albion, and was to be an amphibious landing that also used water and air craft for support. The first action called for *LZ 120*, along with *LZ 113*, *L 30*, and *L 37*, to attack railway junctions in the Latvian towns of Walk and Wolmar, to slow or stop goods and soldiers from coming down from Estonia. While this raid went pretty much according to plan, as did two more flights over the next four days, the weather then kept the airships in their sheds until late in the month. On the twenty-fourth, the weather had improved again, and three Zeppelins, including *LZ 120*, were sent out to attack the guns that were on the island of Oesel, and from which the entrance to the Bay of Riga is protected. Loßnitzer reported afterward that he had been able to that he had been able to bracket the target with a stick of bombs. Defense had been weak at best. On October 2, a similar raid was flown.[1]

The actual attack was to begin on October 12. Troops were to depart Libau on the ninth and the following day, while the troops were underway, *LZ 120* made a flight to Libau, though there isno indication what she was doing there. The following day, three other airships scouted the area around the troop carriers and reported only that there were no enemy ships in the area. Once again, the weather intervened, and while the troops successfully captured Oesel, the airships waited in their hangars. Only on the fifteenth, with the battle now fully engaged, did they again take to the air, to bomb Pernau, a Russian base in the Bay of Riga. Once again, Loßnitzer reported having bombed the target, in spite of antiaircraft fire that was far more dangerous than on the previous attack. By the seventeenth, the attack was over. On that day, *LZ 120* made one more flight—but it was simply for training. They would fly one more mission three days later, a patrol flight that was in no way out of the ordinary—although it turned out to be the Zeppelin's very last war-related flight.[2]

On October 28, 1917, *LZ 120* was flown from its hangar in Wainoden back to Seerappen, where it was hung up carefully. Two weeks later, the crew reported that they had done a motor test on the airship; then the following day it was listed as out of service. *LZ 120*'s war was now finally over.[3]

It would be almost exactly three years before the airship would fly again. In the meantime, the Treaty of Versailles had been ratified. In the course of the negotiations, various of the Allied nations had been promised German war material as reparations. Particularly of interest were those Zeppelins that had survived the war, and *LZ 120* had been turned over to the Italians. On November 20, 1920, *LZ 120* was once again prepared for flight and taken out of the hangar. The flight was a short one—to Seddin. A week later, the second leg was flown to Staaken. Finally, on Christmas Day of that year, the airship would fly south, over the Alps and to Ciampino, a 1,200-kilometer flight.

The first thing the Italians did was to rename the airship. In a solemn ceremony held on January 18, 1921, it became the *Ausonia*, after an ancient name for this region of Italy—and a prewar airship that had borne the same name. The original *Ausonia* had been much smaller than the current one, and had been damaged in a storm. It was rebuilt with a better engine but ended up being damaged in another storm, damage that left it irreparable.[4]

In March, Robert Underwood Johnson was invited to fly on the airship *Roma*, a semirigid airship about two-thirds the size of *LZ 120*, which was in the same hangar as *Ausonia*. He wrote about his impressions later:

It still bore the iron cross painted under one side, but it had been renamed the Ausonia—an ancient name for this part of Italy. It had four boats pendant, one in front, two amidships and one aft, each having motor attached. To communicate between these one had to climb a ladder and walk through the interior, which struck me as a clumsy expedient. It was not quite as large as the Roma, but was of much the same shape.[5]

As *Ausonia* it flew a number of times, with the eventual plan to use it for passenger transportation. Test flights included a flight in late April that took it from Rome to Florence and back. The initial plan for passenger service was to fly between Rome and Cagliari on Sardinia. And so, on May 10, *Ausonia* took off from Rome and headed southwest. Seven hours later, and to the great joy of the masses assembled below, it landed in Cagliari. After a brief stop, the airship returned home. It seemed a great success.

Unfortunately, as people looked more closely at the airship, they realized that all was not well with it. The engines were no longer capable of producing the power they had once been able to. The ballonets were leaking, particularly an issue with them still using hydrogen as a lifting gas. On June 19, the ballonets were deflated—but the Duralumin skeleton was not properly girded for this and collapsed. Nobody was hurt in the accident, but it also left the airship unusable, and so whatever was left over of this once mighty giant of the air was unceremoniously dismantled and discarded.[6]

One of *LZ 120*'s flight records would be broken not four months after it had been set. On November 21, 1917, the navy airship *L 59* took off from Yambol, Bulgaria. Its mission was to resupply Germany's beleaguered garrison in East Africa. Captained by Lieutenant Commander Ludwig Bockholt, the ship carried 15 tons of supplies, but even its structure was meant to be turned into items that the troops there needed. The trip began smoothly, with the airship crossing the Mediterranean and up the Nile. The crew, however, did not do as well, being unprepared for the wild swings in temperature, which eventually also affected the airship's ability to stay aloft. While still over the Sudan, and thus well away from General Lettow-Vorbeck's army, *L 59* received a message telling them to abort. Bockholt turned around, though his crew asked him not to. They landed again on November 25 to Yambol, having flown ninety-five hours—and 6,800 kilometers, achieving a greater distance than Lehmann had managed.[7]

A little less than two years later, the British airship *R34* would beat the time aloft record, but come nowhere near breaking the distance record.

It would be over four years before the time aloft record would be broken again—and the distance record at the same time. Once again, it was a Zeppelin that would do so, but this time flown by a French crew. LZ 114, originally *L 72* in the German navy, was not completed by the end of the war, and was turned over to the French as reparations. The airship was renamed *Dixmude*, and it would be five years before it would fly again, but then the plan was to fly her across the Mediterranean to Dakar. The first flight, of eighteen hours, was followed up by a 2,800-kilometer flight. On September 25, 1923, *Dixmude* left Cuers, crossed the Mediterreanean, then traveled across a significant stretch of North Africa before returning to Cuers via Paris. By the time it landed, it had traveled more than 7,100 kilometers in 118 hours and 41 minutes, both of which were new records, and finally broke the 101 hour record of *LZ 120*.[8] Sadly, after a number of successful, shorter, flights, *Dixmude* was lost over the Mediterranean,[9] presumably due to having been hit by lightning.[10] Fifty people died in that disaster.

Six years later, *LZ 127*, better known as the *Graf Zeppelin*, completed a historic round-the-world flight. In doing so, it also managed to beat the distance record. While the time aloft was essentially the same as Lehmann's 101 hours, it traveled 11,743 kilometers from Friedrichshafen to Tokyo. The whole trip took more than twenty-one days, with an actual flying time of twelve days.[11]

The time aloft record would eventually also be taken by *Graf Zeppelin*, when it took 119 hours to fly from Germany to Pernambuco, Brazil. Although the flight was scheduled to be much shorter, as they approached their destination, they received the message that there was fighting in the area and that the landing field had been taken over by insurgents. After resupplying themselves from a Spanish ship off the coast of Brazil, they landed after having spent slightly more time in the air than *Dixmude* had twelve years earlier.[12]

All these records would be beaten by the 1957 flight by a US Navy blimp. *Snow Bird*, as the ZPG-2 Blimp was called, took off from Naval Air Station South Weymouth, outside of New York City, at 6:30 p.m., on March 4, 1957. On board was a crew of fourteen, which allowed for two complete watches. They traveled first straight across the Atlantic, arriving at the southern end of Portugal. They then swung south, passing between the Canary Islands and the African coast. After this, they aimed southeast toward the Cape Verde islands, then back across the southern Atlantic to about Anguilla. They followed the chain of Caribbean islands back to Miami, turning south to follow the Florida Keys to their final destination of Key West, landing there on March 15 around sunset. This 260-plus-hour, 15,000-kilometer flight has never been bettered.[13]

But in a way, all these records were moot. The real triumph had already come with *R34*'s 1919 flight. While the British had been slow in the airship game, other than their North Sea class, they were happy to learn from anything that came their direction. On September 24, 1916, the navy R-class Zeppelin *L 33* (LZ 76) had been damaged by British fighter craft while attempting to bomb London. In the end, its captain, Alois Bocker, was forced to land in Essex.[14] While the crew—who all survived—was able to burn the Zeppelin, enough remained for the British to make a close inspection of it, and learn enough to copy it.

The result was two airships: *R33* and *R34*. Both flew for the first time in March 1919. Less than four months later, on 2:00 a.m. on July 2, *R34* took off from its airfield in East Fortune, on the Firth of Forth, and headed west. The first stretch had it buffeted considerably by the weather, but the situation improved over the Atlantic, and after two and a half-days, they arrived at the at St. John's, Newfoundland. The next two days were spent flying along the east coast of North America, and thus to Long Island. The idea had been to fly down to New York City before returning to the airfield in Mineola, but a shortage of fuel canceled that plan. Instead, the airship circled the airfield, one of the officers jumped out and landed using a parachute, and at 9:54 a.m. local time, the *R34* landed. They had been in the air for 108 hours, so seven hours longer than Lehmann's flight in *LZ 120*, but had covered only 5,800 kilometers.[15] It was not only the first airship to cross the Atlantic, but the first craft to fly east to west. A few days later, the airship would return in seventy-six hours, marking the first round trip over the Atlantic. The first flight also had the first transatlantic aerial stowaway—one of the crew, who had been cut from the trip for being superfluous and too heavy, hid between the ballonets and the outside hull, only making himself known after they had flown for six hours.[16]

Five years later, a Zeppelin flown by Hugo Eckener would be the first airship to fly from the European to American mainlands. This was LZ 126, named first ZR-3, then USS *Los Angeles*. The flight was to deliver it to the US Navy.[17]

Four years later, the *Graf Zeppelin* (LZ 127) would repeat this flight, on its way to becoming the most successful airship of all time. It would also be the first to cross the Atlantic in commercial service; for five years it would spend the summers flying between Europe and South America for paying passengers. It was joined in 1936 by the *Hindenburg*, who alternated flights from Germany to the United States and to Brazil. The following year, after a successful flight to South America, *Hindenburg* left for its first US trip of the year on May 3. Three days later, while landing in Lakehurst New Jersey, the *Hindenburg* caught fire and burned rapidly. Of the ninety-seven people on board, thirty-five died—plus one of the ground crew.[18]

The disaster marked the end of commercial transatlantic airship service.

One of those who died as a result of the airship crash was none other than Ernst August Lehmann. For Lehmann, the war had ended immediately after their landing in Seerappen. He had moved to Friedrichshafen and joined the Zeppelin corporation, as assistant manager in charge of relations with the German navy. However, on the side he continued to work on the question of transatlantic flights. Baron von Gemmingen took over the Zeppelin Corporation, and after the end of the war Lehmann was made an officer of the Zeppelin Corporation. He would also be vice president of the Goodyear-Zeppelin Corporation of Akron Ohio, though he would work from Germany in this time.[19]

With the end of the war, the Zeppelin corporation fell on hard times. Five Zeppelins that had been planned and had been given hull numbers had to be abandoned under the terms of the Treaty of Versailles. There were no groups within Germany that were capable of buying one of these giants of the sky. It was not until 1919 that they would build a new airship. Conceived as a passenger airship flying between Berlin and Friedrichshafen, it made more than one hundred flights as the *Bodensee*. Just under two years after its first flight, it was turned over to the Italians, as they were owed airships that had been sabotaged by their crew. Renamed the *Esperia*, it continued to fly until 1928. Its sister ship, the *Nordstern*, was built in 1921, also for the DELAG, but never flew for them and was instead turned over to the French.

It was another three years before the Zeppelin corporation was allowed to build another airship. In this case, they ensured that they would be allowed to build it by doing so for the US government. It had hull number LZ 126, but was named first *ZR-3* and later the USS *Los Angeles*. While the previous two airships build were considerably smaller than *LZ 120*, this airship represented a step forward, being more than 50 percent larger than the wartime Zeppelins. It would continue to fly until 1940.

The final three Zeppelins built by the Zeppelin corporation were the *Graf Zeppelin*, the *Hindenburg*, and *Graf Zeppelin II*. Of those, the first was by far the most successful, in fact, it is generally considered the most successful airship of all time. In October 1928, it had its first transatlantic flight. While Lehmann was not in command—that honor fell to Hugo Eckener—he was first officer of this 111-hour, 9,926-kilometer flight. Thereafter, Lehmann would become its commander, a position he held until 1936.[20]

Lehman would also command the *Hindenburg*, a behemoth with four times the capacity of *LZ 120*. On one of its first flights, Lehmann would fly around Germany spreading propaganda via loudspeakers and handbills. The flight had had an inauspicious beginning when it was damaged when a crosswind struck it while it was trying to take off. Repairs had to be made quickly to it could join the *Graf Zeppelin*.

The following year, Lehmann was on board the first flight across the North Atlantic of the season. He was, however, not in charge, though he was the most senior officer on board. Coming in to land in Lakehurst, the airship was running late, and Lehmann requested that it make a sharp turn to land. It was probably this that caused wires within the airship to snap, slashing open the hydrogen balloons and causing the airship to go up in flames.[21] Lehmann waited to the last minute to jump off. He was badly injured and taken to the hospital, where he said to a doctor: "I intended to stay with the ship as long as I could—until we could land her if possible, but it was impossible. Everything around me was on fire. The windows were open in the central control cabin and I jumped about a hundred feet. My clothes were ablaze."[22]

Near him, another to jump from the airship in its dying throes was Alfred Grözinger, the son of August Grözinger, who had been on board *LZ 120*. The younger Grözinger had become a cook, and it was in this capacity that he served on the *Hindenburg*.

Lehmann's last words were, in German, "I am going to live." He was then put into an oxygen tent but died just a few minutes later. He was brought back to Germany and buried in a grave in Frankfurt along with other victims of the disaster. Lehmann had flown 1,075 flights in the course of his life. He was only fifty when he died.

Since their record-breaking flight, Lehmann had seen Professor Pohl only one final time. In September 1917, Pohl had made plans to have his old friend come over, but these had to be canceled when Lehmann was called to Friedrichshafen. At the time, Pohl was still optimistic about the war, that the U-boats and changes in Russia would cause England to capitulate. They would meet again when Lehmann came through Berlin in March 1918 on his way from the airship base in Nordholz to Munich. He told Pohl about his work on airship service across the Atlantic, how they had worked out a way of increasing the speed of Zeppelins by another 10 percent.

Pohl would spend the rest of the war working on non-Zeppelin-related items. He stayed at Tafunk, however, but found himself increasingly in management, now just making sure that the systems that he had worked out for the tracking of radio transmitters were delivered correctly. The most excitement he had in this time was when he had a special train waiting and realized that the systems were almost all missing some parts or another, and had to scrape together the missing parts on the fly. Otherwise, he continued to work on antennas, whether in their setup or repair. Occasionally, he would have the chance to try out the listening posts that Tafunk had in and around Berlin, listening to US broadcasts and trying radios with which they could receive signals from the Dutch East Indies.

The frenetic pace with which he had traveled around to the various fronts slowed, though he was able to take the train once to Insterburg, his father's birthplace, where he had a meeting, and then continue on the 117 kilometers to Gumbinnen, a chance to visit the city his father had grown up in.

But mainly, he planned for the future, whether that of the army or his personal future. For the army, this often meant actively dissuading his people from buying material that would never be used. He had become steadily more disillusioned about the war—and politics in general. He continued to be well informed of the deployment of Zeppelins, though the news was rarely good, including one time when he wrote of Zeppelins being shot down by army troops who did not realize that they were friendly, and that the airships could not be contacted because, as they were navy airships, the army could not radio them.

The more he despaired about the turn the war had taken for Germany, the more he focused on his own work. Along the way, he acquired a three-volume set of the collected letters of Georg Christoph Lichtenberg,[23] who had been at the Göttingen university for the last quarter of the eighteenth century, holding the first professorship dedicated to experimental physics. Pohl felt that he would be the heir to this legacy and hoped that he would be better able to properly continue his work from what he learned in the letters. He also looked forward to his move to Göttingen and the chance to root around the dark corners of the institute's store rooms for equipment that might have been used by Lichtenberg himself.

Above all else he worried about food. He gave ever more elaborate instructions in how to secure his mother's supply, often the bulk of his letters would be give over to that question—what he had received and consumed, what he had found and was sending on, where to acquire sufficient fat to keep body and soul together.

During the summer, he began to be concerned about the war situation, especially tanks he found that the German soldiers simply could not handle. He would spend the final days of the war laid up in bed, falling ill with a fever on the tenth, a fever that continued on all through Monday the eleventh. The rest of the week, while now no longer feverish, he had been so weak that it was not until Saturday that he could again write to this mother. He would regret having missed out on the day that, to him, represented the end of the German empire created by Bismarck.

Exactly one month after armistice day, he would travel to Göttingen to take on his new job. In the meantime, he had dealt with some small matters—a new crown on one of his teeth, buying surplus equipment from the army for his new institute, saying goodbye to his old colleagues.

His new job in Göttingen was perfect for him. In charge of his own institute, his colleagues and fellow full professors were James Franck and Max Born. Over the next twenty years, Göttingen would be the center of a flowering of physics, a time that would end in 1933 with the Nazi takeover. One of their first acts was a law that banned Jews from teaching at universities. Both Born and Franck were therefore soon out of their jobs—Franck could have stayed, as a war veteran, but chose to resign. While Born immigrated to England, Franck eventually landed in the United States.

Pohl was, by this time, a father. He had, in 1922, married Auguste Eleanore Madelung, half sister of his colleague Erwin Madelung. They would have three children, Ottilie, Eleanore, and Robert, the last of whom was born in 1929.

In 1939, seeing what Germany was hurtling toward and, having seen this film and not liked how it had ended the last time, Pohl moved his family away from downtown Göttingen, out of the apartment above his physics institute that he had lived in for many years and into a house that he would live in for the rest of his life. Pohl would expand on his work as a teacher and would use the insights he had gained in his teaching experimental physics to write a series of textbooks. The first was published in 1927 and covered electromagnetism. He followed it with a volume on mechanics and acoustics in 1930 and completed the introductory series with a work on optics in 1941.

After the war, Pohl was one of the lucky ones: he not only had had no contact with the Nazis but had managed to hold on to both houses his family owned—his in Göttingen and the family home in Glücksburg. He was forced to sell the latter to pay the confiscatory taxes all Germans with any wealth were forced to pay in order to help those who had lost everything. Thus his mother came to live with him, bringing with her the letters he had been writing her since the day he left for Heidelberg. She would also bring along the portable desk that her husband had used as a student, among many other family relics.

Pohl in these postwar years also worked together with scientists in many other fields, using his insights from physics to help them get past stumbling blocks. He built one of the first semiconductors, though it was just a first step to what would become the ubiquitous integrated circuit.

He would retire in 1952 and spend the rest of his life continuing to improve his books, with a new edition coming out every few years. In retirement he lived with his wife and eldest daughter, visiting the other children elsewhere in Germany and in the United States.

He would die at home on June 5, 1976; 6,240 kilometers due west, almost exactly the distance that he had flown in 1917 and across the Atlantic Ocean, his son would wake his grandson with the words "Your grandfather has died." The grandson would blink in the bright June sun, attempt to produce the tears that he felt were called upon in these situations, fail, and go about his business of preparing for school.

Zeppelin with hull number LZ 52 being hauled down by the ground crew on November 5, 1915. It was later turned over to the German navy and given the name *L 18*. It burned in its hangar on November 17 of that year.

The front gondola of LZ 52 as it is being walked into its hangar. Professor Pohl can be seen standing in the door of the gondola; he is on the left.

APPENDIX

The text of the epigram on page 3 is is the penultimate stanza of the poem "Justinus Kerner, Erwiderung auf sein Lied: Unter dem Himmel (1845)" ("Justinus Kerner, Reply to His Song: Under the Heavens") by Gottfried Keller.* The original Kerner poem, "Unter dem Himmel" ("Under the Heavens"), was a lament about the possible future industrialization, and thus pollution, of the airs.** Kerner worried that soon the skies above would look like the earth, criss-crossed with railway tracks, and that this would lead to, for example, oil dripping down from clear skies. It was remarkably forward-thinking—after all, the first remotely successful airship would not be launched for another seven years. Kerner's poem was published in the magazine *Morgenblatt für gebildete Leser* (*Morning Paper for Cultured Readers*), which was published as frequently as a newspaper but had content more akin to a magazine.

Keller, one of the most famous German poets of the nineteenth century, wrote his reply the following year and tried to point out the positive aspects of these developments. Keller's poem was originally published in 1846. When it was republished in 1883,*** the "fifty" was replaced with "a hundred," which would do nothing to fix its accuracy. One hundred years, both from the original printing and its reprinting, jumps over the entire age of airships.

The text is from the 1846 edition.

Both poems, with translations, follow.

---

* Keller, Gottfried. *Gedichte von Gottfried Keller*. Heidelberg: Akademische Verlagshandlung von C. F. Winter, 1846.

** Kerner, Justinus. "Unter dem Himmel." *Morgenblatt für gebildete Leser*, September 15, 1845, p. 1.

*** Keller, Gottfried. *Gesammelte Gedichte von Gottfried Keller*. Berlin: Verlag von Wilhelm Hertz, 1883.

Front page of the *Morgenblatt für gebildete Leser* (*Morning Paper for Cultured Readers*) of September 15, 1845, with Justinus Kerner's original antiairship poem "*Unter dem Himmel*" ("*Under the Heavens*"). University of Illinois at Urbana Champaign via HathiTrust

JUSTINUS KERNER *UNTER DEM HIMMEL*
TRANSLATION BY THE AUTHOR

Lasst mich in Gras und Blumen liegen	Let me lie among grass and flowers
Und schaun dem blauen Himmel zu,	and watch the blue sky
Wie goldne Wolken ihn durchfliegen,	as golden clouds drift by
In ihm ein Falke kreist in Ruh'.	And a falcon peacefully circles
Die blaue Stille stört dort oben	The blue quiet is not disturbed
Kein Dampfer und kein Segelschiff,	by any steamer or sailboat
Nicht Menschentritt, nicht Pferdetoben,	nor a footfall, no horse running
Nicht des Dampfwagens wilder Pfiff.	Not the steam engine's wild whistle
Lasst satt mich schaun in dieser Klarheit,	Let me get a fill of this clear view
In diesem stillen, sel'gen Raum:	in this still and sacred room
Denn bald könnt' werden ja zur Wahrheit	since soon could become reality
Das Fliegen, der unsel'ge Traum.	Flight, that unholy dream
Dann flieht der Vogel aus den Lüften,	Then the bird will flee the air
Wie aus dem Rhein der Salmen schon,	as salmon have left the Rhine
Und wo einst singend Lerchen schifften,	and where once the larks navigated
Schifft grämlich stumm Britannias Sohn.	Britannia's son now sails in dour silence

Schau' ich zum Himmel, zu gewahren,	If I look to the heavens to see
Warum's so plötzlich dunkel sei,	why it has suddenly turned dark
Erblick' ich einen Zug von Waren,	I will see a train of goods
Der an der Sonne schifft vorbei.	That sails past the sun
Fühl' Regen ich beim Sonnenscheine,	If I feel rain while the sun is shining
Such' nach dem Regenbogen keck,	I will look first for a rainbow
Ist es nicht Wasser, wie ich meine,	Is it not water, as I suspect
Wurd' in der Luft ein Ölfass leck.	But an oil barrel that leaked in the air
Satt lasst mich schaun vom Erdgetümmel	Let me see look up to the heavens
Zum Himmel, eh' es ist zu spät,	from the earth's chaos, before it is too late
Wann, wie vom Erdball, so vom Himmel	When, poetry has silently left
Die Poesie still trauernd geht.	both from earth as well as the heavens
Verzeiht dies Lied des Dichters Grolle,	Pardon this song of the poet's anger
Träumt er von solchem Himmelsgraus,	when he dreams such horror in the sky
Er, den die Zeit, die dampfestolle,	He, for whom time, love of technology
Schließt von der Erde lieblos aus.	Is barred, lovelessly, from the earth.

GOTTFRIED KELLER: *JUSTINUS KERNER, ERWIDERUNG AUF SEIN LIED: "UNTER DEM HIMMEL."*
TRANSLATION BY THE AUTHOR

Dein Lied ist rührend, edler Sänger,	Your song is touching, precious singer
Doch zürne dem Genossen nicht,	but don't be angry at your friend
Wird ihm darob das Herz nicht bänger,	whose heart is thereby even more scared
Das, dir erwidernd, also spricht:	Which, in answer to you, now speaks
»Die Poesie ist angeboren,	Poetry is inborn
Und sie erkennt kein Dort und Hier!	And knows neither here nor there
Ja, ging die Seele mir verloren,	And, were my soul lost
Sie führ' zur Hölle selbst mit mir.	It would drive me to hell

Inzwischen sieht's auf dieser Erde
Noch lange nicht so graulich aus,
Und manchmal scheint mir, dass das Werde!
Ertön' erst recht dem ›Dichterhaus‹.

Schon schafft der Geist sich Sturmesschwingen
Und spannt Eliaswagen an;
Willst träumend du im Grase singen,
Wer hindert dich, Poet, daran?

Ich grüsse dich im Schäferkleide,
Herfahrend – doch mein Feuerdrach'
Trägt mich vorbei, die dunkle Heide
Und deine Geister schaun uns nach.

Was deine alten Pergamente
Von tollem Zauber kund dir tun,
Das seh' ich durch die Elemente
In Geistes Dienst verwirklicht nun.

Ich seh' sie keuchend glühn und sprühen,
Stahlschimmernd bauen Land und Stadt,
Indes das Menschenkind zu blühen
Und singen wieder Musse hat.

Und wenn vielleicht in fünfzig Jahren
Ein Luftschiff hoch mit Griechenwein
Durchs Morgenrot käm' hergefahren
Wer möchte da nicht Fährmann sein?

Dann bög' ich mich, ein sel'ger Zecher,
Wohl über Bord von Kränzen schwer,
Und gösse langsam meinen Becher
Hinab in das verlassne Meer.

In the meantime it appears on earth
not to be quite so horrid
Sometimes it seems to me that "it will be!"
Will sound in the poet's house

The soul gains storm wings
and harnesses Elijah's wagon

If you wish to dream in the grass,
Who will stop you, poet, from that?

I greet you dressed in shepherd's garb
Driving by, but my fire dragon
carries me past, across the dark heather
And your ghosts watch us go by

What your old parchments
full of magic tell you
That I see through the elements
In the spirit's service becomes reality

I see them gasping, glowing and sparkling
Steel-gleaming, building state and town
While mankind has time
To blossom and to sing

And if maybe in fifty years
An airship full of Greek wine
Flies through the sunrise
Who would not want to steer this ship?

Then I, happy drinker, would bend over
the side, with heavy wreaths
and would slowly pour my cup
Down into the abandoned sea.

ENDNOTES

Introduction

1. "All the Outstanding Events of the War, Briefly Sketched," *New York Tribune Review*, July 29, 1917, 6.
2. "Les origines de la guerre," *Le Matin*, July 29, 1917, 1.
3. "Le troisieme anniversaire de la guerre," *Le Figaro*, August 3, 1917, 1.
4. Ernst Lehmann and Howard Mingos, *The Zeppelins* (New York: J. H. Sears, 1927), 234.

Chapter 1

1. "Fahrtbericht LZ120 vom 26.7.1917," Sammlung Dieter Rühe, LZ 120, Aeronauticum archives, Nordholz, Germany.
2. Ernst Lehmann and Howard Mingos, *The Zeppelins* (New York: J. H. Sears, 1927), 236.
3. Der erste Offizier eines Z-Luftschiffes [pseud.], *Z-181: Im Zeppelin gegen Bukarest* (Berlin: August Scherl, 1916), 46.
4. Lehmann and Mingos, *Zeppelins*, 236.
5. Letter Robert Pohl to Martha Pohl, July 27, 1917, Pohl letters, Pohl Family archive, Göttingen, Germany.
6. Ernst August Lehmann, "Bericht zur 100 stündigen Fahrt des LZ 120 vom 26. bis 31. Juli 1917," Sammlung Dieter Rühe, LZ 120, Aeronauticum archives, Nordholz, Germany. In his books, Lehmann simply writes that they tried both six- and eight-hour shifts, but in this document, written immediately after the flight, he describes how he decided who would be in which shift.
7. Lehmann, "Bericht."
8. "Verlauf der 101-Std.-Fahrt nach Fahrtbericht," Sammlung Dieter Rühe, LZ 120, Aeronauticum archives, Nordholz, Germany.
9. Letter Robert Pohl to Martha Pohl, July 28, 1917, Pohl letters, Pohl Family archive, Göttingen, Germany.
10. Lehmann and Mingos, *Zeppelins*, 236.
11. Letter Robert Pohl to Martha Pohl, July 26, 1917, Pohl letters, Pohl Family archive, Göttingen, Germany.
12. Pohl letter of July 26, 1917.
13. Lehmann and Mingos, *Zeppelins*, 235.
14. Ibid5.
15. Pohl letter of July 26, 1917.
16. John Provan, *The German Airship in World War I* (Kelkheim: Luftschiff-Zeppelin Collection, 1992).
17. Pohl letter of July 26, 1917.
18. Karl Baedeker, *Berlin and Its Environs* (Leipzig: Baedeker, 1908), 9.
19. Pohl letter of July 26, 1917.
20. Ibid.
21. Robert Wichard Pohl, *Pohl Stammbaum*, privately published ca. 1933, Pohl Family archive, Göttingen, Germany.
22. *The Encyclopedia Britannica*, 11th ed., s.v. "Königsberg" (New York: Encyclopedia Britannica, 1910–11).
23. Leonhard Euler, "Solutio Problematis ad Geometriam Situs," *Commentarii Academiae Scientiarum Imperialis Petropolitanae* 8 (1736): 128–40.

24. Wilhelm Grosse, *Unterhaltende Probleme und Spiele in Mathematischer Beleuchtung* (Leipzig: Quandt & Händel, 1897), 125; or Moritz Cantor, *Vorlesungen über Geschichte der Mathematik: Dritter Band* (Leipzig: Teubner, 1898), 603.

25. Karl Baedeker, *Nordost-Deutschland* (Leipzig: Baedeker, 1914), 167.

26. Max Broesike, "Die Bäder und Heilquellen im preussichen Staate," *Zeitschrift des Königlich Preussischen Statistischen Bureaus* 43 (1903): 113–71.

27. Baedeker *Nordost-Deutschland*, 168.

28. Provan, *German Airship*.

29. "Fahrtbericht LZ120 vom 26.7.1917."

Chapter 2

1. Adolf Saager, *Zeppelin, der Mensch, der Kämpfer, der Sieger* (Stuttgart: Robert Lutz, 1915), 21–22.

2. Alexander Bömel, *Graf Ferdinand von Zeppelin: ein Mann der Tat* (Konstanz: Johannes Blanke, 1908), 8.

3. "Ferdinand Graf von Zeppelin," LeMO Biographie Deutsches Historisches Museum, https://www.dhm.de/lemo/biografie/biografie-ferdinand-graf-von-zeppelin.html, accessed July 13, 2021.

4. Saager, *Zeppelin*, 40–42.

5. Ferdinand Zeppelin and Rhoda R. Gilman, "Zeppelin in Minnesota," translated by Maria Bach Dunn, *Minnesota History*, June 1967, 265–78.

6. Samuel Archer King, "Thaddeus S. C. Lowe," in *Appletons' Cyclopedia of American Biography* (New York: D. Appleton, 1900).

7. E.T. Pyle, "The Best Story of the Civil War—How Balloons Were First Used in Battle," [Washington, DC] *Sunday Star Magazine*, May 31, 1931, 10–13.

8. Zeppelin and Gilman, "Zeppelin in Minnesota," 265–78.

9. Ibid.

10. Saager, *Zeppelin*, 48–56.

11. Ibid., 57.

12. Ilse Essers, "Kober, Theodor," in *Neue Deutsche Biographie 12* (1979), S. 244 f. [online version], https://www.deutsche-biographie.de/pnd143155199.html#ndbcontent.

13. Kaiserliches Patentamt, Patentschrift Nr. 98580 vom 31. August 1895, "Lenkbares Luftfahrzeug mit mehreren hintereinander angeordneten Tragkörpern."

14. "A Monster Airship," *Alexandria Gazette*, June 30, 1900, 2.

15. "The Ascension of Count Zeppelin's Airship," *Scientific American*, August 11, 1900, 88.

16. "Count von Zeppelin's Dirigible Airship," *Scientific American*, March 3, 1906, 195.

17. "Vom Grafen Zeppelin," *Wiener Luftschiffer-Zeitung*, November 1908, 271.

18. "The News of the Week," *Herald of Gospel Liberty*, June 30, 1908, 20.

19. "The 'Deutschland' Again Wrecked," *Flight*, May 20, 1911, 499.

20. Douglas Robinson, *The Zeppelin in Combat* (Atglen PA: Schiffer Military, 1994), 23.

21. "Zeppelin Success and Failure," *Flight*, July 6, 1912, 617.

22. "The Work of the 'Victoria-Louise,'" *Flight*, December 6, 1913, 1329.

23. "A Zeppelin in Denmark," *Flight*, September 28, 1912, 881.

24. "Die Tätigkeit der Bezirksvereine im Jahre 1913/1914: Dresdener Bezirksverein," *Zeitschrift des Vereines Deutscher Ingenieure*, May 30, 1914, 1898.

25. Wilhelm Kranzler, *Bezwinger der Luft im Weltkriege* (Berlin-Charlottenburg: Verlag der Schillerbuchhandlung, 1917), 108.

26. Harry Redner, *Die Luftschiffwaffe des Heeres* (Wendeburg: Harry Redner, 1998), 27, 222.
27. Robinson, *Zeppelin in Combat*, 61–63.
28. Redner, *Luftschiffwaffe*, 224.
29. Ibid., 223.
30. Ibid., 221.
31. Ibid., 35.
32. Multiple sources cover the minutiae of German airship raids: Robinson, *Zeppelin in Combat*; and Redner, *Luftschiffwaffe*. See also websites such as *http://www.iancastlezeppelin.co.uk*.
33. Robinson, *Zeppelin in Combat*, 65.
34. Redner, *Luftschiffwaffe*, 225.
35. Robinson, *Zeppelin in Combat*, 83–87.
36. Ibid., 90.
37. Ibid., 93.
38. Ibid3.
39. Ibid., 95.
40. Redner, *Luftschiffwaffe*, 96–97.
41. Der erste Offizier eines Z-Luftschiffes [pseud.], *Z-181: Im Zeppelin gegen Bukarest* (Berlin: August Scherl, 1916).
42. Redner, *Luftschiffwaffe*, 61.

Chapter 3

1. *The Encyclopedia Britannica*, 11th ed., s.v. "Kolberg" (New York: Encyclopedia Britannica, 1910–11).
2. Paul Heyse, *Colberg: Historisches Schauspiel in fünf Akten* (Munich: Deschler'schen Buchdruckerei, 1865). See also Paul Wendt, *Colberg 1807, oder: Heldensinn und Bürgertreue* (Stettin: Dannenberg & Dühr, 1863).
3. Friedrich Maurer pub., *Colberg im Jahr 1807 belagert und vertheidigt: Nach authentischen Berichten von mehreren Augenzeugen* (Berlin: Maurer, 1808). See also Joachim Nettelbeck, *Joachim Nettelbeck, Bürger zu Colberg* (Leipzig: F. A. Brockhaus, 1823).
4. Roger Chickering, *The Great War and Urban Life in Germany* (Cambridge: Cambrige University Press, 2007), 267.
5. Ernst Lehmann and Howard Mingos, *The Zeppelins* (New York: J. H. Sears, 1927), 240.
6. Karl Baedeker, *Nordost-Deutschland* (Leipzig: Baedeker, 1914), 135.
7. *The Encyclopedia Britannica*, 11th ed., s.v. "Greifswald" (New York: Encyclopedia Britannica, 1910–11).
8. *The Encyclopedia Britannica*, 11th ed., s.v. "Rügen" (New York: Encyclopedia Britannica, 1910–11).
9. *Encyclopedia Britannica*, "Greifswald."
10. Karl Baedeker, *Norway, Sweden, and Denmark with Excursions to Iceland and Spitzbergen* (Leipzig: Karl Baedeker, 1912), 429.
11. Ibid., 430.

Chapter 4

1. "Robert Pohl," *Jahrbuch der Schiffsbautechnischen Gesellschaft, Dreizehnter Band* (Berlin: Julius Springer, 1912), 86–87.
2. Ibid.
3. *The Encyclopedia Britannica*, 11th ed., s.v. "Hamburg" (New York: Encyclopedia Britannica, 1910–11).

4. Robert Pohl, "Über das Leuchten bei Ionisation von Gasen," *Annalen der Physik* 322, no. 7 (1905): 375–77.

5. Albert Einstein, "Über die von der molekularkinetischen Theorie der Wärme geforderte Bewegung von in ruhenden Flüssigkeiten suspendierten Teilchen," *Annalen der Physik* 322, no. 8 (1905): 549–60.

6. Robert Pohl, "Über die Einwirkung stiller elektrischer Entladung auf Ammoniak und Sauerstoff," PhD diss., Friedrich-Wilhelms-Universität zu Berlin, 1906.

7. Erich Marx, *Die Geschwindigkeit der Röntgenstrahlen* (Leipzig: Teubner, 1906).

8. James Franck and Robert Pohl, "Zur Frage nach der Geschwindigkeit der Röntgenstrahlen," *Berichte der Deutschen Physikalischen Gesellschaft* 10, no. 3 (1908): 117–36.

9. Max Von Laue, "Erich Marx. Die Geschwindigkeit der Röntgenstrahlen," *Archiv der Mathematik und Physik* 13, no. 3 (1908): 342.

10. Robert Pohl, *Die Elektrische Fernübertragung von Bildern* (Braunschweig: Vieweg, 1910).

11. Robert Pohl, *Die Physik der Röntgenstrahlung* (Braunschweig: Vieweg, 1912).

12. "5. Feld-Artillerie-Regiment Nr. 64, Pirna," *Deutsche Verlustlisten*, October 24, 1914.

13. Kurt Perels, "Seminar für Oeffenliches Recht und Kolonialrecht," *Jahrbuch der Hamburgischen Wissenschaftlichen Anstalten, 32. Jahrgang* (Hamburg: Otto Meissner Verlag, 1915), 211–12.

Chapter 5

1. Karl Baedeker, *Nordost-Deutschland* (Leipzig: Baedeker, 1914), 121.

2. Ibid., 76.

3. Ibid., 122.

4. Ibid., 120.

5. *Die Gesellschaft für Natur- und Heilkunde in Berlin 1810–1935* (Berlin: Springer, 1935), 98.

6. Baedeker, *Nordost-Deutschland*, 113.

7. Der erste Offizier eines Z-Luftschiffes [pseud.], *Z-181: Im Zeppelin gegen Bukarest* (Berlin: August Scherl, 1916), 72.

8. Ernst Lehmann and Howard Mingos, *The Zeppelins* (New York: J. H. Sears, 1927), 240.

9. Baedeker, *Nordost-Deutschland*, 90.

10. Karl Baedeker, *Northern Germany* (Leipzig: Baedeker, 1910), 146.

11. Baedeker, *Nordost-Deutschland*, 95

12. Otto Grautoff, *Lubeck* (Leipzig: Klinkhardt & Biermann, 1908). 51.

Chapter 6

1. Rolf Italiaander, "Lehmann, Ernst August," in *Neue Deutsche Biographie 14* (1985), S. 77 f. [online-Version], https://www.deutsche-biographie.de/pnd11948854X.html#ndbcontent.

2. Ibid.

3. Rolf Italiaander, "Lehmann, Ernst August," in Neue Deutsche Biographie 14 (1985), S. 77 f. [Online-Version], https://www.deutsche-biographie.de/pnd11948854X.html#ndbcontent.

4. Walther Reimer, "Eckener, Hugo," in Neue Deutsche Biographie 4 (1959), S. 288 [online-Version], https://www.deutsche-biographie.de/pnd118528750.html#ndbcontent.

5. Rolf Italiaander, "Lehmann, Ernst August," in Neue Deutsche Biographie 14 (1985), S. 77 f. [online version], https://www.deutsche-biographie.de/pnd11948854X.html#ndbcontent.

6. "Airship News," *Flight*, July 26, 1913, 820.

7. Ernst Lehmann and Howard Mingos, *The Zeppelins* (New York: J. H. Sears, 1927), 6.
8. Ibid., 10.
9. "Hotel Stadt Königsberg," PotsdamWiki, accessed July 15, 2021, https://www.potsdam-wiki.de/index.php/Hotel_Stadt_Königsberg.
10. Lehmann and Mingos, *Zeppelins*, 15–18.
11. Ibid., 21.
12. Ibid., 23.
13. Ibid., 21.
14. Ibid., 25–28.
15. "Zeppelin Renews Antwerp Attack," *New York Times*, September 3, 1914.
16. John Provan, *The German Airship in World War I* (Kelkheim: Luftschiff-Zeppelin Collection, 1992).
17. Lehmann and Mingos, *Zeppelins*, 31–32.
18. Bayerisches Hauptstaatsarchiv, Munchen, *Abteilung IV Kriegsarchiv: Kriegstammrollen, 1914–1918, vol.vol. 18151, Kriegsrangliste.*
19. Lehmann and Mingos, *Zeppelins*, 34.
20. Ibid., 45
21. Ibid., 47.
22. Douglas Robinson, *The Zeppelin in Combat* (Atglen PA: Schiffer, 1994.), 90–92.
23. Lehmann and Mingos, *Zeppelins*, 52–55.
24. Ibid., 55.
25. Ibid., 61.
26. Ibid., 65.
27. *The Encyclopedia Britannica*, 11th ed., s.v. "Allenstein" (New York: Encyclopedia Britannica, 1910–11).
28. Lehmann and Mingos, *Zeppelins*, 70–71
29. Ibid., 71.
30. Ibid., 71–79.
31. Ibid., 82.
32. Ibid., 86–87.
33. Bayerisches Hauptstaatsarchiv, Munchen, *Abteilung IV Kriegsarchiv: Kriegstammrollen, 1914–1918; Volume: 18151. Kriegsrangliste.*
34. Rolf Italiaander, "Lehmann, Ernst August," in Neue Deutsche Biographie 14 (1985), S. 77 f. [online version], https://www.deutsche-biographie.de/pnd11948854X.html#ndbcontent.
35. Lehmann and Mingos, *Zeppelins*, 150–52.
36. Ibid., 169–70.
37. Ibid., 170–75.
38. Ibid., 176–78.
39. Ibid., 181.
40. Ibid., 186–91.
41. Ibid., 195–97.
42. Ibid., 198–99.
43. Ibid., 202–3.

Chapter 7
1. Karl Baedeker, *Nordost-Deutschland* (Leipzig: Baedeker, 1914), 39.

2. Ibid., 39.
3. *The Encyclopedia Britannica*, 11th ed., s.v. "Hamburg" (New York: Encyclopedia Britannica, 1910–11).
4. *Ibid.*
5. Baedeker, *Nordost-Deutschland*, 39.
6. Großherzogliche Statistische Amt, *Groszherzoglich Mecklenburg-Schwerinscher Staatskalender* (Schwerin: Bärensprung'sche Hofbuchdruckerei, 1916), 114.
7. Baedeker, *Nordost-Deutschland*, 85.
8. Großherzogliche Statistische Amt, *Mecklenburg-Schwerinscher Staatskalender*, 114.
9. Karl Lüttgens, "Deutsche Städtebilder: Wismar," (*Die Gartenlaube* 1892): 92.
10. "Die sechste Hauptversammlund des Heimatbundes Mecklenburg in Wismar am 17. und 18. Juni 1911," *Mecklenburg: Zeitschrift des Heimatbundes Mecklenburg*, September 1911, 89.
11. *The Encyclopedia Britannica*, 11th ed., s.v. "Rostock" (New York: Encyclopedia Britannica, 1910–11).
12. *The Encyclopedia Britannica*, 11th ed., s.v. "Rügen" (New York: Encyclopedia Britannica, 1910–11).
13. *The Encyclopedia Britannica*, 11th ed., s.v. "Stralsund" (New York: Encyclopedia Britannica, 1910–11).
14. *Encyclopedia Britannica*, "Stralsund."
15. Ernst Lehmann and Howard Mingos, *The Zeppelins* (New York: J. H. Sears, 1927), 203–7.
16. Lehmann and Mingos, *Zeppelins*, 209.

Chapter 8

1. Joan Patterson Kerr, "What Good Is a New-Born Baby?," *American Heritage*, December 1973.
2. Albert Henry Smyth, *The Writings of Benjamin Franklin* (New York: Macmillan, 1907), 9:79–85.
3. William Baddeley, "Ueber Lennox's Luftschiff," *Polytechnisches Journal* (1836 59 14): 87–92.
4. Gabriel de La Landelle, *Dans les airs, histoire elementaire de l'aeronautique* (Paris: Rene Haton, 1884), 134–36.
5. Ibid., 137.
6. "Navigation aérienne, système de M. Henri Giffard" (broadsheet) (Paris: Imprimerie de Schiller Aine, ca. 1852).
7. Henri Giffard, "Description du Premier Aérostat a Vapeur," letter written to Émile de Girardan on September 25, 1852, in *Mémoires et Compte Rendu des Travaux de la Société des Ingénieurs Civils* (Paris: Siege de la Societe, 1888), 437.
8. Rolla Clinton Carpenter and Herman Diederichs, *Internal Combustion Engines: Their Theory, Construction and Operation* (New York: Van Nostrand, 1908), 239.
9. Hermann Moedebeck, *Handbuch der Luftschiffahrt* (Leipzig: Schloemp, 1866), 124–27.
10. Anatol Murad, *Franz Joseph I of Austria and His Empire* (New York: Twayne, 1968), 194.
11. "Aerial Navigation in France," *Nature*, February 22, 1872, 334.
12. Rudolphe Soreau, "The Steering of Balloons," *American Engineer and Railroad Journal* 67 no. 10 (1893): 473–76.
13. Paul Banet-Rivet, *L'Aeronautique* (Paris: L. Henry May, 1898), 170–71.
14. Alberto Santos-Dumont, *My Air-Ships* (New York: Century 1904), 202–17.
15. Sean C. Dooley, The Development of Material-Adapted Structural Form, diss. École Polytechnique Fédérale de Lausanne 2004, A182-A187.

16. "Neuer grosser Rekord," *Wiener Luftschiffer-Zeitung*, August 1908, 181.
17. "Zeppelins Fahrten," *Wiener Luftschiffer-Zeitung*, November 1907, 236.
18. "Dauerfahrt von Lenkballons," *Wiener Luftschiffer-Zeitung*, December 1907, 261–62.
19. "Die zeppelinschen Fahrten," *Wiener Luftschiffer-Zeitung*, August 1908, 161–64.
20. "Die berliner Lenkballons," *Wiener Luftschiffer-Zeitung*, October 1908, 234–35.
21. "'Zeppelin I' Aloft All Night," *Flight*, April 17, 1909, 229.
22. "Zeppelin's Latest Record," *Flight*, June 5, 1909, 326.
23. Albert Vorreiter, *Jahrbuch über die Fortschritte auf allen Gebieten der Luftschiffahrt 1911* (Munich: Lehmanns, 1911), 14.
24. "'Clement-Bayard IV' on her Trials," *Flight*, July 15, 1911, 617.
25. "Paris to London by Airship," *Flight*, October 22, 1911, 868.
26. John Mackenzie Bacon, *The Dominion of the Air* (London: Cassell, 1902), 25–27.
27. "The 'Adjutant Reau' Trials," *Flight*, September 30, 1911, 848.
28. "Spherical and Dirigible Balloons, 1914," in *The World Almanac and Encyclopedia 1915* (New York: Press, 1914), 418.
29. "19-Hour Trip by 'LZ 19,'" *Flight*, July 12, 1913, 772.
30. "A Record by Italian Dirigible," *Flight*, October 18, 1913, 1158.
31. "Long Tests with the Schutte-Lanz," *Flight*, May 2, 1914, 476.
32. "35-Hour Voyage by the 'L3,'" *Flight*, May 29, 1914, 582.
33. "'Adjutant Vincenot' Beats the Record," *Flight*, July 3, 1914, 715.
34. "New Air Record Set For a Non-stop Flight," *Washington Times*, June 29, 1914, 1.
35. Brian Turpin, "North Sea 3," *NS11: As Bright as Day*, accessed July 15, 2021, http://www.ns11.org/north-sea-3/.

Chapter 9

1. Georg Wilhelm Raumer, *Die Insel Wollin und das Seebad Misdroy* (Berlin: Deckersche Geheime Oberhofbuchdruckerei, 1851), 18, 41, 77.
2. Rudolf Mosse, *Bäder-Almanach* (Berlin: Mosse, 1907), 244.
3. Raumer, *Wollin*, 367.
4. Bertha von Suttner, *Der Kampf um die Vermeidung des Weltkriegs* (Zürich: Füßli, 1917), 48.
5. Mosse, *Bäder-Almanach*, 244, 256, 348.
6. Karl Baedeker, *Nordost-Deutschland* (Leipzig: Baedeker, 1914), 134–37.
7. *The Encyclopedia Britannica*, 11th ed., s.v. "Swinemünde" (New York: Encyclopedia Britannica, 1910–11).
8. "Die Strandung des deutschen Militärluftschiffes," *Wiener Luftschiffer-Zeitung*. December 1908, 307–9.
9. *The Encyclopedia Britannica*, 11th ed., s.v. "Köslin" (New York: Encyclopedia Britannica, 1910–11).
10. Karl Baedeker, *Norway, Sweden, and Denmark with Excursions to Iceland and Spitzbergen* (Leipzig: Karl Baedeker, 1912), 275.
11. Der erste Offizier eines Z-Luftschiffes [pseud.], *Z-181: Im Zeppelin gegen Bukarest* (Berlin: August Scherl, 1916), 63.

Chapter 10

1. "Sitzung vom 6. November 1914," *Verhandlungen der Deutschen Physikalishen Gesellschaft* 19, (1914 no. 23): 1.

2. Max Dieckman, *Leitfaden der drahtlosen Telegrafie für die Luftfahrt* (Munich: Oldenbourgh, 1913) 195.

3. Douglas Robinson, *The Zeppelin in Combat* (Atglen PA: Schiffer Military, 1994), 84.

4. *The Encyclopedia Britannica*, 11th ed., s.v. "Plock" (New York: Encyclopedia Britannica, 1910–11).

5. *The Encyclopedia Britannica*, 11th ed., s.v. "Brixen" (New York: Encyclopedia Britannica, 1910–11).

6. "Zeppelin Kills 6 Parisians, Wounds 30," *New York Times*, January 30, 1916.

7. "French Capital in a Fury," *New York Times*, January 31, 1916, 1.

8. "Crime de Pirates: Un Zeppelin sur Paris," *Le Matin*, January 13, 1916, 1.

9. "Ein erfolgreicher Zeppelinangriff auf Paris," *Rosenheimer Anzeiger*, February 1, 1916, 1.

10. Harry Redner, *Die Luftschiffwaffe des Heeres* (Wendeburg: Harry Redner, 1998), 40–41.

11. Ibid., 231.

12. *Abwurftafel für die 100 kg Kugelbombe enthaltend die Falldauer und den Vorhaltewinkel* (Berlin: Artillerie-Prüfungskommission, 1916).

Chapter 11

1. John Provan, *The German Airship in World War I* (Kelkheim: Luftschiff-Zeppelin Collection, 1992).

Chapter 12

1. Ludwig Dürr, *Fünfundzwanzig Jahre Zeppelin-Luftschiffbau* (Berlin: VDI-Verlag, 1925), 62–66.

2. Otto Speyer, "Handelsnachrichten," *Der Motorwagen*, September 20, 1915, 338.

3. Albert Francis Zahm et al., *The Drag of C Class Airship Hull with Varying Length of Cylindrical Midships*, National Advisory Committee for Aeronautics Report 138 (Washington, DC: Government Printing Office, 1922).

4. Sean C. Dooley, The Development of Material-Adapted Structural Form, diss. École Polytechnique Fédérale de Lausanne 2004, A185.

5. "Duralumin," *Flight*, November 26, 1910, 967.

6. Dooley, *Material-Adapted Structural Form*, A201.

7. Leon Chollet, "Les Etoffes Baudruchees en Aerostation," *L'Aeronautique*, August 1922, 258.

8. "300 Arbeiterinnen," *Berliner Tageblatt*, July 27, 1917, B2.

9. Douglas Robinson, *The Zeppelin in Combat* (Atglen PA: Schiffer Military, 1994), 192–97.

10. Ibid., 201–7.

11. Ibid., 217–19.

12. Ernst Lehmann and Howard Mingos, *The Zeppelins* (New York: J. H. Sears, 1927), 211.

13. Ibid.

14. Ibid., 225–26.

15. Ibid., 233–34.

16. Ibid., 234.

Chapter 13

1. Douglas Robinson, *The Zeppelin in Combat* (Atglen PA: Schiffer Military, 1994), 237.

2. Kenneth Gustavsson, "Venäjän laivaston sotasurmat Ahvenamaalla vuosina 1914–18," in *Venäläissurmat Suomessa 1914–22, Osa 1, Sotatapahtumat 1914–17* (Helsinki: Prime Minister's Office of Finland, 2004), 68–70, 76–80.

3. "Aircraft Work at the Front: Official Information," *Flight*, August 2, 1917, 798.

4. Dmitri Theodor Jarintzoff, "On the Construction of the Military Outport of Libau," *Minutes of the Proceedings of theInstitution of Civil Engineers* (London: Institution of Civil Engineers, 1896), 360–74.

5. "Zeppelin, Bombarding Libau. Brought Down by Russians," *New York Times*, January 27, 1915, 1.

6. August Heinrich Hoffman von Fallersleben, *Gedichte* (Leipzig: Weidmann'sche Buchhandlung, 1843), 57.

7. Friedrich Tischler, *Die Vögel der Provinz Ostpreussen* (Berlin: Junk, 1914), 10.

Chapter 14

1. "Mr. Charles Green's Intended Voyage across the Atlantic in a Balloon," *Mechanic and Chemist*, November 30, 1839, 97.

2. Ibid.

3. "Mr. Green's Intended Aerial Voyage across the Atlantic," *Mirror of Literature, Amusement, and Instruction*, April 4, 1840, 221.

4. Hatton Turnor, *Astra Castra: Experiments and Adventures in the Atmosphere* (London: Chapman and Hall, 1865), 185.

5. Ibid., 199.

6. "Astounding News! By Express via Norfolk: The Atlantic Cross in Three Days!" *New York Sun*, April 13, 1844, 1.

7. Thomas Ollive Mabbott, ed., *The Collected Works of Edgar Allan Poe—Vol. III: Tales and Sketches* (Cambridge, MA: Harvard University Press, 1979), 1063–88.

8. John Mackenzie Bacon, *The Dominion of the Air: The Story of Aërial Navigation* (London: Cassell, 1902), 137.

9. "The Aeronautic Expedition," *New York Times*, July 11, 1859, 2.

10. "Air-Ships to Cross the Ocean," *Cleveland (OH) Morning Leader*, January 22, 1859, 2.

11. "The Great Balloon," *New York Times*, October 25, 1859, 8.

12. "That Balloon Voyage to Europe," *New York Times*, November 26, 1859, 5.

13. "Personal," *New York Times*, August 31, 1860, 6.

14. "Prof. Lowe and His Balloon," *New York Times*, September 10, 1860, 5.

15. "Mr. Lowe's Balloon Again Bursted," *New York Times*, October 1, 1860, 8.

16. "Ballooning in the '60s," *New York Sun*, November 7, 1909, B6

17. "Another Balloon Project," *Scientific American*, February 20, 1869, 116.

18. "Another Balloon Voyage," *New York Times*. June 20, 1869, 8.

19. "A Balloon Ascent Unprecedentedly Satisfactory," *Columbia (SC) Daily Phoenix*, February 24, 1872, 3.

20. Marion L. Amick, *History of Donaldson's Balloon Ascensions* (Cincinnati: Cincinnati News 1875), 64.

21. Ibid., 65.

22. Ibid., 65–75.

23. Rhoda Gilman, "The Balloon to Boston," *Minnesota History*, Spring 1970, 16–22.

24. "A Successful Air-Ship," *Phillipsburg (KS) Herald*, December 21,1888, 2.

25. "Mr. Campbell's Air Ship," *Pittsburgh (PA) Dispatch*, February 3. 1889, 15.

26. "In Command of the Air-Ship," *New York Evening World*, April 11, 1889, 1.

27. "Adrift at Sea," *New York Evening World*, July 18, 1889, 1.

28. "In Command of the Air-Ship," *New York Evening World*, April 11, 1889, 1.

29. "Hogan Probably Lost," *New York Times*, July 18, 1889, 5.
30. "Saw a Balloon," *Maysville (KY) Evening Bulletin*, July 19, 1889, 1.
31. "The Missing Aeronaut," *Maysville (KY) Evening Bulletin*, July 19, 1889, 1.
32. "Plunged into the Ocean," *New York Times*, July 19, 1889, 1.
33. "Andree Off for the Pole," *New York Times*, July 17, 1897, 1.
34. "May Be Andree's Airship," *New York Times*, September 18, 1897, 7.
35. "Airship Line Is Projected over Atlantic Ocean," *Paducah (KY) Sun*, December 31, 1908, 1.
36. "Latest News by Telegraph: Domestic," *Mathews (VA) Journal*, January 7, 1909, 1.
37. "Nixon Will Build First Air Warship," *Washington (DC) Times*, December 31, 1908, 12.
38. "The Air Ship of the Future," *Alexandria (VA) Gazette*, January 2, 1909, 1.
39. "Pennington Airship Back," *New York Times*, June 5, 1909, 2.
40. Ibid.
41. "Pennington Hazy about His Career," *New York Times*, August 28, 1909, 16.
42. "Court Throws Out Pennington Charge," *New York Times*, November 9, 1909, 10.
43. Walter Wellman, *The Aerial Age* (New York: Keller, 1911), 126–67.
44. "Wellman Airship Found Defective," *Washington (DC) Times*, August 24, 1906, 3.
45. Wellman, *Aerial Age*, 174–78.
46. "His Balloon Burst," *Washington (DC) Post*, August 22, 1909, 1.
47. "Planning," *Los Angeles Herald*, March 6, 1910, 6.
48. "Col Walter Wellman," *Washington (DC) Herald*, July 12, 1910, 4.
49. "Just as a Precautionary Measure." *El Paso (TX) Herald*, July 13, 1910, 6.
50. "Advice for Mr. Wellman," *Washington (DC) Herald*, July 13, 1910, 4.
51. Edward Mabley, *The Motor Balloon "America"* (Brattleboro, VT: Stephen Greene, 1969), 68. Note that Wellman and F. Murray Simon tell the story very differently: that they simply tried to lower the cat down to the ship that had towed them out, but were foiled either by freshening seas or the fact that the ship had already cast off. Wellman also explicitly names later radio calls as the first to go between an airship and a ground station. See *The Aerial Age*, 283–84 and 339 for the former, and 287 for the latter.
52. Wellman, *Aerial Age*, 285–334.
53. "Vaniman Ship Bursts in Air; Five Killed," *New York Evening World*, July 2, 1912, 1.
54. "Vaniman's 'Akron' Designed to Cross Ocean, Nearly Ready," *Washington (DC) Times*, September 18, 1911, 15.
55. "Vanniman and Four Aides Killed When Airship Explodes," *Washington (DC) Times*, July 2, 1912, 1.
56. "No Ocean Flight This Year." *New York Times*, May 9, 1912.
57. "To Pilot Airship over Sea in 1915," *Honesdale (PA) Citizen*, July 18, 1913, 6.

Chapter 15

1. Max Broesike, "Die Bäder und Heilquellen im preussichen Staate," *Zeitschrift der Königlich Preussischen Statistischen Bureaus* 43 (1903): 113–71.
2. Karl Baedeker, *Nordost-Deutschland* (Leipzig: Baedeker, 1914), 169.
3. Broesike, "Die Bäder und Heilquellen im preussichen Staate", 113–71.
4. Johannes Richard von Megede, *Das Blinkfeuer von Brüsterort* (Stuttgart: Deutsche Verlags-Anstalt, 1908), 17–18.
5. August Eduard Preuß, *Preußische Landes- und Volkskunde* (Königsberg: Bornträger, 1835), 18.
6. Richard Armstedt and Richard Fischer, *Heimatkunde von Königsberg i. Pr.* (Königsberg i. Pr: Wilhelm Koch, 1895), 265.

7. Baedeker, *Nordost-Deutschland*, 167.
8. *The Encyclopedia Britannica*, 11th ed., s.v. "Hel" (New York: Encyclopedia Britannica, 1910–11).
9. "German Naval Aeroplane Station," *Aeronautics*, February 1913, 67.
10. F. W. Paul Lehmann, "Das Küstengebiet Hinterpommern," *Zeitschrift der Gesellschaft für Erdkunde zu Berlin* 19 (1884): 381–83.
11. *The Encyclopedia Britannica*, 11th ed., s.v. "Stolp" (New York: Encyclopedia Britannica, 1910–11).
12. Martin Wehrmann, *Landeskunde der Provinz Pommern* (Breslau: F. Hirt, 1890), 6.
13. Baedeker, *Nordost-Deutschland*, 141.
14. *Meyers Kleines Konversations-Lexikon*, 7th ed., s.v. "Falster" (Leipzig and Vienna: Bibliographisches Institut, 1914).
15. *The Encyclopedia Britannica*, 11th ed., s.v. "Fehmarn" (New York: Encyclopedia Britannica, 1910–11).
16. Jacob Flohr Brarens, *Besteckbuch* (Hamburg: Salomon, 1852), 19.
17. Baedeker, *Nordost-Deutschland*, 472.
18. *Meyers Kleines Konversations-Lexikon*, 7th ed., s.v. "Panzerschiff," (Leipzig and Vienna: Bibliographisches Institut, 1914).
19. Reinhard Scheer, *Deutschlands Hochseeflotte im Weltkrieg* (Berlin: Scherl, 1920), 207.
20. *The Encyclopedia Britannica*, 11th ed., s.v. "Copenhagen" (New York: Encyclopedia Britannica, 1910–11).

Chapter 16

1. Albert Henry Smyth, *The Writings of Benjamin Franklin* (New York: Macmillan, 1907), 9:79–85.
2. Douglas Robinson, *The Zeppelin in Combat* (Atglen PA: Schiffer Military, 1994), 100–101.
3. Albert Vorreiter, *Jahrbuch über die Fortschritte auf allen Gebieten der Luftschiffahrt 1911* (Munich: Lehmanns, 1911), 70–71.
4. Dr. Hugo Erdmann, "Die Chemischen Grundlagen der Luftschiffahrt," *Deutsche Zeitschrift für Luftschiffahrt*, April 21, 1909, 312.
5. Robinson, *Zeppelin in Combat*, 139.
6. "Helium." *Encyclopedia Britannica*, 11th ed., vol. 13, 233–34.
7. Dr. Geza Austerweil, *Die angewandte Chemie in der Luftfahrt* (Munich: R. Oldenbout, 1914), 8.
8. Dr. Hugo Erdmann, "Die Chemischen Grundlagen der Luftschiffahrt," *Deutsche Zeitschrift für Luftschiffahrt*, April 21, 1909, 317.
9. Ladislas O'Orcy, "The Final Solution of the Airship Problem," *Scientific American*, January 25, 1919, 73.
10. "The 'Deutschland' Again Wrecked," *Flight*, May 20, 1911, 449.
11. "Dethroned as King of the Air," *Washington (DC) Herald*, July 4, 1915, 34.
12. Alfred Mühler, "Mit LZ 37 aus 2000 m. Höhe brennend abgestürzt," *Kyffhäuser Mitgliedermagazin* May 8, 1938.
13. J. M. Bruce, "The Sopwith Tabloid, Schneider and Baby," *Flight*, November 8, 1957, 736.
14. "Black Crosses in the Sky," *Air Defense Artillery*, Summer 1984, 10.
15. "Latest from Europe," *Washington (DC) Native American*, June 8, 1839, 2.
16. "Mauretania Beats All Eastward Records with Trip in 4 Days, 20 Hours." *New York Evening World*, February 8, 1909, 1.

17. "Zeppelin Airship Mass of Wreckage," *New York Tribune*, August 6, 1908, 1.
18. "Zeppelin Airship Wrecked in Gale," *Washington (DC) Times*, April 25, 1910, 1.
19. Robinson, *Zeppelin in Combat*, 39–46.
20. Robinson, *Zeppelin in Combat*, 124–25

Chapter 17

1. Karl Baedeker, *Nordost-Deutschland* (Leipzig: Baedeker, 1914), 141.
2. Karl Peter Andreas Faber, "Das Merkwürdigste aus der Chronik der Stadt und Festung Pillau," *Beiträge zur Kunde Preußens* 6, no. 1 (1824): 44.
3. Friedrich Richter, *Der Ausbau des Königsberger Innenhafen* (Königsberg i. Pr.: Hartungsche Buchdruckerei, 1907), 16–17.

Aftermath

1. Douglas Robinson, *The Zeppelin in Combat* (Atglen, PA: Schiffer Military, 1994), 376–77.
2. John Provan, *The German Airship in World War I* (Kelkheim: Luftschiff-Zeppelin Collection, 1992).
3. Provan, *German Airship*.
4. Ladislas D'Orcy, *D'Orcy's Airship Manual* (New York: Century, 1917), 165.
5. Robert Underwood Johnson, *Remembered Yesterdays* (Boston: Little, Brown, 1923), 577.
6. "Archivio Storico—1921 Il Dirigibile ZEPPELIN 'AUSONIA,'" Scuderio Ausonia Schio, accessed July 15, 2021, http://www.ausoniaschio.it/storia_schio/zeppelin_ausonia.asp.
7. Johannes Goebel, *Afrika zu unsern Füssen* (Leipzig: Koehler, 1925).
8. "French Airship's Record Voyage," *Flight*, October 13, 1923, 630.
9. "Big French Dirigible Was Lost at Sea," *Perth Amboy (NJ) Evening News*, December 28, 1923, 1.
10. "Debris Shows Dixmude Wrecked by Lightning," *Washington (DC) Evening Star*, January 11, 1924, 1.
11. "Graf Zeppelin's Record Flight," *Flight*, August 22, 1929, 904.
12. "Graf Zeppelin—Sky Squatter," *Flight*, December 5, 1935, 580.
13. Frank Maxymillian, "50th Anniversary: Flight of the *Snowbird*, March 4–15, 1957," *Noon Balloon*, Spring 2007, 18–25.
14. Robinson, *Zeppelin in Combat*, 206–7.
15. "The Transatlantic Voyage of R 34," *Flight*, July 10, 1919, 906.
16. George Rosie, "Stowaways, Storms and Suspense on the First Airship Flight to US," *The (London) Times*, June 30, 2009.
17. "ZR-3 Ends 5,060-Mile Flight in 81 Hours," *New York Times*, October 16, 1924, 1.
18. "The Hindenburg Makes Her Last Landing at Lakehurst," *Life*, May 17, 1937, 26–30.
19. "Burns Are Fatal to Capt. Lehmann," *New York Times*, May 8, 1937, 1.
20. Ibid.
21. "Report of Airship 'Hindenburg' Accident Investigation," *Air Commerce Bulletin* 9, no. 2 (1937): 21–36.
22. "Burns Are Fatal to Capt. Lehmann," *New York Times*, May 8, 1937, 1.
23. Albert Leitzmann and Carl Schüddekopf, eds., *Lichtenberg's Briefe* (Leipzig: Dieterich'sche Verlagsbuchhandlung, 1901).

FURTHER READING

Bömel, Alexander. *Graf Ferdinand von Zeppelin: Ein Mann der Tat.* Konstanz: Johannes Blanke, 1908. Biographies of Count Zeppelin, one published not long after the first successful Zeppelin flight, the other during the war—and just two years before Zeppelin's death. These hagiographic accounts do a good job of selling the Zeppelin mythos to the German public and give a sense of the man beyond his work as an airship entrepreneur.

Der Erste Offizier eines Z-Luftschiffes [pseud.], *"Z 181" Im Zeppelin gegen Bukarest.* Berlin: Druck und Verlag August Scherl, 1916. This remarkable document was published during the war and purported to tell the story of a single attack by Zeppelin against Bucharest. Both the name of the author, who claims to be a first officer on a Zeppelin, and the airship itself are pseudonyms; both *LZ 81* (hull LZ 51) and *LZ 101* (hull LZ 71) attacked the Romanian city in early 1916. The author clearly had spent time aloft; the descriptions of the minutiae of flight are unrivaled.

Goebel, Johannes. *Afrika zu unsern Füssen: 40,000 km Zeppelin-Kriegsfahrten; Lettow-Vorbeck entgegen.* Leipzig: Koehler, 1925. Not long after the 101-hour flight, and building on its success, naval airship L 59 (hull LZ 104) took off from Yambol in Bulgaria, headed south to try to resupply German troops in German East Africa. Somewhere over Sudan, they received an abort message and returned to their home hangar. Goebel, who gives every indication of having been on board, is based on his "personal records" as well as the war diary of the meteorologist Walter Förster, and contains a blow-by-blow account of the flight to Africa and back.

Lehmann, Ernst, and Howard Mingos. *The Zeppelins.* New York: J. H. Sears 1927.

Lehmann, Ernst, and Leonhard Adelt. *Auf Luftpatrouille und Weltfahrt : Erlebnisse eines Zeppelinführers in Krieg und Frieden.* Leipzig: Schmidt et Günther, 1937. Ernst August Lehmann wrote two books telling his story. The first was written in English, coautheroed with Howard Mingos and published in 1927. The second was written in conjunction with Leonhard Adelt and published in German in 1937 with an English edition that was published as *Zeppelin: The Story of Lighter Than Air Craft* three months after Lehmann's death, enough time to add a chapter by Charles Rosendahl, reviewing Lehmann's life and describing his death. While Lehmann describes many flights, including the 101-hour one, he does not spend much time on any of them, and some of the details have been forgotten in the intervening years.

Redner, Harry. *Die Luftschiffwaffe des Heeres.* Wendeburg: Harry Redner, 1998. Redner, under the moniker Luftschiffharry, has collected a vast amount of information about German army airship operations during the war. The result was a series of files to be found on his website, http://www.luftschiff-harry.de/, that told, partially in prose, partially as formatted data, the story of the army airships. While today these files are no longer available on the web, they can still be accessed via Redner himself.

Robinson, Douglas. *The Zeppelin in Combat.* Atglen, PA: Schiffer Military, 1994. While now over twenty-five years old, this book still provides the best overview of German naval airship operations in the war. Combining text and pictures with a judicious number of drawings and tables, Robinson presents a complete account of the naval airships, from Zeppelin's first experiments to the final disposition of the dirigibles after the war.

Saager, Adolf. *Zeppelin, der Mensch, der Kämpfer, der Sieger.* Stuttgart: Robert Lutz, 1915.

Toland, John. *The Great Dirigibles: Their Triumph & Disasters.* New York: Dover, 1972. There are many books that tell the story of dirigibles from their earliest days up to the Hindenburg disaster. This book by John Toland, originally published 1957 as *Ships in the Sky: The Story of the Great Dirigibles*, still stands out as one of the better ones. In his usual fluid prose, Toland tells the stories of some of the great airships, from Andree to Zeppelin. While far from comprehensive, the stories he sets down bring the golden age of airships to life as few other books can.

INDEX

PILOT HOUSE R-34 JUST AF